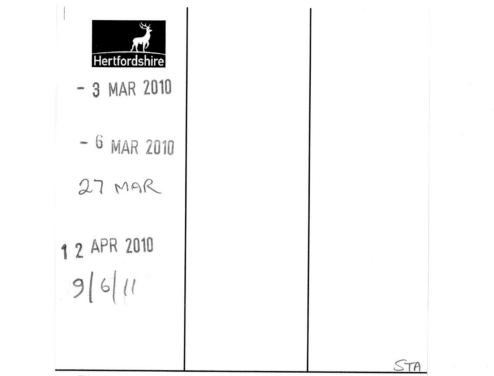

Of Horses
and Heroes

No chance of survival. Spare ride Warren Street *en route* to an early exit in a 31-runner novice chase at Hereford, 13 March 1965. Current safety limit at Hereford: sixteen.

BROUGH SCOTT

Of Horses
and Heroes

RACING POST

Published in 2008 by Racing Post
Compton, Newbury, Berkshire RG20 6NL

A catalogue record for this book is available from the Briti

ISBN 978-1-905156-57-3

Editor Sean Magee
Designer Tracey Scarlett
Printed by Butler, Tanner and Dennis, Frome, Somerset.

TEXT AND PHOTOGRAPHIC ACKNOWLEDGEMENTS

All the pieces collected in this book originally appeared in the *Racing Post*, with the following exceptions:

Sunday Times: Red Rum (both pieces); Grundy and Bustino; Dancing Brave (second piece);

Sunday Telegraph: Warrior; Taiki Shuttle; Castle Mane; Best Mate (both pieces); Papillon; Fantastic Light and Galileo; High Chaparral; Hawk Wing and Coshocton; Denman;

Flat Horses of 2003 (published by Highdown/Racing Post): Falbrav; Dalakhani;

theatre programme for *Days of Wine and Roses* by Owen McCafferty at the Donmar Warehouse, 2005: Arkle.

The author and publishers are grateful for permission to republish these pieces in this volume.

'Mill Reef', 'Hurdlers: The Golden Age', 'Dancing Brave' (first piece) and 'Cigar' were written for this book.

All photographs in the book are used courtesy of the *Racing Post*, with the following exceptions: frontispiece and page 6: author's collection; Jack Seely on Warrior by Sir Alfred Munnings, page 14, reproduced by kind permission of the Canadian War Museum (© Canadian War Museum); Red Rum, page 33: Gerry Cranham; Castle Mane, page 65: Mike King.

CONTENTS

INTRODUCTION
The Legacy of Black 47

HE WAS called Black 47. He wasn't as big or as flash as the other two runners in the last race at the 1948 Isle of Wight point-to-point, but the heroic little way he stomped round the paddock made my sister and I lay out our hearts, and something like half a crown, in support of him.

In those simple days the Isle of Wight point-to-point was, unlike now, run on the Isle of Wight. The course was set around the windy rolling fields just in from the cliffs at Atherfield in the south west of the island. The crowd gathered on a hill with the last fence down to its left, and to my five-year-old self it was a matter of gleeful lavatorial delight to discover that the trench taking away the liquid from the khaki-tented gents urinal supplemented the brook on the landing side of the final obstacle.

From the moment the starter dropped his flag and the three runners came splattering down towards us, it was clear that Black 47 was no match for his two glamorous rivals. His stride was much shorter, his jumping much more laboured than the flowing pair ahead of him, his kit and his rider much more workaday. Looking back, I realise that he was not a racehorse at all.

Quite soon it became clear that completing the course was the best that we could hope for from our straining, dark-coated little friend. He was a good hundred yards behind when jumping the last fence on the first circuit with its potent brook, and by the time the leading pair crossed the third last he hadn't jumped the fence behind them. When he did so, he crashed to the ground and lay very still. Even we little children could understand.

Up front another drama unrolled, although our eyes were still trapped by the motionless shape on the other side of the track. At the second last one of the two leaders pitched sharply, unseated the rider and galloped off, leaving the sole survivor of the original

The author and The Otter on the way to winning the Mandarin Chase at Newbury, 8 March 1969.

intrepid trio the apparently easy task of crossing the natural birch hedge next to which Janet and I were two small and already traumatised witnesses.

Unlike Black 47, this was obviously a proper Thoroughbred. His neck was elegant, his coat clipped, his stride light, his rider lean; he had everything going for him except perhaps quite the right look in his eye. Just as he came into the wing of the fence he jammed his forelegs in front of him and skidded in a muddy refusal to leap. There was a gasping roar from the crowd and dark fury from the rider, who wheeled him off and then, with many oaths, much kicking of the legs and cracking of the whip, crammed him into the fence, only to refuse again. Consternation reigned.

Then over in the rainy distance, something truly magical happened. What had been no more than a sad cadaver was now our little hero back on his feet and remounted. With gallant if weary endeavour he negotiated the third last fence and the second last, but as he ground on towards us we could see that his Lazarus efforts would merely act as a lead to get the 'refuser' over the last and canter off with the prize.

The two unlikely rivals came squelching in. There was no spring in Black 47's stride but there was a plodding honesty that made us will him on. Tired and battered though he may have been, he pricked his ears and with one last heave of his muddied quarters was up and over. Things did not go so well beside him.

'The Refuser' had come into the fence locked absolutely shoulder to shoulder with Black 47, to whom he was quite ridiculously superior. As they came to the wings his rider threw so much resource of voice and spur and flailing whip that even this reluctant partner seemed bound to consent. But no. At the very, very last stride 'The Refuser' jammed on the brakes with such force that while he skidded to a stop, his jockey didn't. With an appalled but perfect arc, the rider soared over his ears and, yes, splash into the foaming brook.

As Black 47 plodded on to glory this little boy thought the world could never be as good. Reality quickly intruded, for by the time Janet and I got our betting slips together the bookie had departed. We had been welshed at the first attempt, but for me that first memory was a defining moment. Back at home in grey, war-ravaged Paddington, the only horses were in the pictures on the walls and pulling milk carts and many other vehicles in the streets. Next to the bathroom there was a picture of my Dad aboard the winner of the Lightweight Race at the North Cotswold in 1922. But that Isle of Wight point-to-point had been the real thing, with colour and life and courage and hope, not to mention a wonderful dollop of raffish absurdity. Looking back now, I realised that I was hooked.

Hooked on the thrill of the racing game, but hooked most of all on the horses. A couple of weeks after Black 47, I was taken to Mr Biles's farm over the downs at Shorwell. Mr Biles's horse had won his first race and now stood gleaming and magnificent in its stable, and as a special treat I was placed on its silky back. Then and now, the Thoroughbred racehorse was to me a thing of wonder, the fastest weight-carrying creature the world has ever seen and England's greatest gift to the animal kingdom. That day a tiny dream took hold that I might get close to Thoroughbreds. This book is a thank you to all those who helped me on the way.

Thanks most of all to those that carried me in the nine marvellous, unexpected racing years that bridged elegant, long-striding short-eared Red Squirrel winging up (and foiling a gamble) at the Bullingdon Club point-to-point in 1962 and big, brave but clodding-clumsy Bonnie Highlander cartwheeling me off to Warwick Hospital and closure on 13 March 1971.

That time and those horses will live with me for ever. A round total of 100 winners was infinitely more than was thought possible when a mere ride in a point-to-point was the greatest ambition, but it was also a source of under-achievement for someone whose early luck saw him turn professional with much higher figures and even championships in mind.

In hindsight the injuries and setbacks were a blessing for me. They put my privileges into perspective. Nobody owed me anything. I owed them.

In 1970, when I was out with a broken leg, racing – and horses – gave me a chance on television. As the first professional jockey to broadcast I prospered not through an Inverdale-calm voice or Balding-sharp intelligence but on the fine old principle of 'If you can't be good be different.' When the riding stopped the writing resumed, making up for a much resented gap when an early arrangement with the *Observer* was terminated because, according to the racing authorities, 'professional jockeys are not allowed to write'.

Over the years I have published three other books of collected pieces, but this one is much more specific in gathering together three other strands written in the *Racing Post* which were always intended for a wider audience. They are firstly a series from 2000 of riding out at fifteen very different stables in Britain and Ireland; then the first-hand account of the glories and final disappointment of Motivator's Derby-winning season of 2005; and finally, written in the spring of 2008, a twelve-strong collection of people who have made an indelible impression on me.

It was after writing that series that the idea of this book was born. For in penning those pieces I realised that the real link between me and those depicted was the horses for whom we shared a passion. So I wanted to begin the project by gathering up some of the horses that have fuelled my imagination in the sixty years, that connect that first bucolic point-to-point with the present day, and hope that some of the excitement they gave me can pass on through the page.

I wanted also to use this opportunity to place a marker for the galloping side of the racing game. It is my firm belief that unless we can make interesting what happens at the heart of things, we might as well all go home. Of course betting is the central dynamic of public interest, and the moment your few bob is on a runner, it becomes just as much 'your' horse as Sheikh Mohammed's. But if we stress betting above all, live racing is only one jump ahead of the 'virtual' racecourse Portman Park and other computer diversions in the betting shops – and a heck of a lot more expensive to put on.

It is no comfort to admit that I feel a touch of guilt about this situation. For as a driving force behind the creation of both Channel 4 Racing and the *Racing Post* I was instrumental in ensuring that we made betting accessible and centre-stage. What I did not want to do was to make betting the be-all and end-all. As the numbers of meetings proliferate, there seems a growing danger that racing and its media outlets increasingly look inward to wrangle over betting disputes and business matters rather than concentrate on putting its most attractive side on display.

If the sport's presence in newspapers is no more than racecards and tips, it will no longer justify its place in the sports pages and less and less on network television. The road to satellite oblivion is a lot closer than many people care to think.

But I want to take you on a journey not of complaint but of celebration – of horses and people worth cherishing in the memory bank. Most of the pieces which follow are taken from what I wrote at the time (with only minor tinkerings appropriate to their new incarnation), the majority of them originally in the *Racing Post* with a few from the *Sunday Times* and *Sunday Telegraph*. (Details can be found opposite the contents page.) Where possible I have kept the sense of immediacy but I hope you will forgive some occasional hindsight and some necessary discursions along the way.

Looking back, I am struck with how lucky I have been in the editors with whom I have worked – at the *Sunday Times, Independent on Sunday, Sunday Telegraph*, and of course throughout my time at the *Racing Post* (where special mention must be made of Edward Whitaker, so many of whose wonderful photos adorn this book). The real criterion for including a piece has been that the words were a true reflection of what I had seen, and that is much easier to do if you know that other eyes are running a quality check.

Which is why the final acknowledgement has to be of the 'without him this could not have happened' kind. Sean Magee is a considerable scribe in his own right – as shown in particular by his marvellous book *Arkle: The life and legacy of 'Himself'* – and his skill has made him an incomparable ally on this project. Thanks to him, and to our designer Tracey Scarlett, the whole process has developed a life of its own.

And so here, as best as I can write it, is what lit my fire.

Old Dreams

*M*EASURING *your life in racehorse shoes may not be as poetic as J. Alfred Prufrock's coffee spoons in T.S. Eliot's poem, but I can tell you it has been a hell of a lot more exciting. Racehorses have given me the most wonderful time, taken to me to all sorts of astonishing places, introduced me to the most extraordinary mix of people, and set a splendid, uncomplaining benchmark of behaviour when the human side seems to be disintegrating. Of course they are just dumb animals, but around them glories as well as disasters cling.*

So many horses, and so much pleasure so often turning to pain: the bitter-sweet addiction of the racing game has taken me from one century to the next, and is just as good – and just as bad – as it ever was.

To choose a handful of horses to express the bite of this addiction has to be entirely subjective, and I have confined it to horses I knew directly and to pieces I either have written or would like to have written at the time.

But there was no question as to with whom we would start. He actually only ever won one race, albeit that in the Isle of Wight point-to-point field where Black 47 was later to star. He was thirteen years old by the time of that success, but he had already played a part in the somewhat wider victory that was World War One. He was bred and reared by my grandfather on the island, and built his courage wading into the breakers from the shore.

In our family he will always be the greatest of them all.

He was a horse called Warrior, and his story has been with me from my mother's knee. My grandfather Jack Seely wrote a book about him, somewhat unoriginally entitled My Horse Warrior, *which with its original Alfred Munnings sketches and simple, unfeigned affection is in many ways rather more attractive than his other 'How I Won the War' books with resounding titles like* Adventure, Forever England *and* Fear and Be Slain.

March 2008 was the anniversary of Warrior's finest hour. It seemed time to pay tribute. Thanks to the Sunday Telegraph, *we did.*

Previous spread: Red Rum and Tommy Stack winning the 1977 Grand National.

WARRIOR

WARRIOR was ready. It was 9.30 on the morning of 30 March, Easter Saturday 1918. He had somehow survived four years of shell and bullet and privation and Passchendale, but now, in the little hamlet of Castel, not ten miles south west of the centre of Amiens, he faced his most dangerous mission of all. He would lead one of the last great cavalry charges in history.

Behind him were the 1,000 horses of the Canadian Cavalry which, in the ten days since the German breakthrough against the Fifth Army at St Quentin, had trekked an embattled 120-mile anti-clockwise loop south from Peronne to cross the Oise east of Noyon and then work back northwards to try and get round the spearhead of the enemy advance.

In Warrior's saddle, as he had been for most of the ten years since he bred the little bay Thoroughbred back home in the Isle of Wight, was my grandfather.

Fifty-one-year-old General Jack Seely was no shrinking violet, and legend has it that he later recommended Warrior for the VC with the simple, if somewhat immodest, citation: 'He went everywhere I went.'

Jack had been elected MP for the Isle of Wight (how could he not be? – his family owned half the island) whilst still serving in the Boer War, but despite rising to be a senior member of the Asquith Cabinet, his political career foundered when, on 30 March 1914, he had to resign as Secretary of State for War over the mishandling of the Northern Ireland drama known as The Curragh Crisis.

He and Warrior had first come to France on 11 August of that year. Since February 1915 he had commanded the bunch of ranchers, clerks, ex-pats, Mounties and Red Indians which made up the three regiments of the Canadian Cavalry. Jack Seely was a popular general. But not as popular as Warrior.

If ever an animal was a symbol of indomitability for weary soldiers to follow, it was this short-legged wide-eyed, star-foreheaded, independent-spirited but kindly gelding who in January 1918 had been immortalised as the first of the portraits painted by Alfred Munnings as War Artist to the Canadian Cavalry.

Warrior was brave but not stupid, fast but not fragile, tough but not thick.

His father Straybit had won the Lightweight race at the Isle of Wight point-to-point in 1909.

His mother Cinderella was so affectionate that she used to follow Seely and his family around like a dog. Warrior did too. It was quite a sight behind the trenches.

Jack Seely on Warrior.
Portrait by Sir Alfred Munnings,
January 1918.

Warrior was a survivor. In September 1914 his groom Jack Thompson had to gallop ten miles across country to escape encirclement by the advancing enemy. In 1915 one shell cut a horse beside him clean in half, and a few days later another destroyed his stable seconds after he had left it. On 1 July 1916, that fateful first day of The Somme, he and the Canadians were readied to gallop through the gap in the German wire which never came. In 1917 only frantic digging extricated him from the mud in Passchendaele, and only three days before 30 March 1918 a direct hit on the ruined villa in which he was housed left him trapped beneath a shattered beam. Yes, a survivor; but could he survive this?

In hindsight it is easy to say that the Germans were overstretched, that the Americans would soon be in action, that the result was inevitable. But that is not what it seemed at the time. Check where Berlin, Paris and Amiens are on the map and remember that the news, from random gallopers and motorcycle messengers, was scarce; and that which came too often spoke of catastrophe. And don't take my, or especially my grandfather's word for it. Take witness from the greatest war reporter, not to mention war leader, that ever put pen to paper. 'Actual defeat seemed to stare the Allies in the face,' he wrote. Winston Churchill was on his way.

As Warrior champed at the bit, ready to cross the river Avre at Castel and gallop up the hill to attack the German positions in Moreuil Wood, Churchill, as a special envoy from Lloyd George, was being briefed first by Marshall Foch of France and then, later, by General Rawlinson, the commander of the beleaguered Fifth Army at his headquarters ten miles south of Amiens. 'The men are just crawling slowly backwards,' Rawlinson told Churchill, 'They are completely worn out.' It did indeed sound desperate. Finally the general was asked if he would still be in position next day. 'He made a grimace,' Churchill records with majestic understatement, 'the dominant effect of which was not encouraging to my mind.'

It was in this climate that Seely took the decision that was to lose a quarter of his men and half his horses before they finally came back to bivouac in the dark up in the Bois de Senecat, half a mile to the West. But the advance had been checked, Moreuil Wood had been taken, and it had been taken because enough of the cavalry had been able to brave the bullets and dismount to clear the Germans, with – and this should cure some of us sportswriters of ever misusing the metaphor again – 'bayonets fixed.'

Cavalry had become redundant in trench warfare. The Germans had disbanded theirs at the end of 1917. Lloyd George had argued for the Allies to do the same after the disaster of the 27,500 horse and tank advance on Cambrai, when Seely and Warrior had trotted behind the leading tank only to see it crash through the bridge into the canal at Masnieres. Horses were desperately easy targets, but a committed group of them could still act as a sort of early day parachute brigade. At full gallop they could shift hundreds of men half a mile in under a couple of minutes.

The signal group would lead it – eleven men headed by Corporal King ready to plant the red pennant with the black C on a white star for the Canadians to aim for. With him was Seely's 35-year-old ADC, the remarkable Prince Antoine d'Orleans-Bragance ('Orleans' as great grandson of France's last reigning monarch, Louis-Philippe; 'Braganza' because his maternal grandfather was the last Emperor of Brazil.) And where was Seely himself? Not for nothing had he named his horse 'Warrior.' The General led the charge.

In fact he could not hold Warrior. 'He was determined to go forward,' said Seely of his charger after they had crossed the bridge and come up out of the hollow, 'and with a great leap started off. All sensation of fear had vanished from him as he galloped on at racing speed. There was of course a hail of bullets from the enemy as we crossed the intervening space and mounted the hill, but Warrior cared for nothing.' Seely, Prince Antoine, Corporal King and six of the others made it. Five didn't.

The pennant was planted. Squadron after squadron came thundering up the hill, taking terrible casualties but going on to exact many of their own. The chaotic sounds of the hooves and the men and the guns was added to by the roar overhead of the wheeling biplanes of the Royal Flying Corps, who dropped 190 bombs and fired 17,000 rounds into the melée. 'One bomb dropped from a negligible height,' records the German official history excitedly, 'places the whole staff of the First Battalion "Hors de Combat". Moreuil Wood is hell.' Especially for horses.

The worst slaughter was to the east . Moreuil Wood was triangular, a mile long on each side. Lieutenant Gordon Flowerdew took his 75 strong C Company of Strathcona's Horse round the northern tip, only to gallop up out of a hollow and be confronted by two rows of machine guns. The Germans had rumours of a tank attack coming down from Villers Bretonneux. Horses did not have a chance. 'Sir,' sobbed Sergeant Watson when he finally crawled back with the news: 'Sir, the boys is all gone.'

Warrior and Seely were now in the wood and what they were seeing was war at its most bayonet-thrusting horrible. In the thick of it was Fred Harvey, a 6 foot 2 inch rancher from Fort Macleod, Alberta, who had made his debut for Ireland eleven years earlier as a fly half on the wrong end of a 29-0 thrashing by Wales at the Arms Park. In March 1917 he had won the VC for single-handedly charging a machine gun. He never ever wrote a word about it, but at a regimental dinner in Calgary many years later confided 'I don't know about 1917, but I think I did a VC's worth at Moreuil.'

The engagement went on into what became a rainy afternoon, and as the light faded an unlikely looking little motorcade came along the road in the valley. 'The Bois de Moreuil lay before us,' wrote Churchill, who was accompanying the French premier Georges Clemenceau at 'Le Tigre's' insistence. 'The intervening ground was dotted with stragglers, and here and there groups of led horses – presumably Seely's Brigade – were standing motionless. Shrapnel continued to burst over the plain in twos and threes, and high explosive made black bulges here and there.'

'A wounded, riderless horse came in a staggering trot towards us. The poor animal was streaming with blood. "The Tiger", aged seventy-four, advanced towards it and with great quickness seized its bridle, bringing it to a standstill. The blood accumulated in a pool along the road. The French general expostulated with him and he reluctantly returned to his car. As he did so, he gave me a sidelong glance and said in an undertone – "Quel moment delicieux."'

It was not so delicious for Seely, Warrior and the other survivors as they held a sad and simple Easter Service next morning. That afternoon another summons came. Seely and Warrior were to report to six miles north to a village called Gentelles at 2 a.m. to plan an attack in the morning. On the way Warrrior lamed himself in the dark and was put out of action. Next day Seely was badly gassed and both his replacement horses were killed. It was Warrior's last great escape.

He was to live until 1941, when Seely felt that the extra corn rations needed to keep the 33-year old hero going could not be justified in war time. On that

Good Friday he wrote: 'I do not believe, to quote Byron on his dog Boatswain, "that he is denied in Heaven, the soul he had on earth."'

After that earlier Easter in 1918 Warrior had recovered to join the victory parade in Hyde Park, and three years later won the same race at the Isle of Wight point-to-point which his sire Straybit had done in 1909. You might have guessed the date of that success. It was 30 March.

Warrior was an absolute. Discussing him sets the bar at a level which few horses at any discipline will be able to match. It was therefore a piece of quite stunning good fortune that in 1962, the very year I first got fully involved as a steeplechase rider, a horse should burst on to the British jumping scene like no other before or since.

In February 2005 the Donmar Warehouse staged an Owen McCafferty reworking of the famous film and teleplay Days of Wine and Roses, *with Arkle as the mystic role model to which the doomed Donal aspires. This was the programme note I wrote:*

ARKLE

ARKLE was an icon. Foaled in County Meath in 1957, he became the best steeplechaser that ever was or ever will be. In 26 races over fences he only lost four times, once when he slipped, twice when conceding stones in weight, and one final time when he broke his leg. But he was not just a four-legged paragon. He became a wider metaphor for invincibility, a shaft of certainty in an uncertain world. And, thank you Father, he was Irish. So Irish he even had two bottles of Guinness in his feed every night.

I remember exactly where I was when I first saw him: standing by the last fence at Cheltenham for the Honeybourne Novices' Chase on Saturday 17 November 1962, Arkle's first race over fences. I was a nineteen-year-old amateur rider already seriously affected by the racing bug and had no defence against the image in front of me.

We had been warned that the Irish thought this lean, greyhoundy, long-eared thing was a bit special, but what happened at the finish just took the breath away. There were decent horses against him, but Arkle just skipped over the fence and sprinted twenty lengths clear as if he was another species altogether. Perhaps he was.

It was all the more remarkable because when Arkle had first appeared at Tom Dreaper's stables, twenty miles east of Dublin, two seasons earlier, he had not been that impressive. 'His action was so terrible behind,' recorded his long-time jockey Pat Taaffe, 'that we thought he would be a slow coach – a slob.' Indeed he did manage only two wins from six races in his opening term over hurdles. But the next winter, over steeplechase fences, Arkle proved to be something else.

As his body matured into its frame, he developed first an athleticism and then a presence that I have never seen before or since. By the time he came back to Cheltenham in March 1963 for the equivalent of the Royal & SunAlliance Chase, he was kicking all other novices out of the way. But when he returned for the Gold Cup next season, it seemed he might have found his match in the massive 1963 Gold Cup winner Mill House, who had given him five pounds and a beating in the Hennessy at Newbury the previous November.

What happened on that cold, clear March day in 1964 became one of the defining moments, both in jumping history and Irish life. You have to remember that we were hailing Mill House as the greatest English trained steeplechaser since the war, a giant of a horse whose spring-heeled leaps used to bring gasps from the crowd as if they were watching hammer blows from a heavyweight. The Irish were insisting that Arkle had slipped at Newbury, but none of us believed them. Then, as they turned for home at Cheltenham and we waited for Willie Robinson on Mill House to put the upstart in its place, we saw the unthinkable: a horse not just as good as Mill House, but quite emphatically, brutally, his superior.

I was a young jockey by then, a 21-year-old undergraduate down from Oxford getting ready to ride in the Cathcart two races after the Gold Cup. In the weighing room we couldn't believe what our eyes had told us. I remember poor Willie Robinson sitting on the bench just as shattered as if he had been taken out by the young Cassius Clay, who had flattened Sonny Liston a month earlier. Willie had thought Mill House unbeatable. He was wrong.

There was a sense of awe around the place whenever Arkle ran. For he didn't just win, he used to destroy his opponents or attempt seemingly impossible tasks in handicaps. In truth his subsequent Gold Cups were little more than exhibition rounds, the most memorable moment when he completely ignored the fence in front of the stands on the first circuit in 1966. So it was what Arkle did in handicaps – conceding two, sometimes nearly three stone – which has seared itself in the memory.

He won the Irish Grand National with 12 stone, two Hennessys, a Whitbread and the Gallaher Gold Cup at Sandown Park with 12st 7lbs, and most remarkably of all finished a close third in the Massey Ferguson at Cheltenham in December 1964 with 12st 10lb, giving 32 pounds to the winner Flying Wild and 26 pounds to the equally talented runner-up Buona Notte. I can see Arkle now, still fighting back, refusing to be anchored by the extra lead. He couldn't do it, but he nearly did.

'Himself' and Pat Taaffe in the 1965 King George VI Chase.

By then Arkle had gathered the most extraordinary aura about him. He used to walk round the paddock with his neck very upright and those astonishing long ears scanning the crowd, the emperor of all he surveyed. On the track he was utterly dominant, sometimes just carting Pat Taaffe to the front, often throwing extravagant leaps merely for the hell of it, once or twice landing on the fence rather than over it. We couldn't take our eyes off him. We used to race back to see him unsaddle. We felt we were treasuring something beyond compare. We were right.

For the Irish he became something much more than a racehorse. He was a symbol, an aspiration, a one-word assertion that all in their world could be right. When in December 1966 he broke his leg and was hospitalised at Kempton after what was to be his final race, there were daily bulletins on the Irish news. When Arkle eventually succumbed to arthritis four years later, there was little short of national mourning.

The 'Celtic Tiger' of the resurgent Irish economy was still a dream in its basket. We were a long way short of today's Ireland with the best educated youth in Europe, with so much building that it is English workers who want to emigrate, not the other way round. There was a yearning for something Irish that was indisputably great. They found it in a horse so famous they honoured him as 'Himself.'

There were books and plays and songs about him. Listen closely and his presence lives on here tonight.

The play was a limited success, but Arkle and his legacy only ever grows, as is brilliantly and evocatively chronicled in Sean Magee's book Arkle: The Life and Legacy of 'Himself', *published by Highdown in 2005.*

For horse lovers around at the time, the truly amazing thing is that another phenomenon was emerging, and from the same stable. Flyingbolt did not last, but March 2005 was the anniversary of his emerging prime. It was only right to pay this tribute.

FLYINGBOLT

FLYINGBOLT won what is now called the Arkle Chase forty years
ago this Cheltenham. He was the best horse never to win the Gold
Cup. More than that, he was probably the second best chaser in the
history of the world. And yet almost everyone has forgotten about him. They
shouldn't have done.

For Flyingbolt was every bit as much of a freak as Arkle himself. At a
time when no contemporary was within two stone of 'Himself', Flyingbolt's
exploits had him officially rated as close as 3lbs to Arkle, two years his senior
and astonishingly also trained by Tom Dreaper in his forty-box yard near the
house at Kilsallaghan, in County Dublin.

Flyingbolt was a tall, gangly, rather washy chestnut with a white face, and
if he never looked very well that was because he wasn't. He suffered from
brucellosis, a debilitating disease which causes inflammation of the joints and
cut his career off in his prime. It is because his owners later decided to soldier
on with the old horse in decline – back first with Ken Oliver in Scotland and
then with Roddy Armytage in Berkshire – that Flyingbolt leaves only a faded
trace in the memory.

When he first appeared he came like a comet across the scene. He won
his first ten races straight, including a division of Cheltenham's Gloucester
Hurdle – what would now be the Supreme Novices'. Switched to fences,
he was even more devastating as a novice chaser, including that effortless
win at Cheltenham. Then in the 1965-66 season he was nothing less than
sensational. Having bolted up conceding lumps of weight in big races over
two and a half miles and three, he came to Cheltenham, hacked up in the
Champion Chase on the Tuesday and a day later turned out to run third in
the Champion Hurdle.

To be honest, that race was not the great Pat Taaffe's finest hour, Flyingbolt
getting pushed wide and the super-stylish Johnny Haine pouncing up the
inside with Salmon Spray. But a month later the astonishing powers of
Flyingbolt in his prime went one step further when this two-mile champion
won the three-and-a-quarter-mile Irish National with 12st 7lbs, giving away
almost three stone to the second.

Sadly that prime didn't last. Brucellosis closed in. Flyingbolt could only
run once in 1966-7 and twice the season after, his final run for Tom Dreaper
being a last place in the Mackeson Gold Cup at Cheltenham. Dreaper
understandably felt such a pale shadow of the super horse should be retired,
but Flyingbolt's owner insisted on continuing.

In 1968 he went to Ken Oliver's yard in Scotland and for two seasons
battled round in big races, his best effort being second in the 1969 King

George at Kempton. His closing victory was in a two-mile chase at Haydock, but in 1970 as an eleven-year-old he moved on to Roddy Armytage's, where his name still caused wonderment but his performances and his sore old joints were on the downward trail.

He was second twice with Stan Mellor aboard. David Nicholson rode him to be third at Cheltenham in the 1971 Cathcart, and then he lasted until the fourteenth fence before crashing out in the Topham at Aintree. He never ran again, and retirement soon faded him from the collective memory.

Forty years on since he first blazed over Cheltenham's fences, 39 since his *annus mirabilis*, it is time we paid Flyingbolt his due as – and let's say it carefully – one of the very greatest of them all.

Hindsight is a dangerous thing, but to have two such champions as opening benchmarks was an unbelievable piece of good fortune for an impressionable enthusiast like myself. What makes my case almost unfairly lucky is that the same thing happened on the Flat, almost more so.

Between 1968 and 1972 there was the chance to get close up to Sir Ivor, Nijinsky, Mill Reef and Brigadier Gerard, four horses who instantly take their places amongst the greatest champions in history. The first two represented the absolute zenith of the partnership between Lester Piggott and Vincent O'Brien, but because of riding commitments I only saw them from afar – although, as related later, I did have an unforgettable drive with Lester to Epsom the day after Nijinsky's Derby. With Mill Reef and Brigadier Gerard it was different. In 1971 I started full time in Flat racing. It was the season they ruled the world.

The next year, backed by Mill Reef's owner Paul Mellon, I got together a team to film the impending Eclipse Stakes showdown between Mill Reef and Brigadier Gerard. Illness meant that the showdown never happened, but the film did – and the times spent at Ian Balding's yard at Kingsclere and at Mill Reef's birthplace at Rokeby, Virginia, are amongst the happiest I have ever had in all my time in racing.

For that reason alone it is through Mill Reef's ears that I will tell the tale.

MILL REEF

M ILL REEF was so small you could put your arm over his withers. He may have measured 15.2 hands, but he was so neatly put together that he seemed even less than that – until he moved. Then there was absolute assurance at every step: at the walk, the trot, the canter and on into the gallop. He was mesmerising.

His secret was perfect balance. This meant the flow of his stride was just as effective on firm ground as on soft. He broke track records in both the Eclipse and the Arc when the going was fast, and when it came up heavy at York for the Gimcrack and Longchamp for the Ganay he did his own version of 'Eclipse first, the rest nowhere.'

When he worked with a stablemate on sloppy sand in Chantilly you could hardly find his prints. No other horse was ever like this – certainly not Brigadier Gerard, who on soft ground really struggled to win his own Eclipse and his first Champion Stakes, although on good ground at Newmarket he ran out Mill Reef's clear superior in that famous 1971 Two Thousand Guineas, the only time they were actually to meet.

I first saw Mill Reef, at his Kingsclere home rather than on the racecourse, in January 1972. He was a little horse in the string with knee boots on for road work. A trainer would not dare risk him amid today's traffic, for at that moment he would have been the world's most valuable racing Thoroughbred. After the Guineas defeat he had carried off, consecutively, the Derby, Eclipse, King George and Arc de Triomphe. In each race, as he did in every one of his eleven career victories, he increased the distance between himself and the second horse in the final furlong. This was partly due to Geoff Lewis' natural, pushy, exuberance in the saddle, but it symbolised a wish to run which was central to Mill Reef's being.

With the great horses the legends swell, but with Mill Reef there is no need to elaborate. The one doubt when he first ran at Salisbury in May 1970 was that he might be as slow out of the stalls as he had been in practice. But he jumped out so fast that he led all the way and trounced the Piggott-ridden favourite. In the Coventry Stakes at Ascot he was so impressive that John Oaksey wrote at the time this was the most perfect two-year-old he had ever seen. That's what we thought of him: a complete, compact, ready-to-run, fast-ground two-year-old. If someone had said then that this was a future Arc winner and one of the unquestioned great middle-distance horses of all time, you would have thought they had been too long at the Pimms.

He looked like a little guy you had to get on with, and blow the consequences. And when he got short-headed by top two-year-old My Swallow in France after a terrible journey over and was then sent to run in the Gimcrack at York in ground that squelched, outsiders could think that Ian Balding was almost desperate to cash in on the colt's precocity. In fact Mill Reef only ran in the Gimcrack at Paul Mellon's insistence, and the sight of the supposed 'fast ground' flyer floating fifteen lengths clear of his field like a speedboat from a bunch of barges remains one of the most remarkable things ever seen on a British racetrack.

But the beauty of the story is that even then there were doubts – and indeed comparisons – to be overcome. Mill Reef wasn't the big story of 1970:

that honour was Nijinsky's. Mill Reef's Gimcrack may have been the most freakish thing of the season, but the most awesome, by some margin, was Nijinsky's majestic victory over 1969 Derby hero Blakeney and others in the King George at Ascot. Nijinsky was such box office because he was the latest and greatest from the O'Brien-Piggott team which only two years before had produced the marvel that was Sir Ivor.

What's more, Mill Reef was not even officially the best two-year-old of 1970. That was My Swallow – a fast, free-going chestnut who had gone unbeaten through the year. He represented the super-efficient David Robinson team. My Swallow had beaten Mill Reef, albeit in arguably favourable circumstances, and his whole aim was the Two Thousand Guineas. When both horses bolted up in their trial races you had to be made of stone not to think that this was a vintage Classic. And that is before you considered the also unbeaten Middle Park winner Brigadier Gerard, whom Dick Hern was bringing to Newmarket without a previous run that season.

Readers should rightly suspect rose-tinted glasses but I relate this through a deliberately harsher lens. Imagine the situation now. Imagine the excitement, almost consternation, when Mill Reef and My Swallow locked horns in the lead only for Brigadier Gerard to swoop past and beat the pair pointless. Imagine the impression on an ex-jock, would-be hack just two months after his final hospital trip. When it came to Guineas showdowns, I had seen the benchmark.

If you accept that, you then begin to see what a wonder the 1971 Flat racing season was to any observer, let alone a fresh-eyed scuffler like this one. Brigadier Gerard, a full-sized beau ideal of the English Thoroughbred, sailed on unbeaten. After the Guineas he won the St James's Palace and closed out in the Champion, but in between he took the Sussex Stakes by five lengths, the Goodwood Mile by ten and the Queen Elizabeth II by a mighty eight, breaking the track record into the bargain. Then and now horses didn't do that sort of thing. Then and now we were being given an inferiority complex by someone called O'Brien at Ballydoyle. Back in Britain here was one who could rout him. And 'The Brigadier' wasn't even the horse of the season.

Unfair though that may seem in view of his clear-cut win at Newmarket, Brigadier Gerard had to bow to Mill Reef in public esteem because his little rival went the braver route. Before the Derby there were acres of newsprint

Mill Reef first,
the rest nowhere:
the 1971 Eclipse.

debating whether Mill Reef's US pedigree, not to mention speedy precocity, would allow him to stay Epsom's mile and a half. Yet in race after race – a record-breaking Eclipse followed the Derby, a record breaking Arc came after a six-length King George – his white nosebanded head hit the front at the quarter mile pole and that zinging stride took him more and more decisively ahead.

Ah yes, that stride. I can see it still. It had a bite as well as a flow about it which brought both leverage and speed. As the Arc field swung into the straight there was a moment when Mill Reef's white noseband was lost behind the tightly packed leaders. Only one British-trained horse had ever won the Arc and that was back in 1948. Was this one race too far? Then, like a ray of sunshine from the gloom, the little horse was through and winging home three lengths clear of the pursuing Pistol Packer.

For Flat racing fans 1971-72 was the ultimate winter of dreams. Both Mill Reef and Brigadier Gerard were staying in training, and both sets of connections were committed to a showdown in the Eclipse Stakes at Sandown in July. With the ignorant bravado of youth, and with unbelievable support from Mill Reef's trainer Ian Balding, who had adored the film *The Year of Sir Ivor,* I re-linked Hugh McIlvanney and Kit Owens, respectively the writer and director of that epic, got the film rights of the Sandown showdown, persuaded racing lover Albert Finney to do the narration, and then, on Ian's prompting, rang Paul Mellon to ask if I could pop over and see him in Virginia.

'When would you next be in America?' enquired Paul Mellon's kind and steady voice on the phone.

'Well, I am probably going to be over in Washington between Tuesday and Friday next week,' I blagged, despite never before having travelled west of Limerick Junction.

'Good,' he said calmly, undeceived by the deception, ' I could do Wednesday. We will book you into Browns. Come to the Bank at noon and we will go to the farm for lunch.'

Elation at the invitation was soon overtaken by extreme nervousness at the utter inadequacy of my qualifications. I had never made a film in my life. I had only been writing for five minutes. I was just a broken-down jock who liked Mill Reef and was a bit of a mate of Ian Balding's. But 'nothing ventured' – and the next Wednesday I stood at the reception of the Mellon bank in Washington and a few minutes later this shy, kind, avuncular figure led me down the steps to the waiting car. 'We should be back at the farm all right for lunch,' he said, and since it was 12 noon and his stud at Rokeby, Virginia was some 200 miles away this seemed an unlikely promise. But the road that led to the Mill Reef film was wonders all the way.

We crossed over the Potomac river in cold and watery sunshine and turned left, the Arlington Cemetery with its Presidents' graves away to the right. We then swung left again towards the crowded, midday bedlam of the airport, got out of the car and walked straight through without anyone noticing. There were no heavy duty Pinkertons, no dark-glassed bodyguards, just the well planned discretion of class and old money. And then we climbed into the Lear Jet. No kidding, there was a 'Blue Period' Picasso hanging by the window.

That was Paul Mellon – wanting the very best but never shouting about it. At Rokeby, the Stubbs painting of Pumpkin, the first picture he ever bought, was in the hall and among the canvases in the dining room were at least three that every schoolchild knows: a Brueghel skating scene, a Van Gogh sunflower, a Sisley beach.

And that was long before we got to The Brick House.

It was a three-storey, nineteenth-century, red brick building set in the centre of the stud. Inside was a treasure trove: the world's greatest collection of English sporting art, topped up with scenes of Longchamp by Degas and, gorgeously, a set of little Degas ballet dancers in bronze and in wax maquette. Through the windows you could see Mill Reef's relatives cantering across the paddock. It screamed for a camera to show others what our eyes had seen.

Which is what we did. The result, thanks to Hugh and Kit, has more than stood the test of time, even if it is sometimes overindulgent with the surroundings and with lingering looks across the paintings. Its climax was not the much vaunted but never fulfilled head-to-head with Brigadier Gerard, although printing schedules of that era meant that a 2,000-word piece I wrote for the *Sunday Times* colour magazine appeared large and loud in the edition before the Eclipse, even though a virus-ridden Mill Reef was already a declared non-runner.

Instead the film made a marvellous virtue out of necessity as it lyrically passed from Mill Reef at his best to an eery unconscious shape on the operating table, to a hero in a plaster cast limping towards his recovery at Kingsclere.

As an introduction to the top end of Flat racing and of the media, it was an experience beyond compare. Yet of all the memories stretching from that Rokeby lunch to long exasperating editing days in a cutting room in Soho's Greek Street once enlivened when two sets of firemen battled at the top of their respective ladders to gain entry into a top-floor window of the 'Cat Shop' opposite, nothing beats Mill Reef's victory in the Prix Ganay in the spring of 1972.

For everything depended on it. Inexperienced or not, I knew perfectly well that plenty of Classic winners, especially those who had been pretty busy at two, did not train on as four-year-olds. If this film was to have any substance, Mill Reef had to show on the track what I had promised in conversation. And knowing that converted TV footage of his three-year-old exploits was both sub-standard and expensive, Kit Owens was taking a whole studio's worth of cameras to Longchamp to pick up every movement of our hero in action.

I booked 22 people into the Hotel du Chateau at Chantilly. (It closed soon after. Wonder why?) A large bus came to ferry us to the Bois de Boulogne, where we set up lenses at every corner and I began to pray. We needed sunshine for our pictures and something extraordinary for our story. Anything less and I was struggling. Actual defeat and the whole project, the whole act of faith granted by everyone from Paul Mellon to Pip, the muscleman lugging the boxes, would be shattered, and I would have to crawl away to somewhere like New Zealand and try and scrape a living as an exercise boy.

It was a showery day but the sun came out. It was not always easy to see, even from high in the stands, but as the field straightened up, even a blind man would have noticed. I was positioned up behind a bearded, hollow-cheeked pirate of a cameraman who was the world's greatest expert on the super-long lens. He was a newly converted, Zen-studying vegetarian who appeared extremely sceptical of all my hype about Mill Reef.

But now right in his lens, right in my binoculars, were the black and gold Mellon silks, the singing hooves, the zinging stride, the bobbing noseband – and Mill Reef not just in front but drawing further and further and further away. It got better and better. Everything now was possible. In an experience I never remember before or since, the hair quite literally stood up on the back of my neck. In front of me the long lens fairly glowed in admiring concentration. 'F***ing hell,' the pirate said.

Naturally the very personal nature of these recollections also demands a more sceptical analysis when it comes to placing Mill Reef and the others in the panoply of champions. For while it's true that Mill Reef was the breakthrough in post-war British winners of the Arc – and there have been only five more since – it's also true that he, and indeed Brigadier Gerard, Sir Ivor and Nijinsky would be found well short of today's top performers on the clock. Mill Reef's Arc record of 2 minutes 28.3 seconds for the mile and a half (2,400 metres) had two full seconds taken out of it by Trempolino in 1987, and ten years later Peintre Celebre lowered it to 2 minutes 24.6, which at five lengths a second means that he would have had 3.7 seconds, or some eighteen lengths, between him and Mill Reef at the finishing pole.

When analysing this, it's worth remembering that Roger Bannister's history making sub-4 minute mile in 1954 was clocked at 3 minutes 59.4, which by 1980 Seb Coe had reduced to 3 minutes 47.33, and the record at the time of writing these words in September 2008, set by the immortal Hicham El Guerrouj in 1999, stands at 3 minutes 43.13. That means that El Guerrouj would be hitting the line as gallant old Sir Roger was entering the straight, making Mill Reef and Peintre Celebre almost close by comparison. But just as no one is suggesting that Bannister was anything but a great athlete trained in very different times, the least we should say about Mill Reef and the other great ones is that they were further ahead of their contemporaries than anything will ever be in today's more intensively competitive era.

This book is but a solo witness, and all I want to log is that while one or two other moments have nearly equalled it – especially when Motivator began to draw clear at Epsom in 2005, as will be described later – nothing for me ever bettered the sensation of Mill Reef sluicing up in the Ganay. In our film Hugh McIlvanney signed off with characteristic brilliance. 'That Mill Reef,' he had Albert Finney say, 'he gave us something.'

In the spring of 1973 I was up to my eyeballs trying to finish production of the Mill Reef film, which we called Something to Brighten the Morning. *Little did I realise that in the jumping game I was about to be a first-hand witness to one of the greatest races ever run.*

On the eve of that year's Grand National I fell into step with Tommy Stack and Ron Barry, who had both ridden Red Rum, the super-progressive seven-year-old who was all the rage for the big race next day. Indeed, as related below, Tommy had actually trained the horse during the brief spell when, as stable jockey, he had taken over the licence on the death of his employer Bobby Renton.

There was no cattiness about it, but neither of them thought – and I recall the phrase – that Red Rum would be 'man enough' for Aintree. As an example of the age-old adage that 'jockeys are the world's worst tipsters', this ranks pretty high.

Some time back I was asked to describe the most exciting race I had ever seen. There was not a lot of time wasted in making the decision. For Red Rum triumphed but only at the expense of a super-hero called Crisp.

CRISP

RED RUM and Crisp's battle in 1973 was the greatest and most agonising National of them all. It was the moment when Red Rum began his career as the ultimate Aintree hero, but on the day the first emotion was to mourn the impossibly heroic Crisp in defeat.

Crisp was conceding 23 pounds, over a stone and a half, to Red Rum, who himself was to carry top weight to those unmatched two victories and two seconds over the next four years. But forget mathematics, the huge Australian was trying to do it the only way he knew how, to blitz his opponents from the front. That might be fine over two miles, and Crisp was a Champion Chase winner at Cheltenham: but how could he possibly last over Aintree's four and a half?

The die was cast at the third fence. Meeting it on a perfect stride, Crisp soared out and clear, and for the remaining 27 obstacles he and Richard Pitman never saw another horse. What happened for the next seven minutes would all but blow the mind and break the heart. Crisp treated the legendary Aintree fences with a disdain never seen before or since. On and on he sailed, a distant black shape a hundred, two hundred yards clear, the 37 other runners just specks in his wake. He had run them absolutely ragged but, as he came up towards the grandstand he had already completed two and a quarter miles. For him that should be race over. Now a whole extra circuit lay ahead.

Crisp at second Becher's.

That's when the enormity of Richard Pitman's problem began to grip the throat. Richard had been one of my best friends in the weighing room. We had travelled together, sweated together, been stretchered off together. Now he was having the most brilliant ride ever seen at Aintree. But he was a passenger on a champion going at two mile pace. Come the finish, win or lose, he was going to be on a horse emptied of every drop of juice.

Tommy Stack was standing beside me. Four years later he would share Red Rum's epic fifth and final National. Now he was an injured, awe-inspired spectator, but one also riddled with doubts. 'Jesus,' he said as we watched Crisp and Richard blazing away towards Becher's on the second circuit, 'there's no way he can keep up that pace for so long.'

But he did, he did – skipping round the Canal Turn, pinging Valentine's, rocking on relentlessly all the way to the Melling Road. The pursuers were all so distant that the only thought was to just how bad Crisp must be feeling inside. He must have built up the biggest oxygen debt in racing history. But there was still no outward sign. Perhaps, just this once, the impossible would happen. But then, at the second last, still a good furlong clear, it showed.

It wasn't much of a mistake. Just a moment of awkwardness, but there was no doubting the split second of stagger as exhaustion clutched.

Crisp and Richard were still clear and galloping relentlessly towards the last. But you knew the tanks were flashing empty. It was a long haul home.

The eyes went back to the pursuers. Leading the pack was a white-nosebanded bay trained on the sands at nearby Southport by a second-hand car dealer called 'Ginger' McCain. Red Rum had been both trained and ridden by Tommy Stack in an earlier life. On National eve, Tommy had told me that for all Red Rum's sizzling five-win streak since joining 'Ginger', he thought his old partner, whose first visit to Aintree had been dead-heating for a two-year-old seller under Paul Cook the day before the Foinavon National in 1967, would be 'too clever' for Liverpool's demands.

On Red Rum, 25-year-old Brian Fletcher already knew different. Red Rum's cunning, his ability to look for landing space whilst still in mid-air, was to make him the most successful Aintree jumper in history. Crisp might be more than a distance clear, but Red Rum always saved something. And Brian – implacable, sometimes contrary Brian – he never gave up hope.

Over the last and on towards us up that pitiless dog-legged 494-yard run-in, Crisp still had a full hundred yards of advantage. He was still galloping, Richard was still pumping. If they could just keep pushing, the huge black car that was Crisp would roll on over the line.

But we knew it was desperate. We shouted for Richard and the voice beside me shouted loudest of all. Jenny Pitman was always a frustrated spectator, and watching her husband's chance of ultimate glory brought extra, even to her fog-shattering voice.

'Riiiichard! Riiiichard!', she screamed. Was that the tipping edge? Down on the run-in Richard, *in extremis*, pulled out his whip in his right hand, cracked Crisp hard on the quarters, and in one fatal moment the game was gone.

Crisp rolled left away from the whip and – much, much worse – away from the right-handed line of the run-in which skirts the Chair fence. Richard pulled him back on to course but now all pretext of momentum drained away. They got to the final railed 100 yards before the finish, but this was much more rocking horse than racer. It was terrible to watch. Fifty yards out and they were still clear but Red Rum was swooping. The dream had become a nightmare. It died only in the very shadow of the post.

It was a race like no other. History made it even grander, with Red Rum and Ginger McCain returning the National to its status as British sport's number one event. Yet the postscript always has to be the sight of that huge sweat-flecked black Australian staggering, hocks buckling, into the second enclosure in 1973. Red Rum became a legend, but it was Crisp's immortality in defeat that made this the greatest day of all.

Poor Crisp. Australia's best ever steeplechaser, star of the Champion Chase at Cheltenham, the tall and mighty 'Black Kangaroo', just about as good a horse as we will ever see, and yet always to be remembered as the weary giant that Red Rum slew in those final fateful Aintree yards back in 1973.

It was both understandable and correct that the first instinct that year was sympathy for Crisp's heroics in defeat. Indeed if that had been Red Rum's only National, he and Ginger McCain would have been a good 'Rags to Riches' story and little more. But the world now knows that this was only the beginning of the most famous and unrepeatable chapter in the Aintree story.

The mere facts of what he did are extraordinary enough. Romping home under twelve stone in 1974, running gallant top-weighted seconds to the Gold Cup winner L'Escargot in 1975 and then to the massive Rag Trade in 1976 before signing off with that record third victory in 1977: simply listing them seems fairly unbelievable, but what made the story unique not just in this sport but in life itself was exactly where all this came from.

In July 2008 I was covering the Open Golf at Birkdale, a place known to the general public as a slightly genteel suburb of Southport whose seaside links have witnessed glory deeds as the world's greatest golfers battle for the claret jug. The thousands who had flocked to see Padraig Harrington finally break Greg Norman's attempt to roll back the years would have long forgotten, or never known, that Birkdale was also the home of Red Rum.

It still seemed scarcely credible. Did he really come out of those scruffy back streets and go through the town and the traffic to use the sands for gallops? Was Ginger McCain really an Aintree-obsessed second-hand car salesman who had once driven the Southport zoo keeper to London with a large lion in the back seat? (It scratched the seats a bit.) Was Red Rum really in the yard behind the flat behind the showroom?

Thirty years on, my feet bent again down the Aughton Road. McCain's Car Sales is still there. The vehicles are better – a gleaming white Mercedes ('only 23,000 miles') stood on the forecourt – but the yard at the back was a weed-overgrown symbol of disuse. Some time, presumably, planning permission will be granted and even this trace will disappear. Maybe somebody will put up a blue plaque, as they do to proclaim that 'Great Men Lived Here.' But we just have to hang on to the memories, and I hope you will come back with me to something I wrote in November 1975. For it was probably the greatest of all the early riding mornings I have ever had.

RED RUM

IT WAS like suddenly finding yourself in bed with a film star. Would she be as fantastic as you imagined? And would you match up to her the way you had in your dreams? The salty rain-swept emptiness of Southport sands at 8.15 last Wednesday morning was a pretty odd place for an assignation with a star, but in racing terms the rest of the comparison was accurate. For I was riding Red Rum.

Red Rum? Yes, the Red Rum, winner of the 1973 and 1974 Grand Nationals, all in all the most charismatic National Hunt horse since Arkle. Yet here he was cantering beneath me, and about a hundred miles of sand ahead for us.

The first feel of Red Rum is a little disappointing. He seems a shade narrow and lightweight, much more ex-Flat racehorse than big strong 'chaser. But then ex-Flat racehorse is exactly what he is, having started out eight seasons ago with a selling-race dead heat at that same Liverpool track he has since taken by storm.

It was old pros' weather on Wednesday morning. Solid Lancashire rain only eased to a threatening drizzle as we left the little yard at the back of McCain's Car Sales, out onto the Aughton Road and through the streets of the Birkdale part of Southport until we finally came to the beach with its warning notice: 'Drivers beware of soft sand.'

You can't imagine a style of exercising racehorses further removed from the traditional Indian-file-up-the-lane-to-the-Downs style. Horses walking in a cluster, Red Rum in front, with his lad Billy Ellison beside us on the big, white-faced Glenkiln, past the pet centre and the Chinese fish and chip shop, over the level crossing and the main road. It certainly works for Red Rum. And in trying to explain it, I remembered another time when, hoisted on well-lubricated words from the night before, I accompanied another champion in training. That was with boxer Chris Finnegan, running round the early morning streets of Clerkenwell. When I eventually gasped back to his door, he told me that he enjoyed the bustle and greeting of the town, and I don't think it all fanciful to say that this equine hero feels the same. So we were safely onto the beach, and after the briefest of instructions were cantering in pairs southwards along 'the gallop', a newly harrowed stretch of sand between seaweed and waves.

At first, the impression of ex-Flat horse remained. 'I'm not sure that I would feel that confident going to Becher's on this' was the way I put it to myself. But then, as the sands swept by, there came a feeling of relentless power about the stride. We seemed to have been cantering for about five miles, and although I hadn't ridden for a few months, I thought I was showing plenty of the old magic. ('What magic?' asked an unkind friend with an all-too-clear memory of my brief career in the saddle.) 'Do we pull up now?', I called across to Billy Ellison. 'Oh no,' came the reply, 'we've got a long way to go yet.'

Suddenly there was a threat of disaster. Alone with a film star, I was going to ruin everything by being sick. Then of all things, on this beach a hundred miles from nowhere there was a hoot on a car horn, and right beside us was Ginger McCain. 'He means us to go a bit quicker,' shouted Billy.

This wasn't going to be funny, for you know that as you release the brake a little the load becomes greater. Far from a beaten-up ex-Flat horse, the length and power of Red Rum's stride made me feel that he might win next year's National pulling a cart, let alone an unfit and panicky journalist. One more notch and we would have gone.

But then an angel in the unlikely form of Billy Ellison saved us.

'Whoa up! That's it!', he called. Red Rum eased, knowing where he was all the time, and in a couple of minutes we were across the sand and into the sea.

Yes, into the sea! All McCain's horses go into the sea, and Red Rum, who had previously suffered from the usually incurable foot disease of pedalostitis, owes much of his dramatic improvement to his regular exercise in sea and on sand. 'He hates trotting on the road, you know,' said Billy. 'When he works he likes to get another horse ahead of him so that he can sort of get it in his sights and then come and do it at the finish. Watch him going home. He always likes to buck opposite the convent.' He did, and plenty more, and having spent one and a half fantasy-come-true hours on Red Rum's back, it is my pleasure to report that his spirit is burning strong.

The openness of Ginger and Beryl McCain cannot be overestimated. They were rightly proud of 'Red' and all that they had done. Everyone was welcome. I even rode him again for ITN, and started the report with the slightly obvious but enjoyable-to-deliver line, 'This must be the ultimate case of "sitting on a story".' At a time when the Grand National was trying to recover from appalling mismanagement, what they did for the future of – don't anyone question it – the 'World's Greatest Race' was a service beyond price.

As were the extraordinary qualities of the animal around which all this revolved. Red Rum lived on to October 1995 and is now, appropriately, buried next to the Aintree winning post. Over the years he became the ultimate in celebrity quadrupeds, opening everything from county shows to betting shops, almost as familiar with the red carpet as the stable yard and, in Ginger's immortal words, 'never once disgracing himself.'

There has never been anything like him, and I don't think we can better the final three words of the report I wrote on that un-foolish first day of April when Tommy Stack brought Red Rum home to final glory in 1977.

We pick the story up as the 15-2 favourite Andy Pandy leads the field towards Becher's Brook on the second circuit. This is a staccato story dictated in a hurry from a house outside the racecourse, as in those days Aintree didn't 'do' telephones. Yet it takes us there ...

Then Becher's once again justified its reputation, taking out first the leader, then Nereo, Brown Admiral and Sandwilan. Who else to take the lead now but Red Rum himself? But immediately a hideous repetition of the Foinavon fiasco loomed as he was hampered by the loose horses at the 23rd.

He was too wily for that, and even though pestered by another loose horse at the Canal Turn he gave Tommy Stack a corner of which James Hunt [then Formula 1 world champion] would have been proud, and suddenly with only six fences left to jump Red Rum was in charge, and a great cry went up as everyone scanned back for dangers.

For a dizzy quarter mile he seemed to be going better than his few pursuers. But then as they came to the third last it was obvious that Churchtown Boy, who had won the Topham Trophy over the same fences only on Thursday, was going with deadly ease. His rider Martin Blackshaw told me afterwards: 'I was really motoring at the time but then I never really jumped the last three.' Up in front Tommy Stack had looked round once, but when he heard the crash of Churchtown Boy hitting the second last he was certain that his only dangers were the loose horses or some terrible repeat of the Devon Loch disaster on the run-in.

From the stands it didn't look so easy, and it was almost too hard to bear as Red Rum safely jumped the last and stormed up the run-in to his place back between the police horses and forever into steeplechasing history.

It was only afterwards that Tommy Stack's complete professionalism began to break. He had us all close to tears as he paid tribute to this incredible four-legged hero. 'You know,' he said, 'he really loves it out there; he looks at each fence as he jumps it, and then looks for the next. On another course he doesn't really bother, but here he knows that he is the king.'

For Ginger McCain, to whom so many people have been free with their 'retire Red Rum' advice, we can't give anything more than complete praise and gratitude for turning out the winner in such marvellous condition.

As the overjoyed trainer ran out to greet Red Rum, he gripped me breathlessly by the arm and just muttered those three words which were echoed fifteen minutes later when the broad blue-tattooed arms of head lad Taffy Williams were scraping the sweat from Red Rum's gleaming but not heaving flanks. Those words were said with a sigh and a wondering shake of the head. They were, quite simply: 'What a horse!'

Any journalist covering any territory needs significant players to help launch a career. It is no false modesty to say that the gods were generous to me. The blazing duo of Mill Reef and Brigadier Gerard were followed by the long-running

Red Rum saga, and in between, in 1975, the flaxen mane and tail of Grundy streaked like a Derby winning comet across the summer.

I wrote reams about him, his trainer Peter Walwyn, his jockey Pat Eddery, work rider Mattie McCormack and head lad Ray Laing. How he had established himself as a star when winning the Dewhurst in 1974. How his future looked compromised when he had the front of his head kicked in by an unruly stable companion next spring. How in the Two Thousand Guineas he still managed to be second to the Henry Cecil-trained Bolkonski, ridden by Gianfranco Dettori, Frankie's father. How he then carried all before him before blowing out in the Benson and Hedges Gold Cup – now the International – at York and having an unprosperous stud career which ended in Japan.

But all that does not matter compared with the one heady day at Ascot in July. Like the piece about riding out at Southport on Red Rum, this has been included in a previous collection. But I make no apology. At the time every instinct told me I was witness to something exceptional. Let's take the writing from the time.

GRUNDY and BUSTINO

G RUNDY'S half-length defeat of Bustino in the King George VI and Queen Elizabeth Diamond Stakes at Ascot was much more than a seal to his greatness. It was the hardest, most implacable, most moving Flat race that I have ever seen.

Bustino's tactics were predictable, but his courage and strength were almost unfathomable. Led by his two pacemakers, first Highest and then Kinglet, Bustino was never further back than fourth and went to the front four furlongs out. The pace was so strong that the field was stretched at this stage and Grundy had already been pushed up close to last year's St Leger winner, and Lester Piggott on Dahlia was also moving through to be a danger. Sweeping into the straight, Bustino and Joe Mercer set for home with a furious determination, and very soon it was obvious that only Grundy, still two lengths adrift, could prevent them taking the £81,910 first prize.

Going to the two-furlong post it was also obvious that it would be no twinkle-toed, flaxen-tailed acceleration that would take Grundy past the outstretched leader, but only grit, power and sheer slogging guts.

Behind them Dahlia was running her best race of the season, but the only question that mattered to the huge crowd was whether the Derby winner could close and beat his year-older opponent. With the whips out, they came to the final furlong just about level, and from high in the stand one had the feel that the older horse's slogging stamina might be too much. But then well inside the final furlong it was Bustino who began to weaken, rolling away from the fence as tired horses do and actually, for a moment, touching Grundy. It wasn't much, but it was the chink in the armour and, with Pat Eddery pressing Grundy like a man possessed, the bonny chestnut battled home to the line amid a crescendo of sound topped, of course, by trainer Peter Walwyn's frantically bellowed, 'Come on my son!'

Dahlia ran on to be five lengths away third, with the two other French challengers, On My Way and Card King, fourth and fifth. All these covered themselves in glory, but they were only supporting cast compared with the two stars. The mile and a half was covered in a quite astonishing time. Grundy finally clocked 2 minutes 26.98 seconds, which is no less than 2.46 seconds within the course record and 3.45 seconds faster than Dahlia's 2 minutes 30.43 seconds in 1973, which is the fastest electrically-recorded time for this race.

Grundy's winnings now pass Mill Reef's previous record total of £312,122. Coming down in the lift to the unsaddling enclosure, trainer Walwyn mopped his brow and said simply, 'They can't take it away from him now.' As he loped past the crush of well-wishers, he understandably didn't want to be drawn on future plans. 'Who cares about the future after that?' he said. Grundy's Milanese owner, Dr Carlo Vittadini, looked similarly blissful and merely said that he favoured his colt bowing out in the Champion Stakes in October. Dr Vittadini added: 'This was a bigger thrill than when Grundy won the Derby or the Irish Derby. He was meeting the best horses in Europe and did it splendidly. There has been common talk that my colt had not beaten much in the Classics, but he's proved that wrong today.'

Among the crush in the unsaddling enclosure, no pair looked more pleased than Sir Desmond Plummer, chairman of the Levy Board, and Douglas Gray, retiring director of the National Stud, who, of course, were party to Grundy's purchase by the National Stud at a value of only £1 million. The word 'only' is used advisedly, as Grundy would now be conservatively assessed at £2½ million.

Walwyn and Eddery pocketed their exotic trophies from the De Beers Corporation, who put up £44,000 towards this race, and trainer and jockey continued their incredible form by winning the next race with Inchmarlo. This completed the most unbelievable fairy story of a day for Walwyn, for he had also taken the first race with Hard Day, ridden by no less a 'cavaliere' than Dr Vittadini's lovely daughter, Franca.

As the horses were led away to be washed down after the big race, the buzz was as much of wonderment as of congratulation. Wonder at the way Grundy's record-breaking speed was so flawlessly complemented by his own and his rider's determination. And, perhaps almost equally, at the magnificence of Bustino in defeat.

When Joe Mercer humped his saddle and weight cloth towards the scales, he said to me: 'It was fantastic. It is the greatest race he has ever run.' Like his two pacemakers, Bustino is owned by Lady Beaverbrook, whose racing manager Sir Gordon Richards was rapt in admiration for the big bay colt.

'It was as good a race as I have ever seen,' he said. 'I wouldn't make any excuses because Grundy is a great horse, but our fellow had to go on half a mile out and, if we had only had something else to tow him just that little bit further, it might have been even closer. But he has broken the track record at Epsom and now they have broken it here, so everyone can see he is a great horse. He will just have one more race, and then the Arc de Triomphe.'

After that Bustino will retire to the Royal Stud at the same time as Grundy takes up his new duties at Newmarket. They are both the most tremendous assets for British bloodstock, bred as they are completely without the often considered essential trans-Atlantic influence.

British racing has many problems, but the riding and the courage and the ability shown by the two heroes in yesterday's race will be something that it can be proud of for as long as man and horse combine.

History agrees that it was the most implacable race of all. Bustino was never able to race again and, although Grundy seemed to have recovered his health and enthusiasm at home, when he did run in the Benson and Hedges at York three weeks later, all his flaxen sparkle was missing, and we never saw him afterwards on a racetrack.

A very hard race does that to a horse. For it is very rare that a combination of the pace of the gallop, the continuing possibility of victory and, above all, the courage of the horse combine into your equine partner giving you absolutely everything. When they do, you know it, and first instincts are best.

In November 1968 I rode a tough, lean, light-coloured chestnut called Oberon in the big Mackeson Hurdle at what is now Cheltenham's Open Meeting. From the third last he was always in the firing line, never quite going to win but absolutely refusing to give up. I drove him all the way and all the way he answered me. When he walked back I could feel him utterly spent and on unsaddling said that he would need a long rest to get over it. He ran three weeks later. He didn't do any good. Seven years later as Grundy walked back into the Ascot winner's enclosure, I recognized that wobble of exhaustion. He too had given his all.

It is about courage. My grandfather, for all his 'How I won the war' hosannas, was never lacking in that area. He said with perceptive authority that in his experience even the bravest man has only a certain reservoir of courage and one day, if you overface him, it will dry up.

It is the same with horses, and the fact is that plenty of them do not actually have the stomach for the fight. Most people access horse racing by TV or at best from the stands and the paddock. Consequently most people miss how hard and tough it is up close. Half a ton of horseflesh is straining heart and lung and sinew, and in jump racing is throwing itself over an obstacle every furlong or so.

That's why the horses that jockeys remember most fondly are those that come up for more. That's why all of us, and so many watchers, will never forget the greatest hurdling era of them all.

HURDLERS – THE GOLDEN AGE

HURDLING is sometimes seen as a lesser sport for failed Flat racers, or for horses without the guts to jump fences. I won't buy that, having been brought up with early TV memories of Sir Ken putting his head down in 1952 and battling through to win the first of his three Champion Hurdles and then being around for what was unquestionably the Golden Age of the hurdling game. It ran from 1968 to 1981 and consisted of Persian War's three consecutive Champion Hurdles and then two each for Bula, Comedy Of Errors, Night Nurse, Monksfield and Sea Pigeon, with only the ill-fated Lanzarote in between.

To ride a good hurdler is a thrilling thing. Meeting an obstacle right may not be as important, but the strategy of a race is. It certainly was in the most satisfying victory of what I will laughingly describe as my whole career. This was on the high-class Flat horse but two-run novice hurdler Persian Empire in the ultra-competitive handicap that was the 1968 Imperial Cup. We were sure we had the pace to win provided he relaxed and hurdled properly. I was only two days back from a broken right arm which was still in a plastic cast. I anchored Persian Empire out the back, and as he cut through the field in the Sandown straight the feeling of mounting, slide-the-knife-home satisfaction lives with me still. We all have our moments.

Four days later I was not far off an even better one. In what was to be the first of Persian War's three Champion Hurdles, I was hurtling down the outside on the 25-1 shot Black Justice, only for his ungainly jumping to let him down, and then only a fantastic effort got him back up again to snatch third place near the line. It was the race of his life. But he had nearly fallen at the first and was very awkward at at least three others. What would have happened if he had really jumped?

Strangely enough, Persian War was not in the accepted sense a good jumper, any more, for that matter, than he was a classy horse on the Flat. I say that as one of his greatest admirers for he, like Persian Empire, was trained by Colin Davies at Chepstow, and when he went over to run in the French Champion Hurdle I rode him every day in Chantilly. He was big enough but there was absolutely no swagger about him. He was just a kind, tough, honest soul who would run his heart out for you. He did not have any spring-heeled jumping technique. He just set off at a gallop that would hurt and rumbled across the hurdles as fast as he could. He had power and my – what guts.

His training had something of the 'shaggy dog' story about it. Colin and Jimmy Uttley, his long-term jockey, were convinced that Persian War needed masses of work, and as the old horse stood the routine the accepted wisdom assumed that this was necessary. I was never persuaded of this, and since Colin and Jimmy won three Champion Hurdles with the horse the jury is likely to give them first hearing. Maybe, but what I had to do with Persian War five days before La Grande Course des Haies still amazes.

Giving more than a stone to two decent French handicappers, we went a good gallop for a full mile and three quarters round the outside of Les Aigles. Persian War was off the bridle after seven furlongs, and under instruction I pushed and shoved him relentlessly – and all the way he strived and answered. At the end he nearly had the other two in trouble, but local trainer Henry Van der Poele shook his head in that Gallic way which says, '*Ils sont fous, les Anglais.*' In La Grande Course, Persian War ran a blinder to be third, up there all the way, only to be outspeeded in the straight. But to this day I believe it was despite rather than because of that final gallop. There have been plenty swifter horses than Persian War and many better jumpers, but I never sat on a braver one.

Looking back at the equine stars that followed him brings a warm glow to the memory. First Bula, the almost donkey-eared brown gelding whose first run was in a race I rode in at Lingfield, where Stan Mellor was issued with the unpromising instructions, 'Hunt him round, we think he's probably useless.' Stan did as instructed until they reached the straight, when the penny suddenly dropped and Bula sprinted up at 25-1.

Bula, so laid back in everything else, then became so quick into and out of a hurdle that Fred Winter had him ridden out the back to make sure he didn't switch off too soon. For stable jockey Paul Kelleway these were tactics which needed no second telling. Poor old Bula got set more and more impossible tasks, sometimes practically half a furlong behind turning down the hill at Cheltenham, and as likely as not still getting there. Another case of 'despite of' rather than 'because of'?

Comedy Of Errors was the biggest and most handsome of this list of heroes. He was a huge black horse on whom Bill Smith looked almost like 'a pea on a drum' when Comedy won his first Champion in 1973, and the big guy might have won three in a row if Richard Pitman had not taken Fred Winter's attacking plan for Lanzarote to his own extreme. 'We had a pacemaker called

Calzado which was supposed to go like hell and tow me to the top of the hill,' remembers Richard. 'But he led to the first and then gave up. I thought I had better push on myself. I think we stole it really but I suppose I would have been butchered if we had got beat.'

Lanzarote was black like Comedy Of Errors, had a kind white-starred face, and suffered from corns, poor dear. He had been so backward on the Flat that his only win in eleven attempts was in a modest heat at Edinburgh. Yet by the

Monksfield (left) and Sea Pigeon at the last flight of the 1979 Champion Hurdle.

time he finally matured as a hurdler he had real pace and class about him, although his jumping technique could lead to some frightful howlers.

When put to fences in the 1976-77 season he showed such promise that he ran in the Gold Cup, only to take a fatal fall coming down the hill. Beforehand John Francome had called him 'the best horse I have ridden.' There were tears aplenty in Lambourn.

Night Nurse was the best jumper of the lot, but also the ugliest. He was a tall, upright sort of horse with a long plain face and big ears out the side. He was ridden brilliantly by the redoubtable, huntsman-like drive of Paddy Broderick, whose best friends, of whom I was one, would never accuse of being remotely stylish. As a Flat horse just about the best thing about Night Nurse was his mother's name. She was by Above Suspicion out of a mare called Panacea, and she was called Florence Nightingale. But when it came to hurdles Night Nurse had wings on his heels. 'He was,' remembers Paddy, 'the best actual jumper I ever sat on.'

Night Nurse did what you always want a hurdler to do: he gained ground and breath in the air. It meant that Paddy could really attack the obstacles, and the pair of them in full flight became as uplifting for those who backed them as it was daunting for those against them on the track. One of those backers was Barney Curley. In 1976 Paddy and I flew over to stay with him before Night Nurse's assault on the Irish Sweeps Hurdle, on which, presumably, Barney was investing heavily. Horse and rider took the locals apart, and to this day on seeing me Paddy always echoes Barney's watchword for that weekend, 'Let there be no panic.'

The beauty of this hurdling period was the way the continuing series of battles saw the torch of the championship handed on from one to the other, and the contests between Night Nurse, Monksfield and Night Nurse's stable companion Sea Pigeon have never been bettered in their sphere. In 1977 Night Nurse and Monksfield even ran a dead heat in the race before Red

Rum's third Grand National, and then in 1978 little Monksfield and Mick Kinane's father Tommy nailed 'Brod' and the champion to take the crown with Sea Pigeon finally taking second. In 1979 Sea Pigeon and Jonjo O'Neill came to the last apparently cruising, only to get outbattled by Monksfield, who was this time ridden by Richard Hughes's father Dessie. It was not until 1980 that Sea Pigeon finally clicked and left Monksfield trailing in his wake.

Of all these Sea Pigeon was much the best as a Flat horse – the idea of Persian War or Night Nurse finishing seventh in the Derby, let alone winning two Chester Cups and the Ebor as Sea Pigeon did, is only in their dreams, even if the thought of 'Brod' rowing away like a policeman on the Knavesmire is a grand one. But over hurdles Sea Pigeon needed to switch off properly, and he never looked more impressive than when John Francome applied his fabled safebreaker's nerve to proceedings in the 1981 Champion and Sea Pigeon coasted up the run-in to pick off poor Philip Blacker and Pollardstown as if he had won the wretched Derby, not finished seventh in it behind Morston in his Classic year of 1973.

What an achievement it was for Peter Easterby and his team to keep two such very different horses on the go – and fittingly both of them are now buried at Great Habton, Night Nurse dying in 1998 and Sea Pigeon two years later. But of all of the great ones of that golden hurdling era, none could beat the story that was Monksfield.

In his whole being and those of his connections, he symbolised the little guy with the biggest heart.

Monksfield was not much bigger than Mill Reef, and was also never castrated, although his subsequent stallion life was not as blue-blooded in the female department as the star of Britain's National Stud. This meant that Monksfield, with his bright bay coat, sharp white star on the forehead and absurdly swinging foreleg at the trot and canter had an extra perkiness about him. Mind you, so did his trainer.

Des McDonogh (father, in the dynastic way of things, of Irish Flat race ace Declan McDonogh) was in his early thirties then. He had bought Monksfield for just 720 guineas. He had himself built the little colt's box up at his small, white-washed yard twenty miles south of the border at Moynalty, County Meath, notwithstanding the minor difficulty that at the time of construction he was himself encased in plaster. With those heavy-lidded eyes and quick fox's face, Dessie had always been original. He had once played the lead in Charley's Aunt.

For four consecutive years he sent out Monksfield to tread the Cheltenham stage. Each time you could not believe that this tiny little entire with that quite ridiculous dishing foreleg could handle the mighty Night Nurses and Sea Pigeons when the whips were up and the money was down. But again and again, the engine, the athleticism and, yes, the courage of the little horse won through. Look once more at the photo of him and Dessie Hughes jumping the last in the 1979 Champion Hurdle and you will see the winning fire blazing out of Monksfield's eye. Sea Pigeon might be faster and classier, an aristocrat of the breed. But 'Monkey' wanted to get it on. As they faced the hill and that huge Cheltenham crowd roared, there was only going to be one winner.

It was indeed the Golden Age of Hurdling, so much so that no look back is complete without Dramatist and Birds Nest, two horses who never actually won the Champion Hurdle but were for long part of the mix. Birds Nest was three times winner of the Fighting Fifth Hurdle for Bob Turnell and Andy Turnell. Dramatist won six hurdles for Bill Smith and the Queen Mother's trainer Fulke Walwyn and took Night Nurse out in a controversial Christmas Hurdle at Kempton Park when the renowned front running champion was harried for the lead by a Dramatist stable companion.

When I criticised this in print, the royal trainer came up to me in the winner's enclosure a week later and started to belabour me so vigorously that the 2008 furore over Ballydoyle's pacemaker in the Juddmonte International seems pale by comparison. In these days I could probably have sued old Fulke for assault. Back then plenty of people thought it merely my comeuppance.

When that hurdling Golden Age began, Guy Harwood was a bright and energetic thirty-year-old garage owner's son just five years into a training career which had begun with me riding jumping winners for him at Fontwell, Windsor and Leicester. Within weeks of Sea Pigeon landing the 1981 Champion Hurdle at Cheltenham, Guy had won his first classic by saddling To-Agori-Mou to win the Two Thousand Guineas at Newmarket and was a Flat race trainer to match any in the land. The transformation was complete.

DANCING BRAVE and the HARWOOD EXPERIMENT

WHAT Guy Harwood did at Pulborough in West Sussex was Britain's most innovative individual racing creation of the twentieth century. Taking an ordinary dairy farm within three miles of where his father Wally had established the original garage business back in 1931, Guy developed the most modern racehorse training set-up that the world had then ever seen.

Back in 1970 people had hardly heard of artificial gallops. Guy had a whole series of them with white rails everywhere, a computerised office system, labour-saving American barns, a private laboratory, a hands on vet and above all else a business mentality.

That was used as a term of disparagement by his rivals, but the key to his success was that he set out to build up a training operation which would make sense in the way a business should. He would take the final decision but he would bring in experts, and their combined skills would make up an unbeatable management team. No one, before or since, has ever done it like Guy.

He already knew a fair bit himself. With his striped colours featuring a flamboyant black 'H', he had made himself a highly effective point-to-point jockey, and he linked a questioning intelligence with a direct, winner's mentality. Giving me complicated instructions to win a 'horse and cart' chase

Dancing Brave's finest hour: the 1986 Arc.

round Fontwell was never going to be enough. But to get where he wanted to go he needed help. And he had the brains to find it.

The gifted yearling judge James Delahooke was drafted in to select the talent; calm and experienced head lad Tommy Townsend came over to supervise the horse care; jump jockey brother-in- law Geoff Lawson oversaw all riding matters; the strong, wise and able Greville Starkey teamed up as stable jockey; and to it all was added the clinical knowledge and informed, pragmatic analysis of top veterinarian Brian Eagles.

When Guy Harwood spoke it was as a mixture of vet and business man. For us in the media accustomed to trainers saying either nothing or such favourite banalities as 'He's a nice horse but will need the race,' Guy was an unbelievable breath of fresh air. He may have been a bit brusque at times, but he told you things based on fact – and never more so than in the build up to To-Agori-Mou's Two Thousand Guineas in 1981.

'The biggest myth,' he said in the February of that year attacking a misconception that is still prevalent today, 'is that a three-year-old is going to be bigger and heavier than it was as a two-year-old. That's nonsense. If you find his best racing weight, you will discover that as a three-year-old it is almost exactly the same. If he is much heavier he is unfit. If he is lighter, he is sick. After all,' Guy concluded with a metaphor from the family business, 'he is the same car.'

On that day To-Agori-Mou pulled the scale at 1,160 pounds, some 70 pounds over his Dewhurst Stakes-winning weight. When he reappeared, and got beaten, in the Craven Stakes on 14 April, he was 1,105 pounds. On 2 May he won the Two Thousand Guineas – his weight was the exact Dewhurst figure of 1,090 pounds. QED.

Harwood was always something of a man in a hurry and you had a feeling that he would not hang around too long, a sense heightened by the news that Harwoods Motors got a Land Rover franchise in 1979, Rolls Royce-Bentley in 1981 and Jaguar-Daimler in 1984. What was needed before the team split up or he moved on – which inevitably would amount to one and the same thing – was a really great horse to crown the enterprise. In 1986, with Dancing Brave, they got it.

Dancing Brave was not a particularly eye-taking individual: medium height, darkish bay and a touch of white on his muzzle. Nothing wrong with him anywhere, but he didn't have much of the swagger you like to find in champions. But oh, could he run! He won both his races as a two-year-old, but they were minor affairs compared with what was to come. The warning was out when he took the Craven Stakes, but it was in the Guineas that we all first saw his truly magnificent finishing kick.

The problem for Dancing Brave, and in particular for his then jockey Greville Starkey, was that next time out in the Derby the whole world marvelled at his finish – but only so late that he failed to catch Shahrastani despite clocking the fastest closing fractions in Epsom's history. Greville had to carry the can but as a rider I can sympathise with his dilemma. Before the race the one doubt about Dancing Brave was whether such brilliant speed would last out the mile and a half journey. So the plan was to drop the colt in at the back of the field and try and switch him off. On a flat course like Newbury there would have been no problem. But in 1986 Epsom's contours stitched him up like a kipper, and by the time Greville Starkey finally got Dancing Brave out on an even keel Walter Swinburn and Shahrastani had flown.

It's worth remembering that Shahrastani was no flukey one-race wonder. He followed up by taking the Irish Derby by eight lengths, and was favourite in front of Dancing Brave when they met again in the King George at Ascot, despite Dancing Brave having won the Eclipse Stakes impressively enough in the interim.

But Dancing Brave had a greater gift of acceleration than any horse in memory. With Pat Eddery on board he sluiced past Shahrastani in the King

George, only to falter a little once he had hit the front. The lesson was not lost on Eddery, whose assets – and he was then at the very height of his powers – included a quite unbelievable ability to stay cool and play late. There is a wonderful story of Pat coming into the paddock at Longchamp before the Arc, touching his hat to owner Prince Khalid Abdullah and looking casually at the other horses in an abstract sort of manner. After a while Guy, who knew better than to try and tie Pat down with any 'orders', can't stand the frustration. 'So what are you going to do, Pat?', he asks. 'Oh,' says the jockey vaguely, 'I think I'll hold him up a bit.'

And he did. At the end of the season the International Classifications gave Dancing Brave a rating of 141, the highest ever recorded. It came from what he did at Longchamp to a whole half dozen of champions who all spread out to battle in front of him in the final straight. Along the rail there was the German superstar Acatenango, next to him the ace French filly Triptych, then the Aga Khan's top class pair Shardari and Darara with his Shahrastani coming wide and the French Derby winner Bering coming widest of all …

It was in every sense the challenge of both the horse and the jockey's lifetime. Pat Eddery did many, many miraculous and daring things in his thirty years in the saddle, but nothing among all those thousands of winners was a match to this.

It doesn't matter how many times you watch the video, it is still a wonder. Here's what it felt like early the following week.

As with all masterpieces, the more you study the better it looks. Pat Eddery and Dancing Brave's victory on Sunday was more than a triumph. It was the most brilliant final trump that racing has ever seen.

To understand fully last week's excitement you must wind back to the 800-metre mark and remember that the unique thrill of top class Flat racing is that a jockey only has one shot. If he moves too soon he gets run out of it; too late and he never collects.

Eight hundred metres out in this Arc there were still plenty of pilots with power beneath them. Eddery had Dancing Brave back eleventh of the fifteen runners. He could see Shardari, Darara, Shahrastani and Bering all poised to sprint. He had to be ready.

With the fastest ever Arc finish about to start, did Pat move out to cover Bering's kick? On a horse whose only defeat was when he got impossibly out of position at Epsom, did Eddery close up for the winning burst? Did he hell! He put Dancing Brave back inside and let the race develop. If he lost, the Seine wouldn't be deep enough.

For a moment you couldn't believe your eyes. He was giving the others a start and, spread eight-wide across the track, they flattened quite furiously for the line. These were crack horses and now Dancing Brave had to move across behind them before even beginning his effort. By any ordinary criterion he had got the cards wrong. But this was no normal beast, no ordinary man. And, as with all greatness, what was seen next will never be forgot.

For about a dozen strides horse and rider went almost desperately to work with little effect on the gap. Then suddenly those sinewy legs bit deep into the Longchamp turf and propelled this gleaming bay wonder towards the others with a momentum which made victory certain long before he knifed past at the death.

He had played last. But he got it right. The trick, the game, the glory was taken.

To do this had needed that astonishing, casual, match-winning cool that makes Eddery one of the greatest instinctive jockeys ever foaled. It also needed a horse with a most extraordinary switch-on of speed, and no praise can be too high for the way that Guy Harwood and his team had brought their colt through seven pressurised big-race months to reach this highest peak on Sunday.

Their training centre down at Pulborough in Sussex has long been a byword for the most modern methods of Thoroughbred assessment – everything from video cameras to muscle biopsy – so it's fitting that Longchamp was able to give statistical proof of the visual wonder of Dancing Brave's finish.

The Paris clock showed that the record overall time of 2 minutes 27.7 seconds for the Prix de l'Arc de Triomphe's 2,400 metres – a mile and a half – included a closing quarter of 22.8 seconds, from the moment that Shardari passed the 400-metre mark in front to when Dancing Brave crossed the line. As Dancing Brave had at least five lengths to make up in that last section and you allow 0.1 seconds a length, this means that he finished as fast as Europe's top sprinter Double Schwartz in the 1,000-metre (five furlongs) Prix de l'Abbaye an hour before the Arc.

The acute pressure in the straight is further shown by the rare fact that this closing quarter was the fastest stage of the race. Even more exceptional for a mile-and-a-half event, the last 200 metres were as swift as any 11.40 on the board, little change out of 11 seconds for Dancing Brave. Compare this with Sagace's last quarter of 11.90 and 12.10 in 1985 or Mill Reef's of 12.10 and 12.40 in 1971 and you appreciate that nobody's done it quicker.

Even by Eddery's standards this was a finish to treasure, and for a moment on Sunday he let slip such phrases as, 'He was terrific, electrifying. When I asked him he really jumped.'

But at Ascot on Friday Pat was back to his usual unexaggerating self. 'I switched to the inside coming into the straight to avoid taking off from the bend,' he said, as if discussing some job in the office. 'Then I deliberately gave them first run because I didn't want to get there too soon. When you come off the bridle it takes a stride or two for him to quicken, but when he does it's very fast, and I don't think any of the others thought a horse could do what Dancing Brave did to Bering.'

It all sounds a bit like yesterday's marketing plan, not the race of the century. But then that's part of the secret.

The memory goes back to just before the start on Sunday. The horses are being loaded, the jockeys frowning in concentration. All except Eddery. He's awake and alert all right, but the way he pats his horse and steps into the stall is devoid of tension. He looks like a commuter wanting a good position on the train so that he can play cards on the journey.

Give him the pack. On this form he could deal with the Devil.

That was in every respect Dancing Brave's finest hour. An ambitious trip to Santa Anita for the Breeders' Cup got fouled by dehydration from a moderate journey and by desperately hot weather. A stud career which produced crack horses like Arc second White Muzzle and Derby winner Commander In Chief was hampered by a rare disease in his second winter, and he, like Grundy, ended up in Japan.

Guy Harwood went back, very successfully, to the family business. The training team had begun to break up and nothing was ever going to equal Dancing Brave, although daughter Amanda Perrett and her husband Mark are now putting new life into the Pulborough operation.

For us in 1986 there was not far to look for excitement to replace Dancing Brave, for on Boxing Day at Kempton Park that year, less than three months after the Arc, we realised that we were into the age of Desert Orchid.

In fact Dessie had been around for three full seasons and we already admired his boldness, but were not quite sure of his ability or of how long he could last. By the time he bowed out, five Boxing Days later, he was a legend across the land.

He died, aged 27 and shaggy, snowy white, in November 2006. It was obituary time.

DESERT ORCHID

H E WAS the warrior we took to our hearts. Desert Orchid was not just good but brave, not just brave but front-running bold, not just bold but fearless and sometimes flawed. He was the grey attacker who put his neck on the line. And the whole world loved him for it.

It was utterly typical of him that he should go out on his shield. That he began and ended his seventy-race, 34-victory, ten-season career with a sickening somersault at Kempton. That the final crash came in his sixth consecutive King George VI Chase, and when he got up and galloped riderless past the stands the whole crowd stood and cheered him just as they had roared home his record four victories in the race.

With Desert Orchid you knew exactly what you were going to get. The tapes would go up and he would charge off to the first as if Prince Rupert had recruited him to the cavalry. In an increasingly evasive and spin-doctoring world there was something wonderfully rewarding in this increasingly white horse who set caution to the winds, and unlike Prince Rupert's one-charge-wonders kept returning to the fray.

Our relationship with him was all the stronger for its taking time to grow. Sure he won six in a row and ended up running in the Champion Hurdle in his first full season. Trainer David Elsworth seemed game to run him in everything, as did the splendidly batty Burridge family. Solicitor Jimmy Burridge had bred Dessie from his headstrong hunter mare Flower Child, while his son Richard was a tall, fit-looking chap who had won a hurdling blue at Cambridge and was a film scriptwriter in real life. They were not quite the Distressed Gentlefolks' Association, but they had to borrow a horsebox to take Dessie to Elsworth's, and it took them two days and much kicking to get him there. They had never expected anything and were having the time of their lives: Richard used to sneak off and jump the fences himself. But after four seasons we thought they had a good horse but not a great one, a character but not a king.

Time for comparisons. As the nine-year-old Best Mate aims to emulate the wonderful third Cheltenham Gold Cup which Arkle achieved at the same age, he brings to the party a record of twelve wins and six seconds from eighteen starts. At this stage Desert Orchid had won eighteen races from 44 starts, had won and been beaten in the King George, had earlier been good enough to run in two Champion Hurdles, had also fallen in three other hurdle races, had been pulled up twice, and had once been ignominiously and unsuccessfully tried in blinkers. Best Mate was the blue-blood, Desert Orchid the hustler.

It was on that foundation that the fairytale took flight. Desert Orchid may have got beaten again in the Champion Chase at Cheltenham, but many people still thought him best as a two miler – and then he won over three miles at Liverpool, followed by a sensational all-the-way, ears-pricked victory in the Whitbread over three miles five furlongs. Being in that happily chaotic Sandown winners' circle with David Elsworth, stable girl Janice Coyle and every offshoot of the Burridge clan was one of the happiest experiences of my television life. But it had only just begun.

The next season he won everything. The Tingle Creek and the Victor Chandler over two miles, the King George and the Gainsborough over three miles, and then – wonder of wonders – the Gold Cup itself over three and a quarter in conditions so rough that all faint hearts advised withdrawal. But

Desert Orchid in his pomp – with Simon Sherwood in the 1988 Whitbread Gold Cup.

being Dessie, he always gravitated to the eye of the storm, and after becoming front-page news at Cheltenham he practically brought the nation to a halt by then having his first ever steeplechasing fall at Liverpool.

By now Dessiemania was a full scale epidemic, and it had a good two seasons to run. He won seven more races, including two more King Georges, and got beat in two Gold Cups – and it wasn't just his colour that was easy to recognize. Everyone had got an inkling of why this was a phenomenon on the hoof. They could see that Dessie did not just want to lead: he loved to rumble. This was no 'Catch me if you can and if you do I will concede' front runner. This was a horse that would race you until you quit.

The memories blur together but two clear images remain : the 'punch-in-the-stomach' certainty of Dessie's jumping as he destroyed his rivals round Kempton in the 1990 Racing Post Chase, and the absolute 'I-will-not-be-denied' set of his head and neck as he saw off Nick The Brief and a 2st 7lb weight disadvantage in what was to be his last ever victory a year later at Sandown.

The legend had invaded the ether and was humanizing into the land of the cuddly toy. One day at Kempton a 'goochie goo' infant in a pram was stationed next to the paddock. As assorted bay and brown brutes filed past, the child gurgled, 'Horsey, horsey.' When a grey finally arrived, the burble changed to 'Dessie, Dessie.' Up close the real thing was never so sweet.

Before that closing King George in 1991, David Elsworth had us all down to Whitsbury. With the extraordinary, intuitive, untutored eloquence which has more recently adorned the Persian Punch celebrations, he talked to us about how the strain of getting the now twelve-year-old hero to racing peak was beginning to get both to him and the horse, of how Dessie 'had to take his coat off at Sandown', of how the end was near.

Dessie himself put up with the hacks and camera crews with plenty of his old swagger right up until exercise was finally over and Janice put his food in the manger. An eager lensman moved forward to get the cosy picture of 'Dessie's breakfast', and the old fighter's patience snapped. The white face came up, the ears laid back and the guy was sent panicking through the door. In six decades with Thoroughbreds I have never seen a horse so clearly express the sentiment, 'Eff off.'

In the search for wider interest, we are apt to drag up all sorts of soft and inappropriate analogies for famous quadrupeds. With Desert Orchid there is no such difficulty. He was the warrior who would not weaken, the horse who led the charge under the banner 'Fear and Be Slain'. That's why we loved and admired him more than any other. That's why his name will live for ever on.

Horses that excite – that's the biggest thrill a racehorse can give. That was Desert Orchid's greatest asset. There was that touch of madness about him. That he was prepared to gallop and attack where no normal horse would go. In a very different way it applied to the dazzling sprinter Lochsong too – well, certainly the madness bit.

Perhaps that was a cheap shot, but anyone at trainer Ian Balding's Kingsclere yard will tell you she fitted the phrase trotted out when horses are a bit nuts – of being 'not entirely straightforward'. The redeeming thing about her behaviour is that as it deteriorated her performances seemed to get better. She was apparently not too bad when in 1991 she finally made it onto a racecourse as a back-end three-year-old, and winning a race with what seemed an unsound filly before sending her back to owner Jeff Smith's stud was at that stage the height of Ian's ambition. But two seasons later he recorded that 'she had become progressively more of a prima donna, and I thought in a fourth year in training she might become impossible to deal with.' She stayed in training and she was indeed difficult – but it helped that she had become the best sprinter in the country.

Whatever her foibles, chief among them were either refusing to go anywhere or then going at a million miles an hour. She took a crash course in popularity in 1992 by landing each of those three impossible-to-win cavalry-charge handicaps the Stewards' Cup, the Portland Handicap and the Ayr Gold Cup. That made her something of a punter's darling, but the next season she became the purists' too when sizzling home in four races – culminating in the Nunthorpe at York and the Prix de l'Abbaye at Longchamp – to be crowned Cartier Horse of the Year.

By 1994, when Ian Balding had thought she might have been best not running at all, she was even faster, even more dangerously explosive, and therefore more exciting than ever. At both Newmarket and York she completely blew up in the parade, and the sight of her and Frankie Dettori setting off down the Knavesmire at York brought a whole new and dangerous meaning to the phrase 'cantering to the start'. Thankfully no harm was done and she signed off (in Europe at least – the Breeders' Cup proved definitely one sprint too far) with another blazing all-the-way victory in the Abbaye.

In that summer of 1994 she was at Ascot for the King's Stand Stakes. There was no parade, and she and Frankie got to the start with his arms and her energy still intact. I was down there too. I wanted to see her speed in close-up. I will never forget it.

LOCHSONG

TEN STRIDES, four seconds, 40 mph. They should re-write Shakespeare. They should say, 'Like a Lochsong from the traps.' She was first to arrive at the start. She had gone past the stands quick enough, but by now she was as calm as a hack. Frankie Dettori had his goggles pulled down but his smile switched up. A stalls handler checked her girth and Frankie jumped down and let her neck strap out a couple of holes. Lightning starters need a longer safety belt.

David Jones, the Kingsclere farrier, walked over to check her racing plates. He wore a straw hat but had a heavy responsibility. The filly picked up each foot as easily as if it were evening stables. 'Linford without the lunchbox,' Frankie has called her. But remember Mr Christie's forbidding mask of concentration. There's no doubt which is the more natural runner.

The first of her rivals was still a furlong away. Starter Simon Morant and assistant Peter Haynes came across and, for a few seconds, there was a little admiring gaggle of professionals united in their admiration of this Queen of Speed.

Anyone who has come into racing was once hooked by the thrill of what the Thoroughbred can do at the gallop. Stand next to Lochsong and you are seeing the ultimate.

She's not the typical massive-shouldered sprinter. She stands ready now. A sensible size compared to the horse mountain that is Blyton Lad. The little sweating midget that is Imperial Bailiwick. But you can see the power in those patterned hind quarters. Most of all you can see the look.

They call it 'the look of eagles'. But with the alertness of the head and the cock of the ears, this is much more gazelle. This is a deer ready to run.

They are loading now. Lochsong got a bit steamed up in the stalls last time out at Sandown and Morant has wisely ruled that she should box up last. Still no sweat on that long bay neck. No jig-jog nerves in the oiled hooves in the grass.

She walks in. The handler ducks under the gates and runs left. Frankie's face is expressionless behind the goggles. The head still but not tense under the helmet. The sprint is going to come from beneath him.

'Jockeys!', shouts Morant as the gates slam open. It's

Lochsong wins the King's Stand Stakes.

a sort of 'God speed', and from stall 4 the speed is God-given. It's not the brutal power you get with some sprinters. Not the forceful jockey-horse reaction you find with others. Frankie leans forward, the reins loose, the fingers in the neck strap. Beneath him she runs, the long limbs bounding her out and racing in an instant. Within seconds she is a receding speck in the distance, her rivals toiling in her wake.

Lay up the treasures. See Lochsong while you can.

There were just three more chances for British racegoers to see Lochsong in action, and at both Newmarket and York, as previously related, she blew her chance by bolting to the start. In between she bolted up in Goodwood's King George Stakes and closed her European career by being walked to the start at Longchamp before rocketing back five lengths clear of her field in the Prix de l'Abbaye.

Finally American race fans saw what Lochsong could do over at Churchill Downs for the Breeders' Cup. Unfortunately their sighting was in a runaway morning workout which amazed local 'clockers' and so burnt out Lochsong's reserves that in the race itself she had to be pulled up ...

That Prix de l'Abbaye success took Lochsong's total of victories to fifteen. Eighteen months later we were in thrall to a horse who was in the midst of scoring sixteen in succession. Cigar was no ordinary moke.

CIGAR

THERE is a way horses look – a way they arch the neck and flare the nostril which says they are ready to go out onto the track and run the others ragged. I have never seen a horse look stronger than Cigar did that first moonlit desert night at the inaugural Dubai World Cup of 1996. He must have known how much was hanging on him.

Which was a lot. As a horse he had the world's biggest reputation to defend. He was on an extraordinary thirteen-race winning streak. He had blazed through 1995, winning ten races from ten, culminating in that astonishing Breeders' Cup Classic in rain-soaked, dirt-sloppy Belmont Park when he hit the wire in a record 1 minute 59.58 seconds for the ten furlongs to the famous Bill Durkan commentary hailing 'the unconquerable, invincible, unbeatable Cigar!' But there was another reputation at stake, and with due respect to the finest colt on the planet it was a shade more important. It was that of Sheikh Mohammed.

It had been exactly a year before that he had the idea. Three or four of us were sitting late into the night discussing the Jockeys' Challenge competition that had been run earlier in the day at Nad Al Sheba. Great riders had been flown in from all over the world. Live TV coverage had been obtained. But somehow it was still not having the impact that Sheikh Mohammed and his vision of an emerging, better-than-the-best Dubai would want.

'We must have a big race,' he said. 'What is the richest race in the world?', he asked me. I explained that it was the Japan Cup, which at that time was worth over £1 million sterling to the winner, almost two million in all. At that time (although it is only twelve years ago as I write) this was an impossibly large sum for even Sheikh Mohammed to top. I should have known better. 'We must do it,' he said. As Cigar stalked the paddock on 27 March 1996, the winner's prize was not a million in sterling, but a million and a half.

The money was the easy bit. For there were the stables to build, the date to fix, the quarantine arrangements to make, and above all the horses to attract. In the last dozen years Sheikh Mohammed has so transformed Dubai that it may be hard for some to realize that it was a comparative backwater back then – and most certainly a backwater on the racing map.

So we all went to work. As a member of the organising committee I can honestly say that it was a wonderfully exciting time, but the further we went the more obvious it became that we needed more than a big event and invited crowds. If we were going to welcome everyone to the world's richest horse race we needed the world's best horse to give it credibility. And with top European contenders unlikely because of the sand rather than turf surface, that increasingly looked as if it was going to be the big powerful bay that owner Allen Paulson named after an aviation beacon, not a tobacco smoke. We thought we needed Cigar to book his ticket. After the 1995 Breeders' Cup Classic, we were certain.

It rained so hard that day at Belmont that any turf course in Europe would have abandoned before lunchtime. The dirt course was deemed to be that silly sounding but brutally testing state of 'sloppy'. That actually means that the top surface becomes a little more than a purée, and the hooves go straight through to the hard surface beneath. The Breeders' Cup Classic field clocked the half mile in 48.3 seconds on their way to that sub two-minute mile and a quarter. Cigar's legs must have been made of iron, but most others aren't. It has been nothing short of an international disgrace that it took the carnage of similar going at the Monmouth Park Breeders' Cup in 2007 for American racing to realise that if they did not put their house in order and put down welfare-acceptable surfaces, the law would do it for them – and pariah them in the process.

But back in 1995 Cigar was awesome, and Belmont Park was the first time I had seen him up close. He was a magnificent man of a horse: powerful and masculine without being heavy and sturdy. He was very composed as an individual in the morning; brutally, arm-tugging forceful in the afternoons. The moment the gates clanged open in the Classic, Jerry Bailey had a double handful of horse on the rein. Cigar had the stride, the power and the will to win. He was completing his ten from ten for the season. He was a certainty for the Horse of the Year. He was box office on the hoof. We had to have him in Dubai.

Quite what inducements were held out to Allen Paulson was not actually my business. But whatever they were, they were worth it. For when we heard that Cigar was coming and that Soul Of The Matter, the Burt Bacharach-owned fourth in the 1995 Classic, was coming with him, we knew that our race would demand attention – provided it was all right on the night.

There is a great moment in all sport when the support teams peel away and the actual participants are on their own. You see it clearest in Formula One, when one moment the pit lane is a crowded market and the next there are just 22 cars with engines revving. You see it in the boxing ring, on the cycle track and of course you see it on the racecourse when the trainer and the owner and the lad and the starter have all had their say and the goggles are finally pulled down, the stalls are loaded and the game is on. In sports psychology they talk of being energised by the adrenalin of challenge, not weakened by the nervousness of pressure. Cigar was adrenalised that night.

So much depended on Cigar. Sheikh Mohammed had given such lavish hospitality that Sir Clement Freud rather unwisely dubbed it 'the Mother of all Freebies'. The then Crown Prince of Dubai had given us carte blanche to bus in as many helpers as trucks would allow, but given the lack of time and of experience there were still some pretty ragged edges as we desperately tried to make this an event to match its billing. It didn't help when the supposedly highly trained, white-dish-dashed security cordon melted into the background at the first sign of trouble.

Cigar had won us over in the mornings as he and his exercise rider stood at right angles to the track next to trainer Bill Mott, every inch lord of all he surveyed. But now he had to run.

And run he did. The floodlights were not so good in those days, but Jerry Bailey was never going to hide him away and do anything fancy. Turning into the straight, the caller was shouting his name. Two furlongs from home he was in front and in command. But then as they hit the final pole Gary Stevens launched Soul Of The Matter, and it was going to hurt.

For a few desperate seconds it looked as if it would even be defeat. We could brazen it out that we had still seen a great contest but the world would mutter that Dubai was a difficult place to come to. We needed a champion to display his crown. Jerry Bailey clamped down behind the mane with increasing urgency and switched his whip from the right hand to the left.

'I saw the other horse coming and range up alongside us ,' Jerry said with lucid admiration afterwards. 'He looked me in the eye, looked Cigar in the eye, and Cigar would not have it. He inched out and ahead again and I truly believe that if they went round one more time the other horse was never going to get by him.'

The winning streak had stretched to fourteen to match that of the legendary Man O' War. The headlines could rightly dub Cigar 'Champion of the World'. But those were just statistics and titles. That night in Dubai a horse had done something for us. By his presence and power and indomitable courage he had put a nation on the map. Since then Dubai has multiplied a thousandfold in every direction. But few things will better that night when the gleam shone in Cigar's eye and the first World Cup was run.

The Cigar show still had a little way to run. Rested and refreshed back in America, he stretched 'The Streak' to fifteen at Suffolk Downs in June 1996 and then equalled Citation's 1948-50 run of sixteen consecutive victories by winning the Arlington Citation Challenge in Chicago eleven days later. Hopes of setting a new mark were stymied next time out when the aptly named Dare And Go outran him in the Pacific Classic. There was one more victory to come, but after finishing third in the Breeders' Cup Classic the racing chapter was closed with nineteen victories, almost $10 million in prize money – a record for an American-trained horse beaten only when Curlin won the Jockey Club Gold Cup in September 2008 – and certainly a lot more in fame.

All sorts of fancy numbers were put on his stud value, but in an ironic twist of fate the horse who was so richly successful on the track turned out to be a stallion who could only 'fire blanks' in the breeding shed. Stud owners and insurance men rent their raiment, but for the general public there was the happy outcome that Cigar was despatched to the Kentucky Horse Park, where retirement is undemanding but visitors can pay homage.

When the Breeders' Cup was at Churchill Downs in 2006 I hooked off to see him, taking Interstate 64 out of Louisville and steaming east for some sixty miles until the domed roofs and the big white railing paddocks of the Horse Park appeared on the left. It was a crisp autumn day. Cigar had a palatial box deeply bedded with straw and his own paddock with an inscription outside detailing his achievements. He was picking away at the grass. There would never be any problem ladies in his life. He seemed content. Was there a message there?

A salutary experience two months after Cigar's Dubai World Cup has taught me to be a bit careful with the quips about the 'sultan's life at stud'. Commenting on the then five-year-old Double Trigger before he ran in the Henry II Stakes at Sandown Park, I had wondered aloud on Channel 4 whether, after all his previous year's excitements of winning the Ascot Gold Cup and the Goodwood and Doncaster Cups to land the 'Stayers' Triple Crown' he might now be beginning to 'think a bit.' Included was a bit of innuendo that he might now be getting keener on the boudoir than the racecourse battle.

Of course, Double Trigger proceeded to make a complete fool of me by coming home miles clear of his nearest pursuer, and a few days later the Racing Post *letters column contained a missive from Middleham purportedly signed by the horse himself, making a convincing case that my comments were way out of order.*

After all, Double Trigger 'wrote', he'd had flu the previous autumn, and the trip to Australia for the 1995 Melbourne Cup had taken a lot out of him.

'I hope I answered your question that I "might just be coming to the end of the line" by winning by seven lengths on Monday,' said the letter before concluding: 'Still, no hard feelings. Come up and ride me at Middleham some time and perhaps I can show you if I've got my mind on other things.'

This was not a challenge I could duck.

DOUBLE TRIGGER

T O BE quite honest I don't think he was that keen to see me. 'Hello big fella,' I said, offering a fatuous pat as Andrew Murphy made the Gold Cup winner ready. The white-blazed head we think we know and love moved with short and instant menace. An awesome set of teeth flashed in the early morning light in his box. Double Trigger does not take fools – or being called a fool – too gladly.

It is patronising as well as silly to ascribe human characteristics to horses one has only watched on the screen or on the other side of the paddock rail. They have their own quirks, their own habits, be they straightforward or difficult. But essentially they are horses. They don't read the papers or listen to idiot commentators like this one querying their enthusiasm on TV ... or do they?

Having accepted the unbelievable honour of a ride on Double Trigger, it was now time to come to terms with what he is really like as an individual. He is not huge, but is much bigger than he looks on the telly. He is 16.2 hands (5ft 6in) at the shoulder. He draws 475kg (1,047lb, over 9cwt) of hardened muscle on the weighbridge. His once bright chestnut coat is now almost strawberry roan in colour. His mane and tail have a dark and tawny look far removed from the flaxen locks of his juvenile days. His demeanour tells you that he is not a pet. He is a five-year-old entire and proud of it.

That acknowledged, it was a relief to be legged into the saddle. I felt a lot safer there. He registered no protest as this new burden was heaved upon him; never felt like taking the unmissable opportunity of two quick bucks which would deposit me in the Johnston equine pool but ten yards from his own box door; never bothered with any skittish wrangling as thirty head of second lot sorted themselves out in the narrow, stone-flagged central yard.

He padded round like an old pro but not like any smiling ears-pricked patsy. This was a training chore. He kept his ears half back and a suspicious eye on the ancient body loaded up behind him.

The strength of his neck is what strikes you. It is of medium length but thickens to a middle-sized tree trunk in the centre. You look down on it and for the first time fully realise what you are sitting on. This is one of the very best horses to have ever looked through a bridle. One of only six in history to have in one season carried off the Ascot, Goodwood and Doncaster Cups, the Stayers' Triple Crown. You run a jolly, placatory hand against that magnificent white-flecked neck. Some horses will flick their ears or toss their head at such blandishments. This one does not take easy pats from strangers.

The string files down out of the Kingsley House yard and begins to wind right towards Middleham's Market Cross. Straight opposite the Kingsley House gates is Warwick House, from where Neville Crump sent out three Grand National winners and where now Mark Johnston stables his seventy-strong two-year-old team. The likes of Ascot runners Hula Prince and Future Prospect join up as sage old Bobby Elliott on Two Thousand Guineas runner-up Bijou d'Inde now leads our little cavalry platoon up through this wondrous old medieval town with the great ruined walls of the castle to the left of us.

Double Trigger is making his own history, but where he is trained goes back long before the Thoroughbred was even thought of. Most of us have some vague idea about Middleham being the northern capital of Britain in the Middle Ages, of Richard III spending his childhood and after 1471 some of his power-hungry years at this castle. But what about Mary of Middleham? Back in the thirteenth century she first made the town 'The Windsor of the

North' and ruled as a widow, her husband dying after what is described as 'punitive castration' performed by the husband of one of his lady friends.

It was castration that Double Trigger seemed headed for just three stroppy summers ago when, with no apparent talent on the gallops, he was so prone to walking around on his hind legs that one morning Bobby Elliott was moved to look at the nearly palomino-marked two-year-old and utter the now immortal condemnation: 'The only place for him is Chipperfield's Circus.'

Now sixteen races, ten victories and £350,000 into Trigger's career, no one around him can forget that first incredible day at Redcar when 'the dunce' suddenly got the message, swept through the field and won by ten lengths in record time. 'We couldn't believe it,' says jockey Jason Weaver, a sharp sky-blue wind-cheatered figure in the string behind us: 'He was just useless at home. Still doesn't do much on the gallops, but he knows just what he is about.'

These words give me a somewhat premature flush of confidence on Trigger's back. We are now trotting between high greystone walls towards the moors in the distance. Trigger has given a couple of canters on the spot but is now jogging along behind Bijou d'Inde with the grudging acceptance of a soccer player in the warm-up routine. I stand up in my stirrups and look back at the horses and riders clattering up in the posse. All's well with the world. Or is it?

For as the countryside now opens out ahead, Bobby forks right and hacks Bijou d'Inde away up the collar of Low Moor between the white markers. Double Trigger follows him and suddenly I am far too acutely aware that with privilege comes responsibility. Just how much of a 'dosser' is Double Trigger on the gallops?

However simple he may be for those who know him, the fact remains that the horse beneath me has picked up the bit and I can feel the power. The moor seems to climb endlessly up ahead. What if Trigger decides to enact his revenge and really test these ageing and unrehearsed jockey reflexes? A small trickle of panic enters my upper arm.

Anyone who has ever ridden knows the rules. Confidence is the key, and the lighter your hold on the reins the better. But it can be easier said than done. A couple of furlongs gone and Trigger is still taking a tug, Bobby and Bijou are only a couple of lengths in front, the moor still climbs on and on. Don't panic – you used to do this for a living. Ah yes, but that was a long time ago: what if cramp begins to set in?

Somehow it didn't. Bobby pulls up and we walk off down to the right. A ridiculous sense of relief floods over me. 'That was great,' I exclaim heartily, like Hancock after the first prick in the *Blood Donor* sketch: 'Shall I ease his girths a hole?'

The reply puts a chill through the blood. 'Oh no,' says Bobby, looking across from the great bulk of Bijou d'Inde: 'We are going over to the High Moor now.' Out to our left the High Moor beckons a thousand feet up in the sunshine. With Welton Fell to the south and Wensleydale green and timeless to the north, it is the most perfect of prospects. But at this end of the reins it could be tempting fate.

No matter that Double Trigger seems a bit more content with life, his ears at last pricked forward. The truth must be faced that I was in quite a funk coming up that long canter. Should I call over Mark Johnston and run up the white flag? Pride won't allow it. Remember what that comes before!

But by some miracle we did it. Deirdre Johnston on the liver chestnut Mattawan leads us at a good canter down towards Penhill Farm. You can feel Double Trigger's strength surging up through his shoulders, but the pace is just quick enough for the brakes not to fail. It's the most dazzling of mornings in one of the remotest parts of the kingdom, so you blink in bemusement as a small man in an elderly Rolls-Royce drives slowly by. No time to ponder, there's to be another canter, a rein-stretching couple of furlongs back homewards and then a right-handed sweep up the High Moor collar.

We are going a bit quicker now, and you can begin to gather what Double Trigger is about. He crooks his head a touch left in a mannerism we know as spectators, but his gallop is straight ahead. The stride is not extravagant, yet has a real relentless flow about it. With that tawny mane in your eyes you can sense that he could keep going long after the others wilt. The trainer's car looms on the horizon. Double Trigger drops his bridle. He's given me quite comeuppance enough.

In fact I have been doubly forgiven. For we then returned for a final couple of spins up the seven furlongs of Low Moor all-weather. Twice again I feel the rolling, tireless power of the best stayer and the best Flat racehorse I am ever likely to sit upon. Double Trigger was unimpressed by my wonderment. He wouldn't have blown a candle out. In November 1975 I had the unique and extremely alarming honour of riding Red Rum bucking and kicking through the streets of Southport and then at an ever increasing gallop along the beach towards Liverpool. It was something I never expected to be matched in my experience. Twenty years on it has been, and more.

Good luck Trigger. You are a real man, my son.

Unfazed by carting me round for a morning, Double Trigger then ran a close second in the 1996 Gold Cup at Ascot and won the Doncaster Cup, to much rejoicing. He soldiered on, winning the Goodwood Cup in 1997 and closing out gloriously by taking both the Goodwood Cup and Doncaster Cup in 1998.

Mark Johnston saddled over 100 winners in 1996 and took more than £1 million pounds in prize money that season – a feat which he, uniquely, has achieved every year since 1994. Anyone wondering why the default position for a Johnston horse is up with the leaders, prepared to make it hurt, should get themselves to Middleham. As I discovered on Double Trigger, Mark's horses don't get galloped hard, but the sheer basic graft of their routine means that they have reservoirs of fitness very few can equal. Johnston's figures do not lie.

Nor do the figures with which the rise of the Japanese as a force in world racing can be plotted. Throughout the 1980s I travelled to Tokyo each November to help organize the Japan Cup as part of the International Racing Bureau team. In structural and organizational terms the Japanese were so far ahead of us it was ridiculous – I remember talking to the TV camera with over 100,000 people in the immaculate grandstand behind me – but could not produce top horses.

It soon became clear that this was the subplot to putting on the Cup itself. It was more than just a prestigious international race, their only one. It was a chance to test their own horses and trainers against the world. For the first few years they found themselves embarrassingly wanting, and if you went around their palatially appointed training centres you could soon see the reasons. However well organized it was, they were treating horses as numbers and not machines. For years they had been sending eager would-be trainers abroad with clipboards and cameras, but when they returned the old guard pooh-poohed them.

When I wanted to have a horse moved across the box at the Miho centre, the lad did not click it over with his voice but got a pitch fork to prod it. When I spent an afternoon at the track I discovered that no horses were gelded, every horse wore a hood, none wore blinkers. I told the authorities that it was not my opinion but the rest of the world's that they were in danger of being a laughing stock. We even made a video of a lad grooming and stroking a horse like a friend, not a tiger. The penny was dropping, but it needed a new guard of trainers to take things forward. Kasuo Fujisawa was one of these, and in July 1998 he brought the big chestnut Taiki Shuttle on the long road from Tokyo to Chantilly, with the Prix Jacques le Marois, one of the defining one-mile races of the season, as his principal target.

TAIKI SHUTTLE

THE HORSE as a symbol has been around since man first started scratching on the sides of caves. Today we have a new one. He's big, he's handsome, he has the whole of Japan behind him, and if Taiki Shuttle wins this afternoon at Deauville, the racing world will shy on its orbit.

But the lessons, as so often with horses, may not be quite the ones we think. The received wisdom is that this, for the Japanese, is payback time. The yen may be crashing but, after years of developing the richest racing nation on earth, they have at last got some runners who can crack it on the international scene.

After eighteen renewals of the Japan Cup in Tokyo have logged a mere four home-bred successes, they are finally receiving dividends on a worldwide investment which has seen five of the last seven Derby winners shipped off east.

After thirty years of overseas failure, the Japanese belatedly tasted Group 1 triumph abroad when Seeking The Pearl won the Prix Maurice de Gheest at Deauville last Sunday. Now Taiki Shuttle, winner of nine of ten races for a cool 490 million yen (more than £12 million) and rated 10lb that filly's superior, can repeat the trick. But a central part of this so-called wisdom is bosh. Seeking The Pearl and Taiki Shuttle are about as Japanese as President Clinton's dog. Both were bred in America, and after nursery days in Kentucky, Taiki Shuttle did all his early schooling at his owner's farm near The Curragh in Ireland, only finally coming under champion trainer Kasuo Fujisawa's care at Miho training centre, near Tokyo, at the end of his two-year-old season.

Fears of this week's Normandy excitements heralding a Japanese-reared superbreed would seem to be somewhat overstated. But the impact of the challenge should not be. Over the years there have been two upsetting themes about continued Japanese failure overseas. One has been the fear that their traditionally flawed methods of horse care would never change, the other that their devoted set of travelling cheerleaders deserve something better. Never more so than when some 100 media and fans followed every move of the big, plain and rather bizarrely over-exercised mare called Hokuta Vega in preparation for the 1997 Dubai World Cup.

After her fatal accident in the race, the sight of the Japanese press sobbing openly contrasted with the much stiffer upper lip British reaction when top steeplechaser One Man suffered a similar fate at Aintree that April.

Being with Taiki Shuttle as he wound up his preparation on the immaculately tended tracks at Lamorlaye was to feel reassurance. Fujisawa was a popular figure when he worked a five-year stay at Newmarket, and his utterances have the simple common sense which is so often the hallmark of champion horsemen. Taiki Farms, started by businessman Yoshiki Akazawa, is an operation whose internationalism has prevented it being tied down by the rigidity of Japanese regulations and whose system of bringing in groups of investors makes Taiki Shuttle, with his 100 shares, the most successful syndicate horse on the globe.

As for travelling support, this is already running at near fever pitch. Before 7.30 a.m. on Friday there were already twenty Japanese media groupies following their hero onto Lamorlaye's exercise grounds. 'It's so exciting,' said journalist Naoko Takahashi: 'You should have been here when he galloped on Wednesday – with all the TV crews there were more than fifty of us around.' Even cosmopolitan Deauville was shaken when Seeking The Pearl broke the oriental duck last Sunday. An extra press room was laid on, the victory made the front pages of all the sports sections back in Tokyo, and the 100-odd Japanese media contingent are already dubbing Taiki Shuttle's bid for the Prix du Haras de Fresnay-Le-Buffard Jacques Le Marois, as 'World Cup Revenge', following their own team's ill-fated visit to the football finals.

Dismiss this as sentiment at your peril. Much has been made of the squillions of yen gambled and invested in Japanese racing. But it's the investment in people and passions that is also now drawing dividends which no other racing territory can match. Ten years back the government-run Japanese Racing Association launched a series of multi-million yen promotions. Anyone who studied the 168,000 – yes, 168,000 – crowd for the Japanese Derby in June will have noticed a dramatic drop in age range and increase in feminine percentage compared with a decade ago. Where else is a champion jockey like Yutaka Take, fittingly in Seeking The Pearl's saddle last Sunday, right up there among the rock stars? It's almost Arrivederci Frankie Dettori. But the stunner is the concentration on the horses. Where else would there be best-selling sportsware featuring as a logo just the outline of the long white blaze which adorns the face of top stallion Sunday Silence?

Taiki Shuttle has got a handsome chestnut head with a fetching leaf-shaped blaze on the forehead. If he wins today it will be pin-up time. At 48, jockey Yukio Okabe is a bit old for the kids but he is also the senior member of the team, whose words and actions are clearly aimed at putting the horses first. Like trainer Fujisawa, he is openly critical of the Japanese unions' insistence on Mondays being a free day for all stable lads, despite the crucial demands of post-race care after Sunday's race meetings. 'We have to think of the animals,' he said: 'This is a nonsense.' Last year Fujisawa saddled 58 winners for some 1.8 billion yen (£7.7 million), but still bridles at being restricted, like all trainers, to just twenty boxes at the Miho centre.

'I'd like more but we have to put up with it,' he said on Friday. 'Just as we do with the need to keep people informed, do the interviews. It's to attract the public.' In that way Japan splendidly leads the world. Every horse is publicly weighed before every race (and Taiki Shuttle draws a massive 510 kilos on the scale). Every horse has a sectional time printed after every run.

Every horse has to pass not just a stalls test but a one-furlong early pace test. When British authorities talk about extra betting revenue and 'self help', they ought to think of these customer services as well as prize money.

Mind you, such aids do not guarantee enlightenment. Before his debut race last season Taiki Shuttle went through the early pace test. Did the future champion sprinter and champion miler, the fastest thing Japan has had in a decade, pass with flying colours? Did he heck. Big, sleepy and apparently uncoordinated, it took him three tries to make the cut. 'I didn't want to press him,' said Fujisawa in a kindly manner: 'You don't need to force these things.'

Well, not as the trainer once did himself. During his Newmarket stay a titled owner came to watch morning work. Just as he passed, Fujisawa was summarily bucked off. Stung by this insult to Japanese pride, the normally genial future hero grabbed his horse by the head, wrestled it to the ground and sat on it. East and West, kindness is best.

Taiki Shuttle duly won the Jacques Le Marois impressively and then took his unbeaten sequence to seven (and his winnings to the Yen equivalent of over £2 million) when running out a five-length winner of Japan's Mile Championship in Kyoto in November. The Japanese have built splendidly on Taiki Shuttle, and in Deep Impact have actually bred and reared one of the best horses of recent times. But if they could extend their culture to Flat racing, taking it as far as fox hunting would be another matter.

For Britain it has been very different. Fox hunting has been part of our culture for centuries, and as times change our legislators and a large slab of public opinion have turned against it. Be that as it may, it is a matter of historical fact that hunting, whether it be fox, hare or deer, has been at the root of jump racing from the beginning. They didn't call it National Hunt Racing for nothing. My own view, having hunted regularly in my early days, is that a lot of the disapproval stems from the arrogance of the past – as in one instance I remember, of a red-faced MFH riding up to some luckless passer-by and shouting in plummy tones, 'Where's my bloody fox?'

But however great the sins of the fathers, class envy is no platform on which to build the law of the land. And if you doubt that this is at the core of things, how come every anti-hunting reference is invariably to 'The Foxhunting Bill'? In my experience, what happens to a hare when the beagles finally catch up with it is just as savage, if no less swift, as what happens to a fox at the kill. Yet no one talks about the 'Anti-Beagling Bill' because beaglers by and large wear scruffy clothes and trainers, or are old men who stand in the middle and watch the hunt develop around them. Unlike the pink coat and top hat brigade, they give you no easy visual targets.

Of course there is also a perfectly earnest wish at the bottom of this: to stop humans harming animals. But the idea that banning hunting with hounds stops foxes or hares or deer suffering at the hands of man is palpably ridiculous, as there has to be culling by other means. If animal protection were at the true root of the legislation I could support it. But the overwhelming impression remains that opponents dislike the hunters more than hunting itself. And banning things just because you don't like the people who do them has no place in a free society.

Which leads us to a pink-coated and velvet-hatted day with the Meynell Hunt in December 1999. Actually I was in a black coat and a black helmet but the man we had come to ride alongside was in full fig. Charles Dixey was making few concessions to political correctness, but he was riding his own horse Castle Mane, whose unbeaten exploits in point-to-points and hunter chases had put him in the betting for the Cheltenham Gold Cup itself in 2000.

This was training as it used to be. I am glad I was there while it lasted.

CASTLE MANE

THERE is preparation, special preparation, and then there is the way Charles Dixey is readying Castle Mane for the Gold Cup at Cheltenham. He is going back to where it all began. Last Saturday I climbed aboard a gigantic former show jumper called Bertie and went along to watch.

While See More Business and Florida Pearl have been with their trainers since July and won their comeback races last month, the still unbeaten Castle Mane only returns to Caroline Bailey's stable tomorrow morning. In the meantime, his 55-year-old owner has been at the reins himself. And how.

Last Saturday morning 1998 Gold Cup hero See More Business, like other top contenders, would have been out for a routine training session as organized and supervised as you would expect for elite athletes on two legs or four. Castle Mane may yet graduate to that elite but, when Dixey retired from 35 years as a City insurance broker a couple of years back, the aim for the light-framed chestnut he had bought in Leicestershire was to hunt, and maybe win a point-to-point. And last Saturday, just as yesterday and every other Saturday since October, a-hunting he would go.

Put aside, just for a moment, any feelings you have about fox hunting, and appreciate what Castle Mane was in for when the Meynell Hounds met at the little country village of Snelston, about ten miles west of Derby. For with Dixey, a slightly over-the-top and unreconstructed figure in scarlet coat and grey hunting cap, Castle Mane's 'qualifying' is not the seven token appearances undertaken by many of the 3,500 horses that run in point-to-points each season. There are big fences in that part of Derbyshire. If the fox breaks cover, the only way you keep up is by jumping them. Mr Dixey talks a good hunt. Now he would have to ride it.

From the 18.2 hands (6ft 2in at the shoulder) elevation of Bertie's enormous back, Castle Mane is not that impressive a sight. He is barely 16 hands, and with his neck set quite low in front of him has none of the upright swagger or glossy muscle texture that one likes to associate with the champion racehorse. No doubt that's why he only cost Charles Dixey a paltry £8,500 two years ago. That was before he won his first four point-to-points and then hit the headlines last March with a runaway win at the Cheltenham Festival. Considering some buyers have since been offering the thick end of half a million, the horse now trotting down the lane on this most gorgeous of winter mornings is one of the bargains of the century.

The business advice is to take the money. The racing wisdom with a horse of this potential is to send it to a Martin Pipe or a Paul Nicholls and see how it measures against the best. But as our fifty-horse cavalcade clopped past Snelston Church and out onto the bank which overlooked the River Dove, with all the glory of the Peak District awaiting beyond the northern horizon, the feeling of being in a time warp was all-pervading.

The first steeplechases were between fox hunters who challenged each other to race across this sort of grass and hedgerow countryside – quite literally from steeple to steeple. Down below us the pack search fruitlessly for the rural predator who, if put to the vote, would almost certainly prefer this to the gun, gas or poison as a means of selective culling.

Ahead of us a four-foot wooden rail blocks a muddy and slippery path. Castle Mane waits impatiently for his turn and then skips gaily over. Charles Dixey, the winner of half a dozen point-to-points in his youth but by his own ever-talkative admission not the greatest rider since John Francome, drops his whip. There is not much scent so the hounds only run in bursts, and the foxes get exercised, not killed. As we gather on the first hill you notice that the Prince of Wales has joined in alongside huntsman Johnny Greenall. It says a bit for the Prince and the other riders that nobody takes much notice, and after a few minutes we all clatter off along another road to the next covert.

Quite soon you discover why. At last there is some activity up front. Suddenly we are in rolling green countryside, with a patchwork of big black fences beckoning ahead. It would not matter if it was the Prince of Wales, Prince Naseem or The Artist Formerly Known As Prince out there. What we need is impetus and elevation. At the second fence Castle Mane does not get enough.

Landing too deep in the ditch on the landing side he knuckles up, Dixey goes overboard and the most expensive horse in the hunting field is galloping loose towards the eastern skyline. When this happens on the schooling grounds, professional racehorse trainers go into rages of cardiac-threatening

nature. Here the wise old figure of
Phil Arthers, at whose stables Castle
Mane boards for his hunting term,
hacks easily over and reunites horse
with breathless rider who then
gallantly gallops on.

It is not the ideal way to prepare
for Cheltenham's greatest prize,
neither for that matter is having
the horse at Dixey's own home and
doing his eight-week pre-season
road work from out of the field.
And while Charles is still adamant
that this season's Gold Cup remains
a target, this does not square with
his avowed intent of sticking with
the very real talents of amateur
jockey Ben Pollock and trainer
Caroline Bailey, whose point-to-
point status does not permit her to
run horses in open competition.

But Dixey only has one life and
in it he will never have another
horse like Castle Mane. When he says that riding him is 'a thrill like no other',
who are we to disagree?

*The Castle Mane glory trail was halted abruptly early in the spring of 2000
when what was later diagnosed as a muscle enzyme problem saw him a weary
and defeated horse at both Haydock and Newbury. But by May his health was
back, and he showed all his old dash to win at Cheltenham and again a month
later at Stratford.*

*Dreams were on for bigger things, but they were not to be. Only a week after
his Stratford success, Castle Mane broke his neck galloping free in his paddock.
Horses are not made to somersault, out in the field or on the track, but it can
always happen. When it does it hurts those closest most. It's a brutal truth with
which to close the millennium, and not one that could be avoided in the next.*

*That final century of the millennium was the one in which the world saw the
end of the horse as the foremost form of transport known to man. It was also the
one which saw the popularity and prosperity of horse racing rise to unequalled
heights in Britain, Europe, America, Australia, Hong Kong and Japan. But as
we move away from the horse, the interest in the game is also on the wane. The
challenge of the new century is to see if the old dreams can live on.*

From the Saddle

*T*HE mornings are best. They always were and always will be. Mornings in a racing stable are when the horses come first. For a few brief hours you all have to believe again. You have to check, to feed, to tack up, to exercise, to school, to decide. In all weathers it is a time of caring, a time of action, above all a time of hope. Even in the most beleaguered and out-of-form yard, hope hangs in the air as addictive as the hardest drug. In truth, it is what you have got up for.

It is half a century since I first got hooked. A golden, late August morning, Frenchie Nicholson's string clambering like a mule train up the steep bank of Cleeve Hill with all of Cheltenham laid out beneath us. A little mare called Thelma's Kuda swinging strong at the canter, in herself pretty moderate as a racehorse, but compared with the hacks and hunters I had been thudding around on, this was a Ferrari at the end of the rein.

An impossibly thin David Nicholson would have been riding all serious-eyed at the head of the string, while his father prodded and teased him about what his own original hawk-eyed mentor, Stanley Wootton, would have said. The bold, blond Terry Biddlecombe would have shone with his instant cavalier brilliance, whatever he had been up to the night before. The 'string' with Keith, and Sam, and 'Thunder' and Ted and Peter would have been barely a dozen. The 'all-weather' was a harrowed strip of plough up the side of a stubble field. But that was then. And hope was everywhere.

The game has changed a lot since that first encounter. Bigger, richer, faster, noisier, sharper, cleaner, infinitely more scientific, yet still dependent on the same early-morning routine. All over the country horses have to be fed and mucked out and exercised and 'set fair', long before most of us have got as far as stumbling through the newspaper.

In the spring of 2000, as the new millennium arrived and as another Cheltenham, another Lincoln, another National, another set of Classics came towards us, it seemed time for an addict to return – to look back at the original inspiration, to visit horses and people at work. What follows are fifteen visits to very different yards in very differing corners of our two islands. The reports are of their time: results, personnel, location, spouses, even professions may have changed. But they were mornings worth waking for.

Previous spread: Ballydoyle.

NICKY HENDERSON
10 February 2000

SEVEN o'clock and the light had not yet come up in Lambourn. The newsagent's window glows bright as you push through the village from Membury; a mile up the Faringdon Road, the huge modern barns of Barry Hills's new empire gleam brighter still. But we dip left between still darkened hedgerows. Another mile, a lodge and a gate on the left, and up a scrunching drive to probably the smartest address in jump racing, to where Nicky Henderson trains at Seven Barrows.

At this hour, smartness and the fact that the Queen Mother, the Lloyd Webbers, assorted adventurers, captains of industry, newspaper editors and superhacks are amongst the 100 head of owners, matters not a jot. There is work to be done. Henderson swallows his coffee, comes out of the kitchen door and threads fifteen paces across the flagstones to where secretary Rowie Rhys-Jones is already beavering in the office. 'All my important decisions,' he says, part pressure, part relief, 'have to be made by 10 o'clock in the morning.'

Some have already been taken. It would have been an hour and a half earlier that head lad Corky Browne and his three assistants set off on their quiet, bucket-echoing vigil of feeding and checking legs amongst the 120-strong equine academy. Thirty minutes ago the place would have begun to fill as other hands arrived to muck out and tack up for first lot. In very different ways, the same little tableau is being played out all over the country. The dynamo of stable routine has been switched on. The place has a purpose.

Which brings us to the ludicrous good fortune of the visitor.

Esprit de Cotte is all bridled, saddled and waiting, his bed of shavings already changed. He is a tall, bay eight-year-old who came from France last season. You may remember him falling when going well in the Becher Chase at Aintree in November, and then disappointing along with stablemate Fiddling The Facts in the Welsh National. He is entered for the National itself at Aintree. But first he and I must follow the others into the famous covered ride where former Seven Barrows maestro Peter Walwyn long preceded John Cleese in his portrayal of Basil Fawlty.

Covered rides are brilliant inventions. Time was, and for many stables still is, when everyone had to circle round an often slippery yard in all winds and weather. For riders and trainers alike, such circumstances are hardly conducive for those vital first checks of tack and action which can avoid so much trouble later. Esprit de Cotte's saddle seems to fit, girths are tight enough, bad luck about his pilot.

Ahead of us, three lads turn to each other and discuss carnal relations. Quite whether they were actual participants or mere watchers on television appears uncertain, but it was ever thus. Into the centre of the ring, Henderson leads a group of owners from Highclere Thoroughbreds, here to see their one-time Derby hope, now Triumph Hurdle-bound, Architect. In the string, one in front of me, Diana Henderson tries to feel good about the thought of scribe and snapper and four more for breakfast.

Racing wives need a book to themselves, some of it with an X-certificate. But when Diana was invented she came with an A-grade. In an earlier life I met her while she and her twin sister Jane and I tried to follow her hopelessly unafraid father, John Thorne, over posts and rails on his idea of schooling practice. On Ben Ruler at Stratford in 1976 she beat her Dad in a hunter chase to become the first woman to ride a winner over fences. In 1978 she signed up with N. Henderson and, along with Browne and travelling head-lad Johnny Worrall, remains one of the four cornerstones who have been there from the start.

Diana is leading the string on the compact little Stormyfairweather. 'He's a bit of a nutter,' she says, a neat, compact figure behind the mane, 'but he fits me.'

Corky has come alongside. He is 57 now but still rides as lean and easy as the youth who did five years' apprenticeship at The Curragh and then spent twenty years with Fred Winter before Killiney's death at Ascot all but broke his heart.

'There's Blue Royal,' he says, one of the stable's three big fancies for Saturday's Tote Gold Trophy. 'He's well.' Yes, the horses can keep you young.

Or age you if they pull too hard. If you haven't done it for a while, there is always an awful moment when the string sets off for a 'canter' and your horse does an early plunge and wants to rush past them at full gallop. All the earlier admonitions – 'He's fine, doesn't pull, just drops his head' – count for nothing as my hand locks needlessly hard on to Esprit de Cotte's reins. For a few horrible seconds I think my strength will fail and I will be ignominiously carted up towards where Henderson waits, a distant speck at the top of this six-furlong, uphill all-weather.

Mercifully, Esprit de Cotte relents. Or, to be honest, Diana Henderson ups the pace a bit. You forget just how quick a Thoroughbred's 'canter' can be. Esprit de Cotte has a marvellous, fluid-rolling stride. His head stretches out, firm but balanced. If he gets his act back together, what a ride he would be at Aintree.

He and the forty others in the string have done this before. At the top they ease down like cars with the ignition switched off. A strangely complicated piece of circling takes place before we all retrace our steps to the bottom and do it all again. Corky is on the chestnut juvenile, Regal Exit. Some in the yard think that Mister Banjo is the Triumph Hurdle horse. Others have taken a price about Architect. But Corky, who only ever goes to Newbury and Cheltenham and has already walked in behind First Bout, Alone Success and Katarino after the Triumph, assures me that Regal Exit will be the fourth.

Architect has now been peeled off with six others to walk back across the Kingston Lisle road for the schooling grounds, where the pale, lean, crumple-faced figure of Mick Fitzgerald is waiting. Three times Architect jumps the four flights of schooling hurdles. Each time he is as neat and bold as an expert.

On his arrival from Newmarket he may have been in a grumpy mood about the various hobdaying and gelding operations he had been subjected to, but this looks like a horse reborn. He is due to make his debut shortly. On the way home I backed him for Cheltenham at 20-1.

Schooling can be the fraughtest of all stable occasions. Trainers can burst blood vessels with frustration. When I rode for Persian War's trainer Colin Davies, his ultimate gasket-blower was to throw his cap on the ground and jump on it. Henderson has had his moments. But not this time. Not even when a talented but gormless novice forgets all that Yogi Breisner and the others have taught him and crashes through the hurdles like a yak.

And not even when a chunky New Zealand chestnut called Demasta does one or two strange-looking leaps in his early tuition for a typically ambitious plan of owner Pat Samuel to pitch for the new multi-million yen steeplechase in Tokyo this spring. It has all gone so well that Henderson even says to me: 'Bet you won't jump those hurdles.' Esprit de Cotte sets off quite sensibly but, after jumping the first, bears down on the second so fast that the resulting jump is a far cry from the peerless poise of Francome in his prime.

'What a place this is,' says Fitzgerald just a touch cryptically as we somehow manage to pull up. 'If you can't get them jumping here, you cannot anywhere.'

Mick's confidence was never better bestowed. That Saturday he chose Geos in front of stable-preferred Blue Royal to win the Tote Gold Trophy at Newbury, and at the Cheltenham Festival he scored on Marlborough, Tiutchev, Bacchanal and Stormyfairweather to become the leading rider at the meeting for the second successive year.

He also got a great run from Architect, who ran a fine race for my ante-post money to finish fourth in the Triumph Hurdle, only to get killed in his next race at Aintree when battling for the lead at the second last.

In the Grand National itself Mick rode Esprit de Cotte, who was putting in the performance of his life before capsizing at Becher's on the second circuit. For such a good jumper Esprit de Cotte was unlucky at Aintree, having also fallen when going very well in the Becher Chase the previous November and failing to finish in that dreadful, swampy National of 2001. Justice was finally done when he completed the course, albeit a distant tenth of eleven finishers, in the Fox Hunters' Chase in 2003.

Testing out Grand National contenders was never the point of this stable tour, but when we shipped up to Scotland the following week another Grand National contender is precisely what we found. Lucky they did not make the actual practice too exact.

LEN LUNGO
17 February 2000

CELTIC GIANT is tacked up and waiting and looking at the view. Not tied up subserviently in a corner, but head out over the box door and big chestnut ears cocked forward as he stares down the green slopes of Hetland Hill to where the Solway Firth stretches, rain-scudded, into the distance. There's an independence about him. Well, he is trained by Lenny Lungo.

Scan the eyes around and you reel in wonder at the achievements of the fifty-year-old jockey-come-entrepreneur-come-trainer who many in racing still pigeon-hole as the answer to the turf trivia question, 'Who rode Martin Pipe's first winner?'

Twenty-five years since he scored on Pipe's Hit Parade at Taunton and ten years since he took out a licence, Lungo has put his own mark on the hillside above Carrutherstown, seven miles south-east of Dumfries, just as definitively as the unique way in which he stresses his Glasgow consonants. This 400-acre, 70-horse, five-barn spread is the 'Empire Lenny Built'. And it's massive.

So, too, is Celtic Giant – 17 hands at the shoulder, 590 kilos on the scales. Last March he carried off the Kim Muir at Cheltenham. Now he has to carry me.

Head lad Roy Barratt comes along to give the leg-up. This is always a moment of slight embarrassment, particularly with a horse as tall as Celtic Giant. Will you waft lithely upwards the moment the lift jerks your ankle? Or will you miss the jump and have to be heaved, sack-like, onto the saddle?

Roy is a short, wise, bird-like figure who left his native Enniskillen when the troubles got bad in the 1960s, and after 25 years with Wilf Crawford, moved to Lungo eight years ago. Roy has heaved up many a sack in his time.

Up above Celtic Giant, the air is good. A shade cockily we walk our way along this first range of boxes, while another lad comes out and vaults on to a big bay horse. Rather grandly I tell him

about early mornings in Argentina, where everyone vaults on bareback. 'Yes,' he says, 'I was out there last year.'

His name is 'JP' Barty and, in true independent Lungo style, he mixes riding out here in the mornings with looking after his own horses nearby in the afternoons. He has also taken Celtic Giant hunting with the Dumfriesshire Hounds in a somewhat unorthodox preparation which will see the massive thing now trotting beneath me run first time out at Cheltenham and then aim at the Grand National, if he makes the cut. 'He's a Christian,' says JP reassuringly, 'he'll look after you.'

After a night spent as guest of the trainer, not to mention the recipient of his distilled wisdom on everything from snooker halls (his wife Barbara runs a twenty-table special in Dumfries) to handicappers (he did not send Phil Smith a Valentine's card) to the magnificently simple secret of his success ('I pull all the strings'), a bit of equine reassurance would not come amiss. As some eighteen of us gather in a vast aircraft hangar-sized sand school, it becomes clear that confidence is what the Lungo team is about.

The trainer comes in on foot. 'This place is a godsend. It gives us the chance to warm up in the dry, to check everything out, to nag the horses a bit. You will see,' he says, waving an arm at us motley pilots trotting around him, 'that everyone here rides as long as Hopalong Cassidy. I think it avoids sore backs and makes the horses use themselves better.'

Indeed, as we finally file out and begin to thread our way past more huge green barns – 'If the training all goes wrong,' says Lenny, 'you could strip the stables out and restore them for agricultural use' – the feeling is not so much of a racing string as a little cavalry posse from the border wars of long ago. We are a purposeful, tousled-maned rather than manicured lot.

We climb up to the hilltop. The rain has eased, but we are grateful for the hard base on the muddied track. We reach the peak and the view rolls away to the left and in front of us. Few racing posses ever came upon such a sight.

Immediately to the side there is a sweeping, wide, railed-off, one-mile circular turf gallop, whose banked turns have been carved out of the hillside. Ahead of us, more rails, a 30-metre diameter circling ring and, sloping easily up, right-handed towards us, the seven-furlong all-weather gallop which, understandably, is Lungo's pride and joy.

'We always used to canter horses up a bank and do it again when I was a kid,' he says. 'It's just that now we call it interval training and, with an all-weather, you can do it with twenty horses, harrow it and do it again.'

Celtic Giant and I are now walking down towards the start alongside young Bruce Gibson on a black, slightly fizzy five-year-old by Phardante. As Mr B. Gibson he had a story-book first ride at Cheltenham on Celtic Giant in March 1999. As B. Gibson (5lb) a recent handicap chase win at Musselburgh was of more pressing importance for the first-term professional. 'Things were a bit slow to start with,' he says with a touch of lean-jawed hunger in his look.

Bruce has pulled his leathers up to jockeys' length. With frigid fingers I do the same, but Celtic Giant does not need much leverage on the brakes.

Roy and JP lead, and the big crest of Celtic Giant settles into a good, rolling stride, his mouth easy on the bit. The gallop bends gently to the right, right again after two furlongs with a slightly steeper pull to the top. Beneath me the great frame lopes lazily along. To think this is already a Cheltenham winner.

Once finished, Bruce and I go down to do it a second time. ' A bit quicker,' he says: 'This one is just beginning and your horse doesn't want too much.'

Born in Hawick 22 years ago, Bruce caught the racing bug and came here via the Doncaster Racing School. 'It was a good grounding,' he says, 'but you need a bit of luck.'

He and Will Dowling share the claiming rides. Robbie Supple is first jockey and later that afternoon is to have a nightmare 33rd birthday at Newcastle, which will include a second, a fall, a brought down and a bucked off after jumping the second. Bruce just hopes for the chance of such humiliation. His horse still fizzes a bit as we step on to the gallop. Way out below us an orange flashing light and a half-mile tailback of traffic signals an accident on the A75.

The traffic that matters now is at the end of the rein.

Celtic Giant may still be 20 kilos over his racing best (but an amazing 150 more than Plutocrat, the stable titch), and may still have another hacking day's hunting with JP to come. But with open space ahead of him and a novice beside, he now remembers he is a racehorse. Out firm goes his head and neck. Keen and hard goes the mouth on the bit. He may be huge, but he has been bred and reared and trained for this. Round the turn and up the last collar he comes with wings on his heels.

Happiness, you remember, is having a good horse beneath.

Celtic Giant certainly brought happiness to Bruce Gibson that year. In April the pair of them lined up for the Grand National, and some ten minutes later lumbered past the line triumphant but exhausted, as the seventeenth and final finishers of the forty who had set out.

That October Bruce and Celtic Giant trekked all the way to Prague and beyond as the sole British representatives in the famous Velka Pardubicka, and were right in contention when exiting at the ninth. For Bruce, who finally stopped riding after just four winners in 2005, things may have never been as good again. But Celtic Giant will always be mighty in his memory.

For me, after visiting two jumping stables, it seemed time to correct the balance and pay respect to the Flat – and in particular to those in the game whose idea of the winter sand is not the beach in Barbados but Saturday night at Wolverhampton races. In 2000, no one was busier than Nick Littmoden.

NICK LITTMODEN
24 February 2000

MAN ON the run, yard on the climb, horses in a hurry. That's the deal with Nick Littmoden on the Hamilton Road at Newmarket. And the winners – no fewer than 61 last year – prove that it works. Whether it can ever work with Mice Design is another matter. He is a tall, lean three-year-old, without so much as a skip in him as we circle around the concrete before filing out on to the track which skirts the back paddocks of this stable, and then those of Rae Guest and Lester Piggott. But from what Nick says, speed does not seem to be among Mice Design's talents.

'He is a lovely ride, though,' the trainer adds, a small, unflash, now 37-year-old figure aboard stable stalwart Cretan Gift – a medium-sized chestnut with a look which suggests he has seen it all before. The reassurance is soon needed, because before we can shorten our leathers, Nick has turned left through the beech trees and led us off at a canter across the vast, and practically horizonless, grass expanse of Southfields.

Out to the right you can hear the swish of the early morning traffic on the bypass, but it is what lies up ahead that is the worry. It is one thing to settle a Thoroughbred into an easy canter when spinning uphill on an 'all-weather', quite another when faced with the largest tract of tended grassland in the northern hemisphere. Memories rush back of arms-out-of-socket days, being run away with on Derek Ancil's horses on Middleton aerodrome when a student at Oxford. But Mice Design, like his stablemates, knows the score.

Despite the early tugs of impending alarm on the reins, he drops the bit and just lobs along behind the horse in front as we scud, seemingly without end, across the turf. A full straight mile it must be, and quite soon it becomes clear you are more likely to have cramp in the back than worry on the brakes.

Routine is the key. Time was when trainers used to torture themselves into finding a different exercise route every day for fear of their darlings becoming bored. Littmoden, like many others, does precisely the opposite. 'They like the routine,' he says, coming up to help resaddle Mice Design, whose tack has slipped alarmingly close to his tail. 'They relax and enjoy their work.'

We are now filing across the Rowley Mile racetrack and towards the still-astonishing bulk of the Devil's Dyke, the eight-mile-long earthwork stuck up by Boadicea's Iceni to try to keep the Romans out. A great pink sun is coming up over the golf course to our left, and the lights are gleaming in the ocean liner-like Millennium Stand which Newmarket will launch in May. But Mice Design is not going to wait that long. He is going to be tested now.

It will not be the greatest gallop since Charles II opened proceedings here four centuries ago. Indeed, it is possible that Mice Design and his stable

companion Mice Events would not give much weight to the Merry Monarch's favourite hack, after whom the Rowley Mile is named. But everything in racing has to find its category. And the Polytrack gallop, which runs uphill alongside the Dyke and then swings left-handed back towards town, is as perfect a surface as any racehorse ever stretched on.

Tom McLaughlin is on Mice Events. Tom is a graduate of the Irish Racing School, Paul Cole's and the all-weather school of hard knocks. He is nursing Mice Events along while, beneath me, Mice Design is going as fast as he can leg it. It is not very fast. The trainer is waiting, a couple of furlongs ahead. It seems a very long way.

Tom has chalked up seventeen winners on the all-weather this winter. 'Not very good,' he says. (Actually, his words are a bit stronger than that, but this is a family newspaper.) He has been with Littmoden ('On and off') for four years. They know about making silk purses from the ears of modest racehorses. Mice Design and Mice Events will be another challenge.

We walk on back towards the yard, where two very different linchpins of the stable are waiting. In the glory days of Slip Anchor and Reference Point, George Winsor cut a familiar figure as travelling head lad to Henry Cecil, before he moved to Southgate when Julie Cecil set up on her own. Soon after 6 a.m., his bungalow door opens, and horses begin to whinny and stamp as feeding begins.

George has a typical racing background. In contrast, 28-year-old Chris Nash comes via the unlikely route of a Cambridge degree and the Southwell training academy, where he first teamed up with Littmoden. As he lugs us up on to our horses for second lot, you guess that if he stays in racing, then this Merseysider should certainly be marked down as one to follow.

Chris is big. Dominic Fox, ex-jockey Richard Fox's nineteen-year-old son, is small, too small at present. 'I have put on a stone in the past year,' he says, a mini-cavalier at the start of our earlier routine. 'I'm working on it. I'm doing weights and things, but I'm still only six stone.'

This time last year, Littmoden was still operating half his string from his former base at Wolverhampton racecourse. At Newmarket, the standard of horse is clearly on the rise, with Flowington finishing third in the Cherry Hinton and Trinculo showing up well in the Champagne Stakes last year. But Nick is not a man to hang around waiting for the bluest of blood. There are races to win, horses to work. This lot, Tom is on Legal Venture, the winner of a seller last year, Jo Fowles is on the buzzy Sounds Lucky, and Blue Star, a winner at Wolverhampton earlier this month, is in charge of me.

Blue Star is a tallish bay by Whittingham and, despite being only four, has already got some of the savvy of his sire's legendary American namesake. He is one of those horses who, even in the sandstorm of an all-weather sprint, is prepared to take a breath. He even took a breath here.

The idea was for the three of us to spin, line astern, to the beginning of the bend and then join up for a quarter-mile of letting them run. Blue Star had switched from relaxed hack lobbing across Southfields to revved-up racer as we came on to the Polytrack, but as we came to the turn he and his rider were left completely flat-footed as Jo released the brakes on Sounds Lucky, who shot through in the centre.

For a few humiliating moments, it looked like a cock-up to test any trainer's patience. But Blue Star got himself sorted and we closed up together. As we came past Littmoden, he was a horse who would win again.

The trainer has to study all three of them. Blue Star he knows about, Legal Venture keeps a bit to himself, Sounds Lucky is a puzzle. A touch jazzed up, but not really firing. Maybe a visor would help, he ponders, as we ease girths and wander homewards.

The form book shows that at Wolverhampton last Tuesday it did.

Sounds Lucky's success in the not too pithily named Bet Direct On 0800 211 222 Handicap (Class F) (Division 1) was worth all of £1,855 to winning owner Paul Dixon and hiked his official rating from 51 to 57. It was a fourth victory in what was already a 26-race three-season career which would stretch on for another 57 runs and eight more wins for Littmoden and Dixon until the old horse was somewhat contentiously claimed by Andrew Reid after running second in a Lingfield seller.

Andrew Reid was of course quite within his rights to claim the horse, but when Sounds Lucky ended his career seven unsuccessful races later by being tailed off at Wolverhampton you hardly thought he had added much to the honour of the game. The same might be said for the connections of Blue Star over their handling of his final days, with the one-time sprinter being pulled up fatally lame in a two-mile handicap at Chester when ridden by Jamie Spencer in September 2003.

After our visit to Nick Littmoden's yard Blue Star had been in fighting form, showing his appreciation of having me as a work rider (only joking) by winning next time out and continuing on for another 44 races over the next four seasons and winning four more races, including three in Dubai when trained by Gay Kelleway.

But by the time of his last success, ridden by Kieren Fallon in a 24-runner Handicap at York in October 2002, his owner had moved Blue Star to the Michael Mullineaux stable, for whom he ran no fewer than eleven times in three months before breaking down at Chester. Racehorses may be there to race, but if Blue Star had been mine he would be on my conscience.

Time to move west, and to change not just the racing discipline but the whole gradient of the training regime. Nick Littmoden is very much a Flat trainer. Paul Nicholls is very much not.

PAUL NICHOLLS
2 March 2000

I T HAS to be the best elevator ride in the land. Lean forward and let the horse run into the teeth of the slope and suddenly, magically, the steep sides of Ditcheat Hill fall away, with the spangled, sunlit fields of Somerset's Blackmore Vale forming a breathtaking backdrop.

Gold Cup winner See More Business is beside us. But he's not here for the view.

We will see and hear a lot about this elevator in the next fortnight. Paul Nicholls has operated an open policy with the media and others have had the chance to sample the woodchip workbench on which Paul measures his horses.

It runs reasonably flat for a furlong, then rises sharply for a good 300 feet over the remaining three furlongs of its journey.

When John Francome rode See More Business up here last year he dubbed it 'the north face of the Eiger'.

But those who undertake this task feel none of the mountaineer's tension. These are fit horses and they love it – and my mount Silence Reigns is an elegant, well-mannered, ex-Michael Stoute Flat horse who knows what to do.

Head lad Clifford Baker is on See More Business and we just follow. No worries about lack of brakes. But no strain either. You can't often use the cliché truthfully, but these would not blow a candle out.

We wander slowly back down the road towards the village; past the lawns of Paul Barber's house, where the crocuses are already pushing up; right-handed below the ever-developing terraced stabling which now houses almost seventy horses; and out for half a mile along the little road towards Castle Cary before turning in and riding the elevator again.

You feel the strength and power of the horse beneath you. It would be easy to say that this hill was the secret. But it would be wrong.

'If you just used this gallop,' says Baker, as we take a turn up the road to the left with the eccentric spike of Glastonbury Tor in the distance, 'you would have very slow horses. The key for us is to be able to use the other gallop down there in the vale.'

You narrow your eyes to make out another dark, five-furlong strip running alongside a hedgerow.

'Down there,' adds Baker, 'they can learn to stretch.'

Baker has had two jobs in racing – 25 years with David Nicholson and five with Nicholls, just a mile from his birthplace beneath the slopes of Priest Hill to the north. He is a cool and easy foil to the trainer's go-getting intensity.

A morning at Ditcheat tells you this is a stable with rather more to it than the gallops.

Rugs, for instance. Three of them on every horse – whoever negotiated the deal with Horsewear in Ireland deserves a medal.

And women. There are 25 staff on the roster and 23 are of the female gender. You can try the kid-in-a-candy-store jokes with jockey Joe Tizzard, in his long brown riding boots but, from the lopsided look of his smile, you get what your eyes have already told you.

The likes of Michelle Hopkins on Flagship Uberalles and Rilly Goshen on Escartefigue are no Lucy Puffington-Fetlocks. These are committed, caring professionals.

But it makes for a slightly calmer, less macho atmosphere than you find in other yards where our old, discredited, I'll-show-him-who's-boss instincts used to come rather too readily to the fore.

These horses have to work hard, but they are clearly among friends. We take the tack off Silence Reigns, and put him into the giant, revolving door that calls itself a horsewalker.

If you were good enough you probably wouldn't mind being trained by P.F. Nicholls. But don't plan on too fancy a breakfast.

Tim Cox has done many sterling services since he also came from Jackdaws Castle two years ago, making bacon sandwiches not the least of them, even if he may never qualify for the special Clement Freud 'Meal of the Day' rosette. Horses have equally unfussy, if more organic fodder. A standard bowl of nuts and a wedge of hay.

Nicholls and Tizzard and Baker munch as they mull over Thursday at Wincanton. Fontwell beckons this afternoon. Second lot awaits and Irbee is being prepared for this spoilt rider.

There is non-slip rubber matting on the downward slope from the higher level stables. In a couple of minutes' time we could do with it on the road, when three kids run across the playground and Irbee bucks with impressive, near-jockey-losing vigour.

The ensuing guffaws might have been tinged with disappointment, but this is a friendly bunch in a friendly village.

It would need to be. Twice a morning, a thirty-strong squadron walks briskly around the farm-pub-church-stable circuit, just like David Nicholson's horses used to parade around the village green at Condicote. We ride two abreast to

make the line shorter and more secure. The lorry behind waits its turn. The driver has seen it all before, and probably backed the big winner on Saturday.

Irbee won a few days ago and you could have guessed it. He's well balanced, his quarters well coupled up behind. His neck and head are quite upright in front of you, in complete contrast to See More Business at first lot, whose low, slightly narrow neck makes him look smaller and slighter than he actually is.

Clifford Baker is now on Call Equiname, a good two inches taller than the Gold Cup winner and far burlier looking in the neck and head and yet, at 520 kilos now, only 10 kilos heavier on the scales.

Incidentally, See More Business clocked a full 580 kilos when weighed for the village fete in the summer, and 520 for his comeback win at Wetherby. Such details are only a guide. But considering Vincent O'Brien went on the record twenty years ago to say that the public should have the right to know horses' racing weights, for how much longer will our racecourses feebly baulk at the simple innovation of setting up a weighbridge and logging each runner's poundage when it enters the stables?

Weights and temperatures and bloodcounts are all part of the checking process. But the real trick is to get the athlete to continue to work with relish. Ditcheat Hill looks steep enough to test him.

Call Equiname has shown fragility enough in the past. But as he sets his big, grey head and drives himself amazingly quietly upwards while the grassy floor slips past, it is not fragility that you think of. It is of Cheltenham.

That's where this elevator is supposed to go.

Call Equiname's problems returned to prevent his running at Cheltenham, though the other horses made it to the Festival. See More Business started 9-4 favourite for the Gold Cup, but on fast ground never had the pace to tackle Looks Like Trouble, and just stuck on to finish fourth. Irbee was fifth in the Grand Annual and Silence Reigns was mildly hampered before finishing seventh in the Supreme Novices' Hurdle: close, but for Paul Nicholls no cigar. For the top trainers, close is never good enough. Paul would not be champion trainer for another six years, but back in 2000 you could already feel the momentum pervading the whole yard.

When it comes to Cheltenham, of course, the momentum in Ireland runs a nation through, and nowhere stronger than the Willie Mullins yard in County Carlow. When we got there in early March 2000 the pride of the stable was Florida Pearl, who had just logged up the second of his three wins in the Hennessy Gold Cup at Leopardstown and who was once again tilting at the Cheltenham Gold Cup, laden down by the heavy tag of 'one of the best Irish horses since Arkle.'

But there were plenty of other stars – and I was legged up on one of them.

WILLIE MULLINS

ALEXANDER BANQUET is a beautiful ride – as easy, elegant and free-flowing as you would expect from a horse who won the Cheltenham Bumper two years ago and may well win the Royal & SunAlliance Chase next week.

But he has a wart on his neck which bleeds if you get the reins tight against it round corners. And with Willie Mullins's gallop up across the road from Bagenalstown you go round corners a lot.

The man who handles Florida Pearl and leads the Irish jump trainers' table has even purer interval training methods than Martin Pipe. His woodchip surface is but two and a half furlongs round. Alexander Banquet and a dozen others hack round it for two full circuits before pulling up and returning briefly to the collecting ring in the centre for the trainer to check them over before the real fun and games begin.

'You do three and three,' says Willie in that quiet but authoritative way of his, not commenting on the incompetence which has rubbed the wart and produced a trickle of blood down the fine, bay skin of Alexander's neck.

Willie was, of course, an extremely accomplished amateur rider, and my greatest memory of his legendary and still-flourishing father Paddy is of the great man watching the wonder mare Dawn Run and the diminutive 60-year-old grandma Charmian Hill lapping alarmingly fast round an equally tight training circle and saying blithely, 'Ah, it will do the old girl good.' Which one?, I remember wondering.

Read Mr Scott for Mrs Hill this morning. No grandchildren but plenty of laps. Alexander Banquet is a lazy sod, so we need to get alongside a workmate to serve his quota. James Nash, the stable assistant and experienced amateur who rode Florida Pearl to win his opening bumper at Leopardstown in 1997, is on the grey Red Moccasin. Two abreast does not leave much room for manoeuvre as we start the carousel and spin round right-handed. And round and round.

It's a good job James was upsides because, after a while, you begin to lose your bearings. Each circuit we flash past a watchful Mullins at the top of the circle, plunge slightly downhill, right-handed alongside a hedge and then face a bit of collar as the turn takes us back up, with the big, green shape of the grandly named Blackstairs Mountains out to the left.

Wart and all: Alexander Banquet and temporary pilot.

Jim Bolger's place is over the brow, but this routine insists on tighter horizons. Horse and rider must balance and turn, just as the other eight or so others are doing in this spinning universe. Finally, Nash says, 'Whoa', and we ease down, the two horses blowing a little, but ready for more.

They can take it, but can this pilot? It is just 12 o'clock on a perfect, sun-spangled, early spring day in County Kilkenny. This is my fourth ride of the morning, and as Alexander Banquet has already done five laps, that makes it 26 (or is it 28?) circuits for me. And we didn't start until 9.30 a.m. 'Ah yes,' Willie had said quietly the day before when questioned as to whether a mount might be available. 'There will be plenty to ride.'

On arrival, the first clue was in the tack room. Most yards have a board with two long lists of horses between which are slotted names to signify who rides what for first and second lot. With Mullins, it is the riders' names that go across the top, with his or her group of horses listed below.

I am lucky to escape with four; Nash, Tracey Gilmour, Jason Titley and current leading jockey Barry Geraghty have five. No time for frills. At the start I had a bridle, saddle and assorted padding in my hand, plus the name and address of my first partner. She is Supreme Schemer across in the red barn, one of five large, standard agricultural barns fitted out with straw-lined concrete boxes which house up to seventy Mullins pupils. Let's go to work.

Traditionalists will flinch at the bald facts of this 'hustle in and out' system, but it doesn't take long to detect a very obvious method in this apparent madness. Plus one central, all-pervading theme. This is a trainer, these are people, who are completely at ease with their animals. And they with them.

On my first visit to Ireland, God knows how many years ago, I have never forgotten the dogs sitting in the doorways in County Carlow watching fools like me drive past. They were pretty sure of their place in the world. So are the Mullins horses, so was Supreme Schemer. She didn't seem to mind while I fitched and fiddled to get the bridle to fit her big brown head. She stood quietly while saddle and pad and girths were adjusted. Actually, she seemed quite pleased to see me.

The odd thing with what was to follow – with her, with a smaller mare called Be My Betty and with a huge young horse named Assessed, before Alexander Banquet did the honours of closing up the morning – was that what on paper looks helter-skelter never felt as if it was a hurry. Mind you, we did not have far to go.

We gather in a little sand ring between the far barn and the road. There are a couple of poles set up in the middle, over which Titley coaxes a rather baffled-looking four-year-old. We cross the road and pause while something like a giant car-park barrier lifts to allow us up the short drive to where Willie's brother George has a house, a large green barn, a paper-shredding business and the small matter of our galloping carousel.

Supreme Schemer may not have raced yet, but she has already cracked the 'merry-go-round'. Within twenty minutes we have done our session and are wandering, nostrils still dilating, back to the car-park barrier and to the second big surprise and brilliantly complementary trick of the Mullins system.

Round the back of the yard we go, off come first the saddles, then the bridles, and with just reins looped round their necks we lead them to the water trough. Then, with no more ado than it takes to write these words, we take them into the revolving door partitions of the horse-walker.

There are two of these great creaking pavilions, one six-horse, the other eight, and they turn throughout the morning. So, whilst Supreme Schemer eases down with her mates, unhindered by jockey talk, the rest of us, including Florida Pearl, potter out for the next session. But thirty minutes later Nash has peeled saddle and bridle from Ireland's much hyped, much maligned hero and, when he has taken him water, exchanges him for one of the first lot on the walker. I once watched the Whitbread Shires walk unaided to their above-ground stables in central London. This bunch look just as wise.

Of course, a central part of the Mullins system is about making a virtue out of necessity. He uses this flat, two-and-a-half-furlong oval because he does not have a hill to recreate a version of the current Pipe-inspired, uphill workbench. He follows the 'fartlek' interval session with the horsewalker, because that's the only way he can get enough horses exercised in a 'Celtic Tiger' economy, where lads can earn twice as much on a building site and have weekends off. But systems only work if they adjust to the horses within them.

By the time Alexander and I pull out, Florida Pearl is already off the walker and waiting for the standard couple of bowls of nuts which make up his lunch. By the time we have all finished and prepared to put our own snouts in the marvellous modern trough at the Lord Bagenal Inn down by the river, Florida Pearl is out in the field rolling, as muddy and happy as any hippo.

Willie Mullins looks over the fence. He is a very modest man with precious little to be modest about.

'I think it works,' he says.

The two stars could not quite make it. Despite that 'best since Arkle' handicap, Florida Pearl ran one of his finest Cheltenham races to finish six lengths runner-up to Looks Like Trouble in the Gold Cup, and Alexander Banquet stayed on to finish within a length and a half of the Sun Alliance winner Lord Noelie.

But the best Mullins system of all, winning the Champion Bumper at Cheltenham – that worked all right. In a seventeen-runner field, Willie ran four: in reverse order, Ballyamber, who was ninth; Ruby Walsh's choice Tuesday, fourth; Be My Royal, on whom James Nash came third; and Joe Cullen, running for the first time since the previous June and on whom Charlie Swan collected at 14-1. It was Willie's fourth Cheltenham Bumper win in the last five years. Yes, the system works. Mind you, so too does John Dunlop's. After Cheltenham comes the start of the Flat. This was the right place to begin.

JOHN DUNLOP
23 March 2000

ENGLAND is at its brilliant best when it mixes old traditions with modern achievement. So too is racing. There can be few more traditional places than John Dunlop's Castle Stables at Arundel. None more efficient.

Driving there in the early morning, you could go back a hundred years or further. The mist was lifting off the Sussex Downs, the great oaks of Arundel Park swished by with the Norman castle and the Catholic cathedral in the distance.

Close up, the stables themselves look like the set of a Victorian TV series. Head lad Eddie Watt seems to have been there since 1852, not 1952. But then

you look a bit closer at the coach-house clock. It says, 'Royal Ascot 1995'. Ah, yes, the championship year.

The records show that, in terms of prize-money, this was the only time the Dunlop team topped the table, but 122 winners in 1999 was once again the highest score in the land.

The location may be strictly aristocratic, you may be able to see your face in Dunlop's toe caps, the young assistant who kindly tacks up your horse may have a double-barrelled moniker, but Castle Stables has thrived for a simple business reason. It is a winner factory.

My winner is called Pairumani Star. He is a big, gleaming chestnut colt by Caerleon, five years old now. His record of six wins from twenty races is typical of the way the Castle Stables academy assesses and develops its pupils. Look back through the cuttings and you see Dunlop quotes about 'slow learner' and 'not being too ambitious'. Last year, well before flopping in the Ebor, he had won three in a row. He had learnt his lines. He was the perfect choice to show us the system.

There is no shouting, but a lot of assistants. There needs to be. There are 170 horses here, almost seventy of them now clomping round the stable yard while John looks on in that laid-back but never lazy way of his. Years ago he explained the need to have the numbers to be able to 'pan for gold', to find the super talent amongst the flood of ordinariness. But to do it you need a system and the people to work it. One of them is beside me now.

He is Gary Hatfield, a part of the travelling team headed by the ubiquitous Robert Hamilton, which shuttles runners not just all over Britain but around Europe too. The three-year-old filly Yazmin is on the ferry and autoroute to Saint-Cloud this weekend.

Gary is on the stayer Fantasy Hill, who won once from five starts in 1999, but he is remembering five years further back. That was when he was riding Erhaab.

'No stars' is the agreed line in Castle Stables this spring. And Erhaab had looked no star that spring. 'He was just another reasonably promising colt,' remembers Gary. 'He got beat on his reappearance at Newmarket, but then he suddenly got it together. He worked brilliantly before the Dante and again before the Derby. This year, there is nothing showing very much yet, but that Sakhee is a really nice colt. He might be the one.'

Sakhee is a bright bay further back in the string. He seems to have presence enough, but then Steptoe's horse would feel good in this place, on this morning.

We are walking up the tree-lined avenue which leads us on to the open parkland. A hen pheasant scuttles out of the bushes and runs towards the idyllic little cricket ground where touring sides traditionally start their season against a Duke of Norfolk's XI. The late Duchess's house, with its sweeping lawn, is now to the left of us and we are about to trot.

Amidst all the badinage there is something of the crack regiment about this outfit. The whole string of us now trot, line astern, up the seven-furlong woodchip gallop which runs beside the parkland's western wall. Halfway up you catch sight of Dunlop, out of the car and watching. He's the colonel, these are the soldiers. He has to watch. And decide.

Whatever the actual routine, the trick about a good trainer is that he and his team tend to make the right decisions and – every bit as important – avoid making the wrong ones. That means management by trust.

We circle among the beech trees and little, apparently inconsequential, checks are made. We then meander back down a path between the trees and Hatfield starts pulling his leathers up and his goggles down. We are going back to the woodchip, but this time for a 'canter'.

Well, it may be a canter to them, but in most people's terms it's a gallop – and plenty. Riding a strange horse, however highly recommended, it's usually advisable to give the one in front a healthy start to avoid brake-failure overtaking. Not at Dunlop's. They don't run away. But their 'canter' is to let them stride.

Pairumani Star may not be the fastest, but he's quick enough for me and better is yet to come. This time, our wander back takes us to the east side of the parkland and to the slightly serpentine all-weather on which the more serious gallops take place. For all his outward traditionalism, Dunlop was one of the first to give the lie to the idea that turf gallops were essential to racehorse training.

Lincoln winner Right Wing leads off the pairs of 'workers' in the clearing sunshine, and Sakhee goes off four pairs ahead of us. The instructions are that I should follow a length behind Gary and join him at the four-furlong marker. 'Don't come earlier,' he says from beneath the goggles, 'because these two will never last home.'

We do the best we can, but even getting level is quite a struggle. There is a wonderful smell of fresh woodchip. The grass is flashing by, yellow-green to the left of us. For a few blissful strides Pairumani Star flattens out to his maximum, but once we have passed Dunlop you can feel him ease off as his lungs take a great heave for oxygen. Staying is his game. Trust his team to make it another successful season.

There is that word again. Back in the yard, a full eighty minutes since we left it, 'trust' is echoed by two very different ends of the age scale. There is the youngest employee, sixteen-year-old Donna Heath from Hastings and fresh out of the Racing School, her face a picture of idealism which you pray the more venal parts of the racing game will never break. And there's Ken Butler. Nobody knows how long Ken has been at it, but you can bet he was riding work when the old king was alive.

Ken has some strange ear muffs under his helmet, but he has clear views on what a racehorse needs. 'They have to understand what is wanted,' he says, his face weathered by countless windswept mornings. 'This lot do. With this man's method they accept we are all in it together.'

Gary Hatfield was right. Sakhee was indeed 'the one'. That season he won the Sandown Classic Trial and the Dante as well as running a length second to Sinndar in the Derby itself. Next year under the Godolphin banner he was a seven-length winner of the Juddmonte International at York and a six-length destroyer of his Arc rivals, and he only got inched out of the Breeders' Cup Classic by a nose by Tiznow and an inspired Chris McCarron.

As for Pairumani Star, he continued on his admirable way, winning photo-finishes at Goodwood in May and Leopardstown in July. He was a typical product of the oiled and classical Arundel scene, but up north an equally unforgettable tableau awaited.

SUE SMITH
30 March 2000

STEPTOE AND SON meets the Brontë sisters: just when you think that Harvey and Sue Smith's operation high up on the crags of Ilkley Moor above Bingley is troublingly wild, comedy intervenes. Get too deep into the joke and you are pulled up short by some strange new truth from one of the greatest horsemen ever. Craiglands Farm is a place like no other.

Horses in every cranny of the two sets of barns huddle against the weather, few concessions are made to aesthetics, and old bits of trailers, ploughs, rollers and every other sort of agricultural hardware are parked around the top field butting on to the moor. Being the archetypal Yorkshireman, Harvey can't bear to part with anything, be it machinery or horses. Not for nothing does Sue Smith call this place 'Magpie's Castle'.

There used to be a parrot who sang 'God Save The King' in a broad Yorkshire accent. Mind you, there also used to be a big bull who bossed around the yard. 'Ah yes,' says Harvey, looking up at a huge set of horns on the wall, 'but he chased t'missus down't lane one day. So I put him up 'ere.' Once the wall was all show jumping pictures. By last Friday's visit all the recent photos were racing ones. Outside you can see why.

An elderly-looking horsebox has its back down ready for loading the four-strong party for Kelso which will produce the 37th and 38th winners of the Smiths' most successful season since they started as a hobby almost ten years ago. Harvey and jockey Seamus Durack will follow in a couple of hours' time. But Sue will stay back with Grand National runner The Last Fling and the others. She likes it that way. You see, she does the training.

Harvey's a presence, of course. He's crafted this hillside, these gallops, that schooling paddock. He has views on everything, none of them too deferential. He has an insight into horse psychology which, with his wrestler's strength and stopwatch timing, made him the unique show jumping figure of his or any era. But he's 62 now. He sits on a horse only occasionally. Sue Smith is on The Last Fling. Don't doubt that, in the saddle, she calls the shots.

Not that she or any of us are displeased with Harvey's inventions. This is a strictly functional place, where people and, above all, horses, adapt and relax. While in some yards work-riders file out in an orderly queue to be legged up one by one, here you will probably have to find your own way aboard. That's what that little mounting block is for. Lord Fortune stands. I heave myself on.

There are half a dozen of us wandering down from the top yard. Sue and The Last Fling have gathered another ten or so and we drift across the Otley Road, which climbs over this high saddle of moorland between Bingley and Guiseley, with the faded Victorian industrial backdrop of Bradford's original dark satanic mills way over beyond Baildon Moor to the south.

Sue is a calm and confident rider. She was a pretty good show jumper in her own right. 'Not up to Harvey's standards,' she says, 'but I rode at Hickstead and plenty of the big international shows.

'As for racing, my Dad [the late Henry Maslen, news of whose death was to come through later that morning] had horses with Arthur Pitt and Mick Bolton and I was always interested.

'When I joined Harvey up here we started getting them ready. And after a bit he said, "You'd better take out a licence."'

The training system they have devised is very much their own. For instance, all the horses, The Last Fling very much included, do their two-month conditioning while still spending nights in the field.

'Yes,' says Sue. 'Because we go over the moors, rather than the roads, we can leave

their hind shoes off so they can all go out in the field together.' What about a rug at night, you enquire timidly. 'Oh no,' she scoffs, in fair imitation of her husband. 'That's in summer time.'

Last week it was only early spring, but the weather gods were merciful and you could understand what a place this is to prepare horses.

'We don't do much fast work,' says Sue as The Last Fling and Lord Fortune break unprompted into their routine trot. 'We wander round these moors and they train themselves a lot. And of course,' she adds with the amused smile she keeps for all of Harvey's pet projects, 'the gallops are good.'

They are; they scrunch light and well-cushioned beneath Lord Fortune's hooves now. And they are utterly original, too. More than two miles of all-weather strips laid out around the wall-strewn, lamb-sprinkled fields. While others spend thousands on effective but expensive trademark companies, Harvey has made them himself from stuff he gets virtually for free – filler sand, plastic and, of all things, pig's hair.

'Yes,' he says when we have cantered back up to where he sits on his quadbike, 'the pig's hair holds it together.'

The head is still jaw-juttingly proud, but is now silver-haired and almost benign as he continues: 'Jockeys say it's the best surface they have ridden on. But 'ere, come and look at this job. Time we got things changed.'

Down we go to a little walled-off schooling paddock packed with fences and, germane to this discussion, with the French-style 'mini-fence' hurdles used at Southwell.

'Horses love to jump these,' says the man whose innumerable Hickstead Derbys and John Player Trophies inform his opinions. 'The old-fashioned sheep hurdles are barbaric, skin their legs, don't teach them anything. By next year every track should have these. We should be in the 21st century, not the bloody 1800s.'

While committees ponder, Harvey and Sue go their own super-practical way. One day he worked out that, with fifty horses, their team were spending 500 minutes a day, 50 hours a week, washing off horses after work. So he built a sort of water viaduct just outside the yard along which we slosh and emerge clean as whistles.

Inside, he has patented a new doorless front to the boxes where horses can lean out between pipes and take their water and food from buckets in the passage. 'It relaxes them,' says Harvey, 'ever seen 'osses as relaxed as ours?'

The Last Fling takes his cue by having a second extremely muddy roll in the paddock. His long face and narrow chestnut neck look lean after his uninspiring effort in the Gold Cup, when he was pulled up behind Looks Like Trouble. 'It was a big mistake to run him,' says Sue with typical candour, 'but we have a fortnight to freshen him up for Aintree and he just could suit the place.'

Which Sue obviously does here. Harvey has gone to Kelso where one of the winners (and for the third time) is a horse, Misty Class, whose main previous claim to fame was refusing to start and kicking Charlie Brooks in the paddock. Sue has a horse to ride and another sore-backed one to lead. Next year Errand Boy could be a major star, and bumper animals like Diceman and King Of The Light could be anything.

'I have told Harvey he has got to get rid of some the lesser ones and some of this stuff,' she says, looking across at the giant Steptoe booty in the field, 'but he's not getting rid of me.'

It is easy to think that the Smiths and the Grand National are destined for each other, but sadly The Last Fling proved not to be the horse to put them together. In 2000 he ran pretty well to finish seventh behind Papillon; in the swamped-out 2001 National he departed at the fifth fence; and while he ran his best race in 2002, his name proved all too prophetic. After leading for much of the way he crashed out and was killed at the Canal Turn on the second circuit.

But the famous Will Ogilvie line that 'Danger beckons yet to daring' still rings across the land at Aintree time, and despite the risks, yards all over the country preen, prepare and pamper their 'National horse'. This adds a special frisson to a stable visit, for the mind knows that in a week or two's time the horse up ahead of you could be not just under your eye, but out in front of the greatest global audience a horse race ever draws.

Then again, our visit to see the then Grand National favourite Star Traveller at Henry Daly's stable in Shropshire was never going to be on the dull side.

HENRY DALY
6 March 2000

CHEERFUL ASPECT by name and by nature. He is a jolly brute, who started life as a Sheikh Hamdan hopeful and whose speciality is bucking you off at the canter. He did it to Walter Swinburn on his very first run as a two-year-old, at Newcastle in August 1995. Now he is trying to do it to me. Laugh? – the lads at Henry Daly's are nearly dying.

Suddenly, serious thoughts, rather than me, need chucking out of the window. Up ahead on the woodchip, leading Grand National hope Star Traveller is moving sweetly under Jenny Macdonald.

Out to the right, the wooded hillside opens to reveal Ludlow racecourse, neat and idyllic way below in the clearing. After a few more leaps Cheerful Aspect forsakes the bronco act. Normal service can resume.

This part of Shropshire, hard by Mortimer Forest and the Welsh border, is a hidden arcadia which our motorway world has mercifully not reached. It seems almost too beautiful, too much of the past, to be capable of housing something as purposeful as a Grand National-winning stable. But the trick is not to be awed by the setting, but to use it.

At first sight, Daly, Micky Wiggin and Star Traveller are figures from another era. But what is happening at Downton Hall is not just up to speed. It is turning history on its head.

To look around, as we follow Star Traveller and his stablemates down the drive, is to go back almost two centuries.

The big house and its tended lawns look down across the green fields of the valley and on up to where Titterstone Clee stands to the east, 1,700 foot high, wild and jagged.

Downton Hall and its 5,000 adjoining acres on the ancient Rose-Boughton estate is the archetypal country seat. It seems to be Regency Shropshire alive and well in the year 2000.

So how come Star Traveller and his team will take Saturday's spotlight – and have earned it? Because they are all professionals now. Horse, trainer, owner, stables, the house itself.

Without the focus Daly's success now gives it, this would be just another relic without a future. In Star Traveller's saddle 25-year-old, Shrewsbury-born Jenny Macdonald is not interested in the tale of how, nine years ago, Tim Forster's long-time friend and owner Wiggin inherited this huge pile from one of those amazing foxhunting maiden ladies straight out of P.G. Wodehouse.

It is cold. It is one week before the National. She has a job to do.

Industry is what unites. The outlook, unless you are a techno-billionaire or a hotel and golf course complex, is notoriously bleak for country estates. These fields are already strewn with lambs, but all sheep are nearly valueless. And if you do stick to farming, it is machines, not people, who do the work.

Enter racing. There are twenty of us about to turn and jog back up the drive. Its inherent heavy labour count is usually seen as training's biggest drawback. In rural Shropshire it is a godsend.

Daly, like the horses, fits the place like a native. A couple of generations back he would have been another young sporting gent doing the social round.

At 33, he still has some of those trappings and plenty of easy, self-deprecating charm. But he gets up early. So he should. No inheritance, not even taking over where the late Tim Forster so memorably left off two seasons ago, guarantees anything in racing now. But Star Traveller and 36 winners this term show that Daly and his team have got a system that clicks.

It is an odd mixture of ancient and modern. On the one hand you have the old house's stable block once ringing with coach horses and hunters; above it there is a sixteen-strong yard aligned in the current thinking, a seventy-head capacity in all.

Outside there is the sweep of some of the most tempting-looking grassy hillside in the country. But what we are now approaching is a five-furlong strip of woodchip gallop up a bank.

The traditionalist Forster, with Grand National wins from Well To Do, Ben Nevis and Last Suspect already to his name, never believed he would cope with the gallop's limitations when he moved in July 1994. A best-ever 52-winner, Champion Chase-lifting final season four years later was his ultimate, albeit soon to be posthumous, salute.

David Cooper came with him from Letcombe Bassett. A head lad's life has made him leaner and more country-vowelled than his brother Andrew of Epsom and Sandown fame.

But the two sons of the head dairyman to the Overbury herd near Bredon are very much the same in their cool response to crises. David's came when Forster's head lad John Humphrys died suddenly fifteen years ago.

'I was at Nicky Henderson's when The Captain rang,' says David. 'I suppose I would still be second travelling head lad there now. It was easy to accept the challenge at Letcombe, more difficult moving the family. But we're wonderfully settled. It's a marvellous place for children-and for horses.'

The current equine pride and joy is a couple of places ahead of us, a light, lithe little bay much more like the Flat-racer he tried so unsuccessfully to be as a two-year-old (ninth of nine, tenth of thirteen and eighteenth of nineteen) than the big joker I am on. The story has been often told of how he later became a point-to-pointer, winning his last two and then his first five chases under Rules. Of how his continued improvement has seen him rise 35lb in the ratings.

What matters now is the glow of his coat and the tribute he pays to the way Cooper with Forster, and now with his young successor, has adjusted from old ways to new.

Well, slightly new. The surface may have changed but not all that much else. The two exasperations of riding for Forster, which I was lucky to do for six or so years, was that everything, from the season to the actual cantering, would go so slowly. Nothing was winning until practically Christmas, every canter would test your arms to the sockets. With all-weather gallops and young

Henry at the helm, presumably we are into a rapid-fire, twelve-month, Martin Pipe-type system. Don't hold your breath.

Whatever happens to Star Traveller this weekend, Daly is well on the climb. But what he offers is all the fun and excitement of jumping, pure and simple, in the most beautiful environment imaginable. If that means this season's first winner did not happen until October 29, well, that goes with the territory.

And if you think that when we hit the all-weather you can let the animal run in the 'half-speed' canters beloved of Flat-race trainers, dream on. Get your anchors out. Or, if on Cheerful Aspect, get the parachute ready.

The truth is that this steady camber work is a perfect platform on which the stable builds its fitness.

The one snag is that if you have not switched your horse off after half a mile you are then confronted with a slightly downhill last furlong. A couple of years back the brakes failed on the ill-fated Coonawarra, who then jumped a large hedge into the next-door field. His promising pilot was so unnerved that he quit the game almost immediately.

No dramas this time. Only an appreciation of the place and of the little bright-eyed, so-aptly-named horse who could follow Cheltenham winners Dublin Flyer and Martha's Son in putting it indelibly on the map.

Simon White is the bearded son of Ken White, who won English, Welsh and Midlands Nationals in his riding days with Fred Rimell and will be driving Star Traveller up to Aintree on Saturday. Simon is in charge of the second yard at Downton, and has inherited much of his father's unaffected wisdom.

'He's a star,' he says of the leading Grand National light, 'a star in every sense.'

Looking back at all these moments of hope humbles me with the attrition of the consequences. For while Star Traveller went off 10-1 second favourite for the 2000 Grand National and put up a brilliant display of jumping to lead for much of the way, it still proved to be his last race. A bad mistake at second Valentine's jarred an old injury and he had to be pulled up.

Hope is one of racing's greatest assets, and for a long while Star Traveller and Aintree had seemed a dream come true. But reality had still got its man, and after doffing our cap to little Star Traveller we had to move back to the Flat. For April means Guineas time, and trying to switch one's mind from hardened old chasers to flashy young colts hardly past their third birthday.

In 2000 the leading British contender for the Two Thousand Guineas was the Barry Hills-trained Distant Music, whose unbeaten three race sequence as a two-year-old had ended with the Champagne Stakes-Dewhurst Stakes double. It seemed a great idea to go and have a look at him. But actually seeing him proved easier to say than do.

BARRY HILLS

13 April 2000

ROBERT CAPA was the bravest and most brilliant war photographer of the twentieth century. Fog would hardly have fazed him, and it doesn't worry the horse who carries his name. But it does the man on top.

Barry Hills's first lot is coming onto the long canter to the left of the Faringdon Road, but, with the fog and mist heavy on the grass, we can't see twenty metres. Capa and I are last in the file and, as the others kick off, he momentarily lugs over to the right. In a second we are hot in pursuit, but the tail in front is disappearing. It belongs to Distant Music.

Capa is a grand, big, good-fronted colt by Salse with strange white roan patches behind the saddle. He was second in both his races as a two-year-old, but middle distances will be his forte.

Even at this spinning, natural canter, he takes his time to get going. Distant Music doesn't. He's Guineas favourite. For a few dreadful fogged-out seconds, he shows us why.

Being lost in the fog is one of the worst imaginable experiences on a galloping racehorse. It happened to Keith Barnfield and me on the top of Cleeve Hill with two of Frenchie Nicholson's a fortnight before one of them ran in the National.

Back then, I remember there was a quarry somewhere up ahead. What may happen off the track up the Faringdon Road is a mystery I do not want to solve for anyone. Especially not for Barry Hills.

The weather is about the only thing that this most meticulous of men cannot organise. But, as we see later, he is working on it.

The immaculate, but highly functional massive four-barn Faringdon Place complex which Barry has created a mile out of Lambourn on the road to Wantage is, in every sense, a living, working monument to his half century in the game.

'It's incredible,' Capa's owner Bob McCreery says later. 'When Manton [which Hills had rented from Robert Sangster] went wrong and he had to move back to South Bank he was in his fifties and considering retirement. But he borrowed a million pounds, built this place and now, at 63, has 150 horses and is going better than ever.'

At seven o'clock you can't see Barry, but then you can't see anything. Not outside, that is. Inside it's different. Inside is how the Hills team operate. These horses are luxury goods.

These big barns with their controlled ventilation, their rows of pristine boxes, their tack rooms and, praise heaven, their 'old-stagers-turn-in-the-

grave' state-of-the-art toilets, are Fortnum and Mason compared with the normal stable's standard store. Yes, Barry is working the top of the market.

This means the best conditions for people as well as horses and, as some forty of us gather in the huge aircraft hangar of a covered school, it is no surprise to see some familiar and, let's say it, old faces atop this year's class of racing hopefuls.

Few more familiar, none older, than Ollie Brennan. He's lean and light and 63. He's ridden all sorts of good horses, including Brigadier Gerard and Slightly Dangerous, the dam of Warning. Now he rides Distant Music.

The first glimpse of the Guineas favourite is one of racing's most heady rites of spring. Of course, everyone always says the same thing.

'He's done really well through the winter, we're really pleased with him,' etc, etc. But this time the tribute and where it comes from is particularly potent.

'He has never,' says Ollie, patting Distant Music's neck with a grey-gloved hand, 'raised hoof nor head to anyone. I have never had a nicer colt to deal with.'

Racehorses are an athletic commodity, but they are also sentient creatures for whom confidence is key.

As we file out across the road you notice the easy poise and the elegantly cocked wrists of the ageless little man aboard Distant Music. Confidence flows down the reins. Horsemanship never had anything to do with calendars.

But it's time to concentrate on one's own inadequacies. Ollie and the others are pulling their leathers up.

No preliminary trots – in a minute or two we'll be off into the murk. Terry Sturrock is two ahead on last year's Ascot winner Elmutabaki. Now he's disappeared, and Distant Music after him. Capa may not win the Guineas but, believe me, he is trying.

Everything gets exaggerated in the fog: the sense of speed, of distance, almost of reality itself. At the end of the canter you suddenly wonder what all the fuss was about. We get back to talking up the season and picking over the last and the tenth and twentieth and thirtieth that went before.

'He's more refined than power house,' says Sturrock of Distant Music, 'real speed. Remember the Champagne.'

Brennan wants to remember the 1963 Bunbury Cup. He did a Matt Feakes horse called Songedor and he is still bollocking Jimmy Lindley for coming too soon.

Barry Hills is on a little chestnut pony called Conroy. He's not a great one for early-morning conversation, but those narrowed eyes don't miss a lot as we file past fifty-odd horses to be brought to racing pitch.

So many imponderables. So many easy ways to mess things up. The winners have already started, but the weather is changeable. 'You have to be careful you don't set them back,' he says.

He won't talk about 'secrets', but of 'doing things right'. The place is modern, but not faddy. He feeds just twice a day, after exercise and in the evening. He gets his hay from Hertfordshire, not Washington State.

He weighs everything, but does not panic about it. He knows that the system has to work. That the team, from assistant Kevin Mooney to teenage Robert Naylor, are professionals who want success just as much as he does.

'It's much more efficient here,' says Barry, as we get second lot started, with breakfast to be taken later. 'When we were trailing all the way over from South Bank I was always chasing my tail.' They are the words not of contentment but of a competitor who, no fewer than 31 years on from his first licence, could well have his best year yet.

Attention to detail is not just necessary, it is a life force in itself. For it questions as much as it answers.

At breakfast he rattles off the horse, jockey and race (Acropolis, Doug Smith, Winston Churchill Stakes, Hurst Park, 1956) in a picture, hanging in the South Bank loo, which also features as stable lad a young trilby-hatted B. Hills.

After breakfast we step outside and up into the converted loft command centre, where three secretaries beaver away.

One of them comes across with a printed chart from the local meteorological centre, and she and B. Hills then get involved in an animated discussion about their ability to put a computer pattern to the climate.

Yes, he is trying to fix the weather.

'This man,' says McCreery admiringly, 'is a real pro.'

Distant Music proved to be a good horse but not a Classic winner. Just beaten in the Greenham (run that year at Newmarket), he was some eight lengths off King's Best in the Two Thousand Guineas, and although after a long summer break he got things back on track with a good third behind Kalanisi and Montjeu in the Champion Stakes, his four-year-old career did not fulfil that promise.

But his trainer still keeps pressing on. In 2006, Barry Hills' 70th year, he trained 103 winners and clocked up a record £1.8 million in prize money. Yes, training can keep you young – particularly, as our next stop confirmed, at the beginning of the week.

PETER HARRIS
27 March 2000

THERE is nothing like a Monday morning squeal. It happens at the trot and runs right up through a horse like lightning in reverse. From hoof to head the whole body quivers and flexes with a sudden rush of explosive, cork-popping well-being. Inigo Jones was like that last week.

He is entitled to be. The sun has had come out between the showers in this beautiful and historic corner of Hertfordshire, eight miles west of Aylesbury, with the great, wooded bank of Ashridge to the north-east.

Inigo had started his four-year-old season with a victory under Walter Swinburn at Haydock. He was to return there three weeks later, this time fourth under Pat Eddery in a bigger field.

Up ahead of him in this trotting ring is Primo Valentino, the little chunky star who will carry the Peter Harris stable banner in the Two Thousand Guineas.

Inigo squeals again. He's not very big, but his bright bay neck gleams with condition and the limbs beneath have champagne fizz. Like most racehorses, he and the others spent Sunday resting in the box. But they are born to run – and on a Monday, given half a chance, to buck.

The horse behind suddenly plunges left into the centre of the circle, to the whooping delight of the rest of us. But we had better be careful. We are on camera.

At Church Farm, Aldbury, you nearly always are. The famous open-house, syndicate-owning philosophy perfected by Harris means that a staff of four are constantly on hand to mind owners who come to call. A splendidly equipped clubhouse lounge overlooks the yard, and at this moment Peter Mason, who joined the team after a career in, of all things, local government, is lensing away to make sure all the pictures are up to date.

There is plenty to look at. For as we finally file off the trotting ring and pass the chuckling vet, Bob Baskerville ('Ah yes, the Monday-morning squeal,' he says approvingly), you are already struck by the central Harris trick of mixing ancient and modern. The gates to Church Farm may swing open automatically, but in the old-style yard there is plenty of hard-won wisdom.

Jimmy Miller may not be exactly ancient, but he was 21 years with Clive Brittain, (and took Bold Arrangement to the Kentucky Derby in 1986) before he and his partner Jenny Morris came to Aldbury seven years ago. Jimmy and Jenny know the score. And it shows.

Mind you, at Aldbury scores were settled rather differently in the old days. Beside the picture-postcard duck pond in the village green there is a still healthy looking set of wooden stocks, into which mediaeval miscreants were put and pelted with tomatoes.

Pat Eddery may yet be in danger of similar treatment if things don't work out on the racetrack, but as our fifteen-strong string winds to the right through the village, the lane in the opposite direction is called Stocks Road. Thereby hangs a tale.

For the lane leads to Stocks mansion, now the centre of an impressive country club but formerly the home of Playboy supremo Victor Lowndes. Time was when Victor used to ask a well-known racing figure round of a Sunday morning. At the front door the butler's habitual greeting was, 'Mr Lowndes is in the bath and asks you to join him.' But this was a Playboy jacuzzi. This one used to have 'Bunnies' beneath the foam.

Whether such revelries were prompted by trotting alongside the startlingly glamorous, blonde pony-tailed, blue-and-mauve-riding-suited Sally Skyrme, I will leave to your imagination.

Sally is the former wife of David Skyrme, who rode many jumping winners for the yard and still employs his jockey skills here every morning before doubling up working for horse suppliers Dodson and Horrell in the afternoons. Sally and David know that the Harris horses, and indeed the Harris treatment – most staff can be found free housing in this most expensive of areas – are too good to miss.

The most expensive horse is ahead of us now as we trot south-westwards towards the railway line and the Grand Union canal. Primo Valentino is not very tall and has no great front and shoulder on him, but he's a runner and has proved it. His five-win sequence, culminating in the Middle Park, deservedly won his twelve-person syndicate the Racehorse Owners' Association Award for 1999. After a setback with some unseasonable snow, he now goes straight for the Guineas.

The experienced Colin Williams is in Primo's saddle. Colin came from Peter Chapple-Hyam's last season, but he, like the rest of us, will have been both amazed and impressed at the originality and effectiveness of the Harris system, which sees the fifty-strong bunch of two-year-olds housed at Pendley Farm, a mile away up the Tring road from Aldbury, and which has every horse being turned out before Christmas.

'I had never seen anything like it,' says Colin. 'Primo was out for six weeks among eighteen colts and geldings. You'd think it would be a disaster, but they soon settle down.' Between lots – I had ridden the charming but, from his form, rather aptly named Rogue Spirit first lot – Peter Harris takes me to Pendley, the magnificent spread formerly owned by the famous 'Voice

of Show Jumping', Dorian Williams. In ten wonderfully lucid minutes this absurdly young 66-year-old soon makes everything clear.

He shows me the seventeen-acre field which was Primo's holiday home. He explains that the horses quickly get a pecking order, but this in no way relates to racecourse performance: Primo was middle of the road. 'You don't save on food,' he says. 'They eat nearly 18lb a day, but their heads get a rest.' He shows the stud paddocks next door where Primo was bred, and then we return down to the two-year-old yard which Robert Eddery now runs with the efficiency of his brother Pat in the saddle.

Before Robert came in 1991 there were just thirty Harris-trained horses. This year there are a record 104, but time and motion fits them all. There is a six-furlong hill gallop at Pendley for early work, but in full season everything is done on the one-mile woodchip, which Primo and Colin, Sally and her horse Volontiers and I are now approaching. The two-year-olds use it between the older-horse lots. Getting there is quite alarming because a Virgin train whizzes by about ten yards away. In this case, horses scare a lot less than people.

Nothing scary about Inigo on the gallop. This is supposedly just a canter, but the Harris horses don't hang about. He wings away beneath me. Somewhere up front Primo is powering along in his Classic preparation, but for a few brief moments Inigo and I, plus Sally and Volontiers, are the only world that matters. The gallop bends left and upwards to where Harris and an owner have a sunlit grandstand view.

Way out on the northern horizon you can see the giant column erected in 1832 by the Earl of Bridgewater. You don't have to be an aristocrat to share in what this corner of Hertfordshire now has to offer, but riding or watching the likes of Inigo sure makes you feel like one.

I guess we would all squeal to that.

Every spring there is a three-year-old who has shown such dazzling pace as a two-year-old that lucid appraisal suggests he is unlikely to last out the straight mile of the Guineas. But every year those closest to him get infected with a sense of belief which waves such sense aside. In 2000 such a horse was Primo Valentino.

Much as we all wanted to will him stamina that Pendley morning, come Guineas day his sprinting pace never looked like lasting home, and he finished seventh behind King's Best. Thereafter he did not race over further than six furlongs, coming a close fourth to Agnes World in the 2000 July Cup and taking the Abernant Stakes at Newmarket first time out the following season.

A new horse can be bought at the sales; a new man to take on the training burden can be more difficult to find. But for Peter Harris there came a family solution. Walter Swinburn had married his daughter Allison, and as Walter came to terms with life after being a three-time Derby-winning jockey his original insistence that 'I would never think of training' began to turn.

Gradually he became more and more involved, and at the end of 2004 Peter Harris handed over the licence, and the official trainer at Pendley Farm is now one W.R. Swinburn. There have, as yet, been no superstars, but with Peter revelling in the title of 'assistant trainer' the family firm continues on the climb.

However much success he has as a trainer, Walter Swinburn will never lose the tag of 'The Teenager who won the Derby on Shergar'. But it should not hang heavy round his neck, because the glories of the past are only a burden if you refuse to face the future, and training racehorses forces you to face forward every day.

Our next visit was to Britain's greatest living proof of this. Training Desert Orchid made David Elsworth part of the nation's family. He was the means by which we understood what made 'Dessie' tick. He was almost as much ventriloquist as trainer in all the television interviews we did together down the years. 'He's like a ship under sail,' David said at Kempton one day, as he explained why Desert Orchid galloped so much better right-handed (as there) compared with left-handed (as at Cheltenham.) 'He just seems to catch the wind better on that side.'

It was a great and illuminating image, and the possibility of such insights added extra magnetism to an Elsworth stable tour. But with Dessie retired there was always the danger of David becoming a transatlantic echo of American legend Charlie Whittingham's warning: 'What would I do without training? Just become an old drunk?'

That possibility will always beckon many of us, but during the spring of 2000 David was on a roll.

DAVID ELSWORTH
4 May 2000

AT WHITSBURY the sap is running, and so are the horses. Hundreds of them – mares, foals, stallions and, of course, the biggest racing squad ever seen in these parts, aiming to put David Elsworth back at the top of the tree.

Among them is a grey horse to ride. Benatom feels proud to pace the same yard as Desert Orchid.

Dessie's box is the one on the corner with a blue plaque on it. The inscription says: 'Winner of 34 of 70 races.' Ten years ago, Dessie had just cruised home in the Irish National, Barnbrook Again had won the Queen

Mother Champion Chase at Cheltenham, and In The Groove was about to start that extraordinary roller-coaster three-year-old career which would see her win the Irish Guineas, the Juddmonte International and the Champion Stakes. But that was then. This is seven o'clock on the Tuesday of Guineas week. This is now.

We file out through the arched gateway, and start walking up the lane of what is a tiny village but a big name. Whitsbury Stud, with Cadeaux Genereux, Magic Ring and Compton Place plus this year's harem of visiting mares, is over the bluebell bank.

Elsworth's two top yards are dispatching some of their number to join us. There is another blue plaque: it is for Reform, winner of the Champion Stakes for Sir Gordon Richards back in 1967.

Benatom has his own perfectly honourable history. He's seven years old now, quite a dark grey with still quite a bit of shaggy winter coat. He started off with Henry Cecil, winning at Thirsk, Goodwood, Newmarket and York. Two years ago he came to Elsie and won at Wincanton before running a good sixth in the Supreme Novices' Hurdle at Cheltenham.

Last year he ran eleven times on the Flat, was a bit unlucky in the Northumberland Plate and then won the Reg Day Memorial at Newmarket for a second time. Even trotting up this specially watered lane, well balanced, no extravagance, ears half interested, you can feel that he has seen it all.

But history is needed for inspiration, not relaxation. And the familiar grey-haired, ruminant-faced figure pedalling two-wheeled beside us has quite literally got on his bike to find it. After unhappy hiccups both to his training and to his personal life when he moved west to Whitcombe in Dorset, Elsworth has 'retired' from driving, and is back to the rolling downs and those deep-hedged Hampshire lanes outside Fordingbridge where he once showed something close to a genius touch.

So, most importantly, are almost all of the main players with whom he has made this not so much a standard training operation as a sort of country commune. Peter Vaughn, Ross Arnott, David Croft, Seamus Brady, Dick Brown, Paul Holley and, of course, up ahead of us on Indian Blaze, the neat but now 64-year-old figure of Rodney Boult.

We are walking down towards the gallops with the cow smell of the milking parlour strong on the breeze, but with the famous open expanse of Whitsbury stretching away in the distance. It was the sight that used to drive Dessie wild.

Except with Rodney. 'The old horse could be a real bastard,' remembers Alan McCabe, himself no mean performer in the saddle, 'would hook his head up and cart anyone. But Rodney could just give him a long rein and relax him. Hack him round here easy.' They like horses to enjoy themselves here.

We have reached the two-furlong woodchip circle on which all thirty of us trot and hack happily round. Benatom does it like clockwork, just quickening after the first circuit as a little rush of well-being brings a couple of little bucks out of him. The breeze has sharpened a bit, and on our final turn a three-year-old filly called Toleration suddenly won't tolerate it and whips off to the right, dumping the nimble Kevin Parsons who, in moments, has vaulted back on board.

Maybe Toleration had taken her cue from a couple of out-of-character pieces of early morning bolshiness up ahead. To much junior amusement, the great Rodney had a problem making Indian Blaze leave his stablemates, and then yesterday's Ascot sixth Premier Prize decided that she would make life difficult for young Neil Pollard.

Order is soon restored, albeit at the expense of a bit of Elsworth cussing, and soon we are trailing down into the valley where the hurdles still stand as tribute to the once-a-year, speed-of-sound schooling sessions to which Dessie used to subject Richard Dunwoody and Simon Sherwood. Pollard was in Dubai during the winter, riding some twenty winners for Paddy Rudkin. But this is his stable, this is the season when he needs to convert promise to big-time performance. The signs suggest that the indicators are on green.

That's exactly the feeling when we walk in right-handed and let our six-strong pack spin their way half a mile up the grass to where the trainer is waiting. The old turf has already dried out beautifully. Benatom and the others have the spring of a thousand winners beneath them.

On the way back the silver-haired cyclist checks over each of us, but you sense that his mind is already on the next lot. Once in the yard his enthusiasm shows you why. Into one wood-shaving-lined box after another he leads you. 'Just look at this,' he says, patting the chestnut frame of yesterday's Ascot second Persian Punch as the first of a whole series of infectious introductions. 'We will aim for the Melbourne Cup again. Should have won two years ago.'

On past Pawn Broker – 'He's a good horse, and that thing of Dunlop's who beat him [Sakhee, in the Classic Trial at Sandown Park] must be decent'. Past the giant, white-legged Alfini 'He can go, and he'll do well in the Guineas', to the tiny, almost pony-sized Scarteen Fox, whom Pollard is about to tack up. 'Now this is a star,' says Elsie. 'He has got all the gears. He ran a cracker at Newmarket.'

Deadly Serious is unlikely to be given much of a star rating on his public efforts so far, but he makes a smashing mobile grandstand as the sun comes out and we all wend our way back up past the stud, the cow parlours and on to where the skylarks sing.

This time we follow the first hacking circuits with a wander further down the lane before turning right and breezing back an uphill, dog-legged five furlongs to rejoin the ring. Deadly Serious whizzes scratchily along as a would-be sprinter. Up here even the ordinary horse comes to believe he can run.

That's the lesson this team has at its core. Elsworth plays the instinctive game. Sure Jean Hunt, Mary McCabe, Michael Meredith and Chris Hill make sense of things in the office, and assistant Tony Charlton has been an important import from Toby Balding. True, the whole ventilation of the top yard has been redone over the winter. But at root this all stems from a country, not a computer, brain.

The sun is warm now. We have taken the saddles off to let the horses roll and pick grass in the paddock. Next to us is a lovely, long-striding chestnut two-year-old by Cozzene called Giza. He is one of nearly fifty, by far the best batch Elsie has ever had. The trees are in blossom. All the instincts say that this place will be, too.

Plenty of good things happened to the Elsworth yard in 2000, most notably Persian Punch's wins in the Henry II Stakes at Sandown and Prix Kergorlay at Deauville, and the season came towards its close with that horse's runaway Jockey Club Cup in October.

Persian Punch was then seven years old, yet incredibly was to compete in another 35 races, and notch a further eleven famous victories, before that unique career came to a tragic end in April 2004 in the Sagaro Stakes at Ascot – the same race in which he had run so well the day before my visit.

And as ever, many hopes of the early morning sunshine in May 2000 ended up on the dark side of the moon.

The two year old Giza never made it to the racetrack. The giant chestnut Alfini moved menacingly up to the leaders in the Two Thousand Guineas, only to break a hind leg and have to be put down.

My second ride Deadly Serious never won a race and my first one, Benatom, ended a long and honourable career a week after our visit and then had a happy retirement with his owners at the Lordship Stud.

David went on to train his 1,000th winner at Salisbury in August 2000, and in 2002 he and his team moved on to historic Egerton House near Newmarket, where a by then almost completely white Desert Orchid finally left us in April 2004.

It is possible to twist oneself into all sorts of anthropomorphic knots about the fate of current and former racehorses, but the truth is they are sentient beings without imagination. Therefore they should be treated with care and respect, but we should recognize reality. If a horse is healthy physically and mentally he or she may easily have a second life in another equestrian discipline, but if not, euthanasia is often the kindest option. We human beings have brought them into this world, and it is sometimes our duty to take them out.

Such thoughts are prompted by the memory of the next stable tour and the horse I rode there, who after his racing career came to the Moorcroft Welfare Centre (of which I am a trustee) and was quickly reorganized as a thoroughly enjoyable hack. Not bad for a sprinter for whom speed was once the only thing. But then he was always a good guy to be with.

TERRY MILLS

11 May 2000

W HO SAYS they can't talk? Mitcham stopped and looked at the pheasant. It was strutting through the undergrowth dragging a great, sweeping tail of almost peacock dimensions. It was 6.15 on Tuesday morning and the other horses were moving ahead of us into the mist. But Mitcham would not budge. 'Quiet,' he says to my suggestion that we should follow them. 'Can't you see I am watching it?'

It is the ears that tell you; they are refined and pointed and flick back and forth as he takes in everything around and, in this case, on top of him.

Mitcham is a big black colt whose finest hour, you will remember, was when he won the King's Stand Stakes for Terry Mills at Royal Ascot last summer as a three-year-old. He has a wide bull's neck that rises bold and upright in front of you and he has such a composure about him it would be almost embarrassing to ask why he finished a disappointing twentieth out of 21 in his Palace House Stakes comeback on Saturday.

There's no stroppiness about colts like Mitcham. Indeed, all those around Loretta Lodge love him to death, and you don't doubt it when his lad Matt Venn says that Ascot 'was the happiest day of my life – I was not ashamed to be crying.' There's no need for arguments and little point in them. Mitcham has good manners, he has got the ability, but he needs to do things his own way.

You could say the same about Mills, except that he is in rather more of a hurry and that at 61 we are unlikely to get any overseas offers for stud.

At 5.45 he had been sipping coffee in his cramped little office, already planning the day with son Robert, assistant Richard Ryan and jockey Tony Clark. He remains the cockney-vowelled Londoner who began with one rubbish truck and developed A. & J. Bull into a multi-million-pound waste disposal business, which he cashed in big-time two years ago but still runs for the new owners. He didn't get here by lying in bed of a morning.

Loretta Lodge is on the Headley Road on the southern side of Epsom, but reaching it at that time of morning had taken less than half an hour from Battersea. On the Downs the mist might make most things seem asleep, but back in town, the 44 bus from Tooting to Vauxhall had been through the Wandsworth roundabout, and the commuter rush hour had well begun. First lot at Mills's had a much greener feel. We may be close to the city, but threading our way up past the buildings and paddocks which adorn this 150-acre spread you can appreciate how well Epsom has fought to keep much of its country virtue.

There are a dozen of us – the two leaders fluorescent-jacketed to get us safely down the 200-yard strip of road – and in a few minutes we have turned left to wander down the straggly, thick-wooded lane they call 'The Sheep Walk'.

Soon after Mills bought Loretta Lodge from Brian Swift's executors, the Great Hurricane of 1987 looked to have spread enough trees across the Sheep Walk to stop Hitler's invasion itself. Terry scoffed at the task. This was the man who, thirty years ago, was knocking down houses in Battersea for £200 that are worth £200,000 today, so a few trees were not going to stop him.

On Tuesday there was fresh woodchip laid, a path proud enough for an Ascot winner. Or a pheasant.

After a minute or so, Mitcham decides that he has seen enough of Chinese plumes and tails, and wanders off after our guide, who is in a much more nervous condition.

Torrid Kentavr is a Trempolino three-year-old who last week had his first run for the stable when a good third to the Cumani colt Trumpet Sound at Brighton. He's had some time off and now it's back on the gallops again. It's sending him sweaty and fidgety.

However bad the worry, he's lucky to have a calm pilot. Ken Hartnett is the sort of spare, light young Irishman you see in paintings of horse fairs in Dingle. Now 26, he left County Kildare at sixteen to seek his fortune and had his own fifteen minutes of fame when he and David's Duky won the Eider Chase in 1992. He's been through a number of jobs, but is very impressed with the staff house Mills has provided. As Torrid Kentavr jig-jogs towards the start of the Wax Track artificial gallop at the bottom of Six Mile Hill, he justifies the wages.

Hartnett's grandfather was wheelchair-bound after a pile-up involving Pat Eddery's dad Jimmy at Dundalk in the 1950s. Racing is full of such intricate bloodlines, but when Mitcham begins to float along in the misty wake of Torrid Kentavr there is only one family tree that really matters. For, however ridiculously unbelievable it may be, an extension of both horses' pedigrees would take you back to the greatest of all founding fathers who, no fewer than 231 years ago this month, first ran across these Downs to land the most famous bet in history. Eclipse first, the rest nowhere.

Epsom has been through a lot of highs and lows since Eclipse's day. On the training front they looked like hitting rocky times a couple of years back when three big stables closed together. But with Running Stag flying an international flag, with Simon Dow heading an Epsom Trainers' Association application for Heritage money for stable staff, and with more gallops than ever before, things are on the go.

So is Mitcham, though so cool and easy that you wonder where he gets the fire in him to run through a thundering field of sprinters. So is his trainer, although in his case you can see where the fire lies.

Mills is a man of appetite who knows how to get hungry men around him. For him, what has happened so far is good – but not good enough.

Back in the yard Matt Venn greets Mitcham with undisguised relief, head girl Karen Latchford hoses off muddy legs and Paddy Duddy appears to remind you that it was he who led up Lester Piggott that day when Indigenous broke the world speed record at Epsom in 1960. But Terry Mills is the presence. And Terry has a plan.

The achievements of the likes of Mitcham, Bobzao and All The Way are not enough. They were successes, but bargain buys. In the last two years he has upped the ante and there are classically bred, later-maturing horses among the forty-strong team.

Barathea's son Norton cost 300,000gns as a yearling and was seen as a live candidate for this year's Derby until a series of niggling setbacks. Among the two-year-olds are horses by Cadeaux Genereux, Ela-Mana-Mou and, maybe most coveted of all, the 160,000 guineas son of Sadler's Wells called Tender Trap.

This lot don't gather on the Downs until the mist has lifted and the sun is warm. They are only hacking, but there's no doubting the promise they show, no avoiding the enthusiasm they generate.

'We have done well,' says Mills, changed and showered before returning to the day job in Merton. 'We have won big races. We have got our own swimming pool, lunging rings, paddocks and circular five-furlong Polytrack. We have had everything except ...' He pauses and his voice goes very gravelly South London: 'Except that Classic winner. And there's going to be one among this lot. I promise yer.'

Yes, horses can talk. The trick is to listen. Some ears are being cocked pretty cute down at Epsom.

Norton did not make it as a Classic hope, any more, sadly, than Epsom has progressed as a training centre. But the horse's 57 runs for Terry Mills included a true glory day when he had the top hats raised by winning the Hunt Cup at Royal Ascot in 2002. He battled on as a much liked member of the stable for another four seasons. Forget about the original dreams, or even that 350,000 guineas price as a yearling. He was a racehorse. He had been found his level. That is what a trainer is for – be they at Epsom or rather further afield.

Many parts of Britain seem to lay claim to the title of 'God's Own Country', but Yorkshire appears to do it most – and not just because it can boast eight racecourses to its name. Travelling north from York towards Malton and beyond, there is a more appropriate title. It should be called 'Easterby Country'.

A couple of years back I tried to persuade Mick, the master of Sheriff Hutton – and of several thousand acres and quite a few horses into the bargain – to write his autobiography. 'I can't do that,' said this earthiest of millionaires, 'I have done some terrible things.'

Five miles north-east across past Castle Howard and into the Habton Vale, Peter Easterby admits to no unbridled naughtiness, but some of the chuckles around his stories suggest that he was not always the loser. What he, his brother, and now his son Tim exhibit is a deep, uncomplicated knowledge of the game and its creatures. That's why it's always good to go there for education.

TIM EASTERBY
18 May 2000

THEY don't hang about between canters at Habton. At most stables you get a full ten minutes while you circle around, receive instructions and get reorganised. With Tim and Peter Easterby, you are lucky to get ten seconds.

But then they don't hang about over anything. What this astonishingly well-balanced father-and-son operation are up to in the flat lands between Castle Howard and Kirkbymoorside is as good an example of controlled hurry and organised chaos as you will find in any business anywhere in these islands.

Peter Easterby was the first we saw on Monday morning, wandering out to open a paddock gate with a fat black Labrador at his heels. In his habitual flat cap, gumboots and old maroon sweater, you might think his biggest task of the day would be selling a few cattle at Malton market. You would be a hundred horses and a thousand acres in the wrong.

Tim is little different. At 34, and very much his own man rather than any boy to a dominant dad, he is still pretty difficult to spot as the obvious boss as you get into the maze of boxes, alleys, barns and store rooms that make up the original Easterby yard.

Mind you, it is pretty hard to locate anything here without either psychic knowledge or years of experience in what is only one of a series of farms and barns and boxes scattered around adjoining fields.

'I was trying to move a horse yesterday,' says the genial Grainger Morgan-Evans, long-standing box driver and general factotum. 'It took me three tries to even find the thing.'

In fact, Tim is the guy in the most controlled hurry of all. He does not shout; indeed, he rarely raises his unreconstructed Yorkshire voice. But his muttered asides are always worth catching.

He moves with hard-to-follow swiftness around the Easterby horse warren. He goes to the tack room and grabs a bridle and saddle, and then we are in a straw-filled box, where he greets a slender-faced three-year-old filly and, with a

few deft movements, wipes her
over, tacks her up and brushes
out her tail with a big, soft,
yellow bristle brush.

'She's It's Allowed,' he says.
'She's tough.' And he's gone.

So the filly and I are left
alone and very soon it is
obvious that It's Allowed is as
sweetly feminine as she must be
heroically tough. At home, we
have a little mongrel bitch whose
multimix bloodlines have given
her the most magically cheerful
temperament. She loves nothing
more than to play games with
her nose. It's Allowed is a bit
like that. Except that she's a
Thoroughbred. And boy, hasn't
she worked for her living!

Last season, as a two-year-old,
she ran no fewer than sixteen

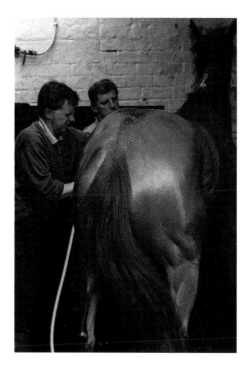

times, winning three and being placed on seven occasions, while switching
stables from Mick Channon to Easterby midway through the campaign after
sharp-eyed Ian Armitage claimed her for a bargain 10,000 guineas at York.

She was to return to the Knavesmire on Tuesday for a highly satisfactory
first run of the year. Monday was just the warm-up.

Outside it is close and hazy. We are legged up and led through a brick alley
to walk out past a large straw-lined barn and down the drive to turn right on
to the Great Habton road. Horses are coming from all directions, some thirty
in all.

On the right, there is a long, green paddock with a set of eight thick tree
trunks alongside the hedge, used for schooling purposes and serving as a
reminder that they have trained Gold Cup and Champion Hurdle winners
here. They may well do so again. On the left, there are twenty fat and satisfied
newly shorn Sussex rams.

But this is not a place for reverie. Some 400 yards down the road, we turn
left through a gate and circle about at the top of a biggish, dead flat cornfield
with a little old barn stuck in the middle of it. Tim and Peter are already there
with a Labrador or two.

With a minimum of fuss, we are sorted out and told to do our 'couple of
canters'. My group includes a square-butted two-year-old called Cumbrian

Casper, who has just been castrated to clarify his aims in life, and French Fellow, who certainly won't be receiving the same fate, despite his defeat in the Two Thousand Guineas.

There is a sandy path, followed by a woodchip one, round the edge of the cornfield. We hack off down the side of the hedgerow which, until recently, used to hide rows of pig sheds on the other side. The pigs' honking used to have a bucking effect on fresh horses of a morning. Cumbrian Casper does a buck and a kick regardless, French Fellow coasts along calmly, and It's Allowed sails in their wake, her silky, narrow neck beautifully balanced, her mouth easy and receptive on the bit.

After five furlongs, we get to the end of the cornfield and ease down to a trot and, for a few brief moments, a walk. That's when you imagine there would be some turns and talk and general retuning. But that's when the shout comes – 'Ready?' – and we are on towards home. And winging it.

Of course, in the jargon, it's 'only a canter', but the horse is being allowed to stretch and as we come spinning alongside the far hedge to where the Easterbys are watching you are reminded of the old line, 'If this is a half speed, I don't know where the other half is coming from.' It's Allowed is a flowing delight.

She may be a mere 83-rated handicapper, but she reminds you that 300 years of selected breeding have defined the Thoroughbred into the ultimate running machine.

Machines need maintenance, and this lot are soon wandering back past the rams and the logs and into the horse warren, where buckets and hoses await.

At exercise, It's Allowed has been a model professional, but now, at the washdown, she wants to play again. She pushes her nose and stamps her foot. If she were five feet smaller, you could roll her over like a puppy.

Lorcan Wyer comes over and takes It's Allowed through the alley and into the barn, where seven other horses are already hitched to the horse-walker.

It's Allowed goes happily on to join the others for something of a 'cool down chat', and we go back to the tack room and start the whole game again. Simple, quick, what's-all-the-fuss-about horsemanship – that's at the heart of the Easterby phenomenon. Five-furlong sprinters or three-mile chasers, they all get treated the same.

No fancy foods, special bedding or extravagant imports from far-flung lands. They get Baileys horse mix and oats which are home grown, just like the straw on which they sleep, and the processed nibbles on which they pick.

For second lot, I am on a filly called Castanea Sativa ('I call her Italian,' says Peter bluntly), and we do the same thirty-minute routine. She comes back to the same washdown and a spell on the walker.

After the much-treasured Marjorie Easterby's boiled egg breakfast, Tim takes me on a whirlwind tour of the two other yards up the road. Along with the hillside boxes at Easthorpe, they provide him with a 100-horse capacity.

The facilities come with complementary paddocks, like the one in which Pipalong is now happily taking a turn in the sun.

Soon we are back in the cornfield watching some two-year-olds winging past, each in their own way enjoying their run. Each being watched unfussily, but expertly, to find a place where they can shine.

Tim Easterby sums up the family horse secret with one of his trademark muttered asides.

'Confidence,' he says.

There was only time to visit one more trainer on this journey, in Britain at least. Fittingly, it was in Yorkshire where this man began his racing career, when coming over from Barbados in the middle of winter, way back in 1965, to knock on the door of Malton trainer Pat Rohan and be told: 'The Rohans are out, but you had better come in or you will die of cold.'

More than forty years on Michael Stoute has long outgrown the desperately eager young man who only became Pat Rohan's best ever assistant because his original ambition to be the BBC's racing correspondent was thwarted by one Julian Wilson. But it's worth remembering that Michael was quite an awkward, earnest chap when he started. He got on all right with the more party-going public school chaps at Newmarket, but he wanted you to know that not a single stone would be left unturned any day, any hour that he was with his horses.

It is entirely a compliment to say that not all of that outlook has been rubbed smooth. The biggest danger of big-time success in any profession is that the blade that has harvested glory for you is also blunted by it. Stay around Stoute for only a short while and the only sense you will get is that of the sharpener's stone. You even feel sharpened by your visit.

In May 2000 the stable was once again riding high, with King's Best as Derby favourite after his dazzling defeat of Giant's Causeway in the Two Thousand Guineas and former Dante winner Greek Dance just back from running second in the Prix Ganay at Longchamp.

MICHAEL STOUTE
25 May 2000

BEING a Michael Stoute horse, you have the best of everything. Best food, best care, best comforts. But you have to work for your corn. Ask Alva Glen. On Tuesday he was on overtime. He was carrying me.

He is a big, bay three-year-old colt by Gulch who obliged in his maiden at Nottingham last October and who ran all right in his comeback behind Pawn Broker at the Craven Meeting. At 6.45 a.m. he is tacked up and ready in his high Victorian box in Freemason Lodge. King's Best is a few doors further along, Greek Dance over on the other side, but Stoute is not at the top of the trainers' table once again by having just a one- or two-horse operation.

On the face of it, the sheer numbers of what, after the Aga Khan influx, is now the country's largest stable, seem daunting. Some ninety in Freemason Lodge, another eighty or so across the Bury Road at Beech Hurst. But as Alva Glen and I join some thirty of his fellows in the circular covered school there is a classroom intimacy about it. Two abreast we wander round, the swimming pool and horse-walker in the centre partially obscured by the plastic rain-shield that comes down to a rider's shoulder level.

Rodney Bowker is beside me on Sir Alex Ferguson's Chinatown, who finished one in front of Alva Glen in that race at Newmarket. Rodney was a long-time linchpin of the John Gosden team at Stanley House and knows how good stables should be run. 'Cut no corners,' he says firmly. 'We do things properly.'

That includes resaddling a horse whose rider has allowed his girths to go back too far. 'They will need to come a couple of inches forward,' a watching Stoute says to me as we file into the paddock. In a minute or so head man Stuart Messenger reorganises this latest recruit and we are walking quietly out

to file across the Bury Road, and then advance right-handed towards the end of the great grass expanse of the Warren Hill canters.

Everything very calm, long-leathered and easy. But these are high-mettled racehorses. And in one bucking, whirling instant the leading horse shows how.

Not King's Best: he is three or four back and as calm as the starter's hack. This leader is some chestnut thing with temporary adrenaline overload. How Charlotte Preston sits on him only heaven and her breeches can know. If it was ice-skating it would be a triple lutz, and now here he is backing threateningly towards us. 'Derby favourite in kicking shock' is not the headline you want to read. Good job the others don't panic.

How King's Best handles the razzmatazz at Epsom is something that only the day will answer. But if he is half as cool as he is here you ought to get on the phone to the bookmaker at once. Ignoring our pirouetting friend, King's Best and his regular rider Gary Foster trot past to head us out on to the bottom of the Warren Hill canter.

For everyone else it is just the most routine of exercises – goggles down, hack off a length apart, spin up past the white discs and various roadside watchers, pull up and stroll back down for a second go. But to me it is the privilege of being not the observer but the observed.

Stoute has just been across the other side to see Greek Dance, Beat All and three others in final workouts. King's Best is two ahead of us. Alva Glen and his ageing partner can hardly be priority number one.

Only one thing of any note happens in the canter. Halfway up Alva Glen flinches a bit when a little divot smacks his face, and hangs right for a few strides before changing legs back onto his near-fore and finishing well. 'He's better when he changes back,' says Stoute as we come past his hack: 'He gets into his rhythm. He's got ability, but he needs to pull himself together. To graft a bit.' Don't ever think the headmaster isn't watching.

'Big stable, but little groups,' Bowker had said earlier – 'That's one of his secrets.' For the second canter ours is reduced to just four: King's Best and Chinatown upsides front; then Alva Glen and Shablam, a Lear Fan three-year-old you might remember being fourth in the Dee Stakes. Irishman Martin Courage is on Shablam, and for two furlongs he and I do quite well, sitting a couple of lengths off the others. Then, imperceptibly, Foster lets out a notch on King's Best and daylight spreads between us. Alva Glen and Guineas pace don't quite go together.

After pulling up we walk off, girths loosening, leathers lengthening, to join the whole group in the plantation. Stoute rides up talking to each of his four-legged pupils and their two-legged minders in turn. When he gets to us, he decides more homework is needed.

Out onto the Side Hill canter. Six furlongs of left-handed grass gallop circling back past Warren Place. Alva Glen keeps up easily and is better organised. Extra lines can help pass examinations.

From here it is a gossiping stroll back over Long Hill, the Maktoum wonder of Warren Towers to the right of us, an errant loose horse hollering up the gallop to the left. By the time we get back to crop grass on the wide, green square at the centre of Freemason Lodge it has been a good hour and a half of exercise.

After breakfast, a little unraced chestnut colt of the Aga Khan's carries me with five others for an equally lengthy trek past Moulton Paddocks and twice up the lung-stretching mile of the Al Bahathri gallop. Stoute's horses may start with advantages, but they have to work.

'The challenge is greater than ever,' the man himself had said while ticking off details such as Australian oats, Canadian hay and the need to keep consistent high standards, 'what with Godolphin and Ballydoyle always there. So you have to concentrate, but the essential is to create a good ambiance, to have a staff who can really work together.'

Back on the square, Jock Brown returns the compliment. Jock has been around top horses for what seems a hundred years. He took Jupiter Island to win the Japan Cup for Clive Brittain in 1986. He doesn't need to ladle the syrup, but as Greek Dance digs away at the earth to make a good rolling place he looks around the sweep of Freemason Lodge and puts the place into perspective.

'This man,' he says, his voice reverting back to his native Scotland for emphasis, 'doesn't miss a single trick. There are a lot of horses, but he treats them all as individuals. Classic horses, handicappers, older horses, two-year-olds, colts, fillies – all of them different.'

'I tell you,' he adds, not unaware of the enormity of the remark, 'the man's a genius.'

Tribulations don't pass Stoute by. Training problems prevented King's Best making the Derby field and the colt's Irish Derby attempt ended sensationally when Kieren Fallon had to pull him up lame before halfway. He never ran again, but his name lives on as a successful sire at the Kildangan Stud, not twenty minutes from The Curragh.

And so to the last stop in this saddle-carrying journey – and although Ballydoyle was not originally planned as the final port of call, it was wholly appropriate serendipity that it should so become. For nowhere else in the world so completely captures the necessary mix of natural setting and technical mastery. You never doubt you are in green and timeless Tipperary but you are a long, long way from folksy pictures of donkeys and jaunting carts.

It was a wonder to visit it in Vincent O'Brien's time. It is even more so now in what historians will presumably call 'The Age of Aidan'. At the time of our tour Aidan O'Brien had yet to follow Vincent into the Derby winner's circle at Epsom. But in the Racing Post Trophy and (albeit disqualified) French Guineas winner Aristotle, they had the horse we were all taking about – and there was to be plenty of that.

AIDAN O'BRIEN
1 June 2000

W E always knew they were meticulous at Ballydoyle, but this is getting ridiculous. On the dot of 7.45, Pat Keating is at the main gates to greet us.

The hushed voice of Aidan O'Brien is at once on the walkie-talkie and we are into the jeep, past the Nijinsky statue and left up the drive to where Aristotle, Ciro and all the rest are walking towards us. One has an empty saddle. This is Glyndebourne. This is for me.

He is a neat and handsome Sadler's Wells three-year-old who won under Michael Kinane at The Curragh last Saturday.

Truth be told, he puts his ears back a bit when this lump lands where 'Mickey Joe' had been, but his manners are otherwise impeccable.

Good job too. Aidan has driven up with Alex Ferguson in the front seat. Two great managers don't need a joker to make their day.

They don't joke a lot at Ballydoyle. They are quiet and ordered and with their new black and maroon riding-out kit, more immaculate than ever.

Out in the distance lie the untamed heights of the Galtee Mountains, but all around us is nature under care.

Paddocks are topped, trees doctored, brambles banned and nettles a sin. The long miles of white railings alongside the gallops have green, rugby post-style padding whenever a corner protrudes.

One does now. It is on the turn of the wall as we walk across the bottom of the drive and on to the woodchip all-weather canter. Even at the best of places, this can be a signal for a bit of whirling around, pre-gallop anticipation as your horse sees the others thunder away.

At Ballydoyle they have thought that one out. Just before the canter, we file behind a thick hedge so the lead horse is always out of sight.

That's just one of the multitudes of tricks started by one legendary O'Brien and continued now by another. Every horse has its own wooden tack cupboard outside its box, every detail of its development from shoeing to body weight is constantly monitored. A closed-circuit camera watches the likes of Aristotle's every move and, as we go up the gallop, an electronic eye at each furlong post clocks off the sectional times.

Vincent O'Brien installed this system back in the 1970s. Twenty-five years on, only Newmarket among the racecourses has followed where he led.

King Of Kings was once clocked up three furlongs in a barely credible 32 seconds and, in this Epsom countdown, Aristotle has been putting in comfortable seven-furlong sessions at an even twelve seconds a furlong. Mercifully, Glyndebourne is being asked to stroll along at hardly half that rate for what is the standard loosener O'Brien gives all his horses.

After four furlongs, the gallop goes through a clump of trees and we ease down to walk out into the sunshine, and a breathtaking view of the Slievenamon mountains out to the south.

Aristotle, Ciro and some others move off to do rather more serious exercise, including the Derby hope's regulation rounding of Ballydoyle's own version of Tattenham Corner. The rest of us wander down another plastic-railed walkway for a second canter.

Aidan and Sir Alex come alongside in the jeep, accompanied by Demi O'Byrne, who is a linchpin of the Coolmore racing empire, and Mike Dillon, Sir Alex's confidant and adviser, whose empire merely encompasses Ladbrokes.

No complicated instructions. Just the mention of a name, and a one-line summary for each – 'He can keep going, Finbarr … Just a steady swinger, Anita … Okay, Grainne' – until every one is done.

Anita Harvey and I are to do a 'steady swinger' back up the five-furlong woodchip. She is on Columbus, a Sadler's Wells three-year-old who cost a tidy million at Newmarket. Anita has worked in several places, but is still in awe of this. 'There cannot be anything like it anywhere,' she says.

Up front, Evan Henley takes instructions on a walkie-talkie. This is another Aidan innovation which seems so obviously helpful that you wonder why more trainers don't do it.

We walk round the big hedge for our hidden take-off once again. Glyndebourne's target is the Queen's Vase at Royal Ascot. He cost some 650,000 guineas at Newmarket.

He may never reach the brass-plaque immortality of the likes of Royal Academy and El Gran Senor but, with the possible exception of having to lug me around yesterday, no-one can say that he has had anything but a millionaire's treatment.

The sun is shining, the rooks are calling just as they did in that gorgeous Kit Owens/Hugh McIlvanney film, *The Year of Sir Ivor*, way back in 1968. Glyndebourne is a beautifully balanced mover. As we skim up behind Columbus and on towards the canopy of shade at the top, the holidaying Sir Alex is not the only one with a song in his heart.

Sloping back to the paddock, reins are taken out of the rings of the martingale so that the horses can pick easily and roll if they want.

Aidan comes over and has time to pick and chew with each in turn. We are just nine days away from all the Epsom madness, when time will be so short. But now there is still time. Time to take trouble …

On second lot, there will be forty-odd two-year-olds swinging up the all-weather, a delight to the eye and a tug at the punting heart. Sunday's impressive winner Darwin will come up and we will nod our heads in appreciation of what might be to come.

His is the first name to conjure with for now, but Aidan can rattle off the families of so many amazingly well-related animals that the mind goes into pedigree spin. Racegoers will not have long to wait.

The two-year-olds are housed across the valley in the yard from which David O'Brien trained Assert and Secreto before turning his skilful hand to the vineyard game.

Aidan, Anne-Marie and their four young children live closer by, and somehow can take all of us in for breakfast without flinching.

As we wolf down the sausages, bacon and delicious brown bread, Sir Alex talks of the sort of pasta foods that Manchester United eat on match days, and of the need to keep up the body fluids even after the warm-up. Aidan's bespectacled head tilts, birdlike and inquisitive.

For a few brief moments, you might think his mind had quite turned away from his horses. But then he pauses.

'Keep the fluids up,' he says. 'Yes, that's interesting, we never take water away.'

Then he reaches across and flicks on the TV remote control. Up on screen comes the Ballydoyle closed-circuit system. Another flick, and we're watching Aristotle drinking too.

We described Michael Stoute as a genius. One of the definitions is having an infinite capacity for taking pains. How better to describe Aidan OBrien?

Aristotle did not click in the Derby, finishing a distant tenth to Sinndar and then winning fame as the most expensive horse ever to be exported to Singapore. Glyndebourne, on the other hand, refused to be belittled by my brief presence in the saddle, winning the Gallinule Stakes impressively a week after my visit and then running second to Sinndar in the Irish Derby.

Sir Alex Ferguson, of course, trained on even better, although sadly no longer with Ballydoyle connections. It was at The Curragh in April 2001 that Rock of Gibraltar began the ten-victory, dual Classic-winning spree which was to take Alex into the great temples of racing in true Manchester United style, only for the relationship to end acrimoniously in a court dispute over stallion rights.

Happily Ferguson is again a much welcomed figure on the racetrack, even if his invitation to the Coolmore open day may have to wait awhile. What is undisputed was that the mutual respect shown between him and O'Brien over the breakfast we shared was one that was fulfilling and challenging to them both. Manchester United's subsequent Premier League and Champions' League double does not suggest that he has gone backwards, and results only say the same thing about Aidan O'Brien.

For while Ballydoyle seemed pretty amazing at that visit, since then Aidan and his Coolmore backers have re-written the record books, culminating in the 'Annus Mirabilis' of 2008, when there were times when it seemed that only the intervention of the Monopolies Commission could prevent the big prizes going over to Ballydoyle.

The Coolmore/Ballydoyle operation has raised the bar. 'The future' – as Colin Hayes wrote on the Lindsay Park gate back in South Australia all those years ago – 'belongs to those who plan for it.'

Others must plan to compete.

*　　　*　　　*

WORKING with racehorses – still the best and the worst job in the world. What a ludicrous and honoured pleasure it was for this aged hack to have a dozen trips when only the best was on show.

Not for me long slogs up the motorway to see runners fail, fall or, worse still, never return. No drudgery around the muck heap, no miserable empty afternoons when the last winner seems an age away and the next one hardly a dream. Heck, for me the luck was so good that in these fifteen different visits during the rainiest spring since records began we never once got wet. 'Jammy' must be my middle name.

In many ways, it was a journey of a lifetime. From Arundel to Dumfries, from Suffolk to County Carlow – fifteen very different places, fifteen very varied ways of handling the four-legged athlete, but a wonderful welcome in every one. For me it was a fascinating experience, as well as a thrilling opportunity to step back in time – to realise again that stable life is still the best of all ways to start a morning. Old Disraeli wasn't far wrong when he said that 'a canter is the cure for all evils.'

To say I was – and remain – grateful would be something of an understatement. To all the trainers, lads, and families who gave me so much help and hospitality, I can only say that whatever admiration I had in advance was in every case only enhanced by visiting.

To all the horses, there is the biggest thank you of all. They more than gave me pleasure. For a few brief hours, they made me young again.

Motivator

*I*N OCTOBER 2004 Motivator winged home in the Racing Post Trophy at Doncaster and automatically became favourite for the Derby the following June. As Michael Bell and his wife Georgina sipped celebratory champagne with me afterwards, an idea formed which could only ever be put to such a famously good-natured couple. Could I come and log the road to Epsom, with the Two Thousand Guineas on the way?

The colt had the credentials. He had only run (and won) once before Doncaster, but the quality of that victory and of his subsequent homework had always suggested this was a horse of the highest possible class. He was by the hot new stallion Montjeu, and so after that Racing Post Trophy everything was possible for him. And for me, if I could get alongside.

It was something I had always wanted to do. Normally big-race previews are written as one-offs, but this way the readers would get to know everyone from the burly farrier to the five-foot-nothing apprentice. Most of all they would get to know the horse. And we all might get to understand what is entailed in that long journey to the first Saturday in June.

The odds were always that the whole thing would end in tears long before anyone got near the Derby. But month after month Michael Bell was happy to welcome us in. And at Epsom on 4 June 2005 there were indeed tears – of the kind that we all hope to shed.

We started in January 2005.

Previous spread: Motivator, ridden by Dalibor Torok, on Newmarket Heath, February 2005.

Getting started – *30 January*

THE DAYS lengthen, the clock turns, and inside Motivator the bomb ticks. From time to time, something akin to a mini-explosion goes off as he trots along, and he gallops instantly on the spot, letting out a couple of lightning bucks while the power surges through him.

Newmarket's Derby favourite is fresh – very fresh.

To be exact, there are just 89 days to the 2,000 Guineas, 124 to Derby Day itself. Not even two school terms for Michael Bell and his Fitzroy House team to take their scholarship-winning pupil through to graduate at Epsom's most demanding test of all. For them, the long haul ahead as the horse hardens, the worries magnify and the pressure intensifies will be the best and worst months of their lives. Eighteen weeks is a long time to hold your breath.

It's Tuesday morning. Richard Simpson gets up at 4.30 a.m. and goes out to feed Motivator his early-morning bowl of bruised oats at 5 a.m. On Tuesday, the colt had eaten up his overnight feed. All was well. Another ninety horses to check. Richard has been at Fitzroy House for fifteen of the sixteen years that Bell has trained there, and has been head man for ten. His father worked for Peter Cazalet in Kent, Arthur Stephenson in Durham, and David Robinson in Newmarket. Richard had thirty rides as a Luca Cumani apprentice, and fourteen years with Jeremy Hindley, where he was work-rider for Dewhurst winner Huntingdale and led up Muscatite to be third to Lomond in the 1983 Two Thousand Guineas. Good horses, but Motivator bids to be better.

That's the Derby dream that already pervades everyone at this handsome, traditional yard, which stands proudly behind its high walls off Black Bear Lane, just as it did when Bahram (1935), Mahmoud (1936) and Tulyar (1952) were trained there to win the Derby for the Aga Khan.

At 6.30 a.m., James Cronin walks across the High Street from his home in Tattersall Crescent. He takes the 200-yard trip up the hill to Fitzroy House, collects his grooming kit and pitchfork and makes his way to Motivator's box to muck out and groom him.

'He usually stands in the same place on the far side,' says 26-year-old Dublin-born James, whose father is now handyman at Bell's father-in-law's Mount Coote Stud in County Limerick. 'He will have eaten some of his feed, and when I have finished he will pick at it again and then finish it after exercise. I only came here last year [after a lengthy spell with John Gosden and a shorter one with David Loder], and am so lucky to have this horse.'

James keeps fit by going to the Bedford Lodge Spa in the afternoons and is a good rider. But Motivator is a special case, very quick on his feet, a touch fast to react. Of a morning, it is Shane Featherstonehaugh, another Dubliner, who takes the saddle. Shane's late father Brian worked for the Irish Press and took his son with him to the races. Shane went to a local trainer in the holidays. He came over and rode at Simon Dow's as an amateur. He worked for some time for Richard Hannon in Wiltshire. At 27, he's a bit quieter than the more extrovert Cronin. He is very quiet on a horse too. When he joined Fitzroy House in 2004, he was just what Motivator needed.

As Shane takes the rugs off the horse, you see a very differently conditioned animal from the tightly muscled runner who walked the paddock before the Racing Post Trophy in October. After continuing cantering until Christmas, he is finishing a four-week break when mere trotting has been the routine. At this stage he is noticeably fleshier behind the girth, less defined along that nicely crested neck, on which a few pimples have come up with the easier workload. He is a good 16.1 hands (5ft 5in) at the shoulder, has elegant but still powerful hindquarters, and an alert medium-sized head with a small white star between the eyes. Look hard, because we might be seeing a lot of him.

By the time Shane has Motivator tacked up, a ubiquitous, smiling, silver haired figure has appeared. Sixty-year-old Roy 'The Bombardier' Thorpe lives on a houseboat in Ely and gets his nickname from his days with the King's Troop Royal Artillery. He has been with Bell from the beginning and has

April 2005: Shane Featherstonehaugh on Motivator, centre.

delayed ending his duties in charge of travelling so that he can take Motivator to Epsom on the first Saturday in June. He legs Shane into the saddle with practiced ease as the trainer looks on.

Bell has his computer with him. It is eight years old, chunky, portable and about to be dispatched to school. It is called Nicholas Bell, and on command can spew out details of every four-legged friend in Fitzroy. It can also twist its father round its finger, and now gets a paternal lift to catch the waiting bus while mother George Bell, a former three-day event champion, rides over to join the waiting string. This is the easy time for Flat racing stables, but the good mood here is not a seasonal thing.

'Michael is wonderfully laid-back,' says Richard Simpson. 'Jeremy Hindley was a good trainer, but a dreadful worrier. He would smoke eighty cigarettes a day when a good horse was running. This man lets us get on with it. Makes sure we do the sensible things. Lets us all work through the plans together.'

The project they are undertaking is just about the most fascinating challenge in sport.

Motivator has run (and won) just twice and is not three years old until next month, but by 30 April needs to be ready to tilt at Two Thousand Guineas glory, and by 4 June to be primed for the Epsom roller-coaster itself. He is a born runner, a purpose-bred athlete whose huge potential has already showed. The task is to get his mind and muscle through the increasing workload ahead.

But now the thirty-strong posse of first lot has journeyed down the Rowley Drive horsewalk, through the middle of Newmarket and out to trot beside the Bury Road and up the west face of Warren Hill. Not for the first time, you wonder how some trainers can still defy common sense by sending green horses on to the streets without a companion, how long it will be before Newmarket follows Chantilly with a traffic-avoiding tunnel between stables and gallops.

The grey Shabernak, a big, talented but fragile-legged stayer, makes a fine mobile interview post as we follow Motivator down the Bury Road with first Luca Cumani's and then Bedford Lodge on our left.

As we get level with Sir Michael Stoute's house, a huge car transporter lumbers up the opposite lane with a swish of tyres and a hiss of brakes.

Suddenly, Motivator decides that's enough. In a blink of the eye, he flicks his whole body into a complete 180-degree left-handed turn, so fast that you wonder how it happened. Shane Featherstonehaugh's long legs turn with him like a ballet partner.

'It's all right,' Shane says afterwards as we trot up the frozen side of Warren Hill. 'He always goes in the same direction.'

There are no more dramas on our seventy-minute trip, but James Cronin still finds it hard to keep his eyes off his charge.

'In some ways he's a hard athlete,' says James. 'In other ways he is our baby. I couldn't sleep for three days before he ran in the Racing Post Trophy. What's ahead is going to be awesome for all of us.'

Motivator will upgrade to cantering next week, and there will be a shift in his diet from bruised to the more concentrated crushed oats, and to the green vitamin-rich American hay rather than golden, less power-packed English variety.

'The four weeks trotting break has been good for him,' says Shane with the shadow of worry in his eyes that is unlikely to leave until the horsebox draws away from Epsom. 'But he has got pretty fresh. I can't wait for Tuesday when the cantering starts.'

A month later the temperature had dropped sharply and a short blizzard hit Newmarket. Photographer Edward Whitaker had long waited for this, and was out of the blocks like a sprinter to get a 'Winter Wonderland' picture of Motivator coming up Warren Hill – which duly made a beautiful page in the Injured Jockeys' Fund calendar for 2006 (as well as the opening of this section).

The temperature had dropped – but expectation hadn't ...

In the snow – *27 February*

I T WAS Motivator's birthday on Tuesday. He was just three years old on that bitter-cold, snow-clad Newmarket morning, but is already hardening into a gleaming jewel some nine weeks and fifteen weeks before his Classic dates in the Guineas and the Derby. Pity we can't say the same about his trainer and his rider.

Michael Bell broke his collarbone on one of the very last days of traditional hunting with the Cottesmore two weeks ago. Shane Featherstonehaugh smashed his wrist when a two-year-old flipped its lid on the walk back down Warren Hill a week before. At 7 a.m. on Tuesday, the wounded pair stood in Motivator's box as if to draw strength from the shining muscle packs of their hope and inspiration.

'He has now done three full weeks of cantering,' says Bell, wincing slightly as he adjusts the sling on his left arm, 'and he is such an active, clean-winded horse that if you got excited you could begin to pick up with him straight away. But we know we want him to run on 30 April, not a day before. We won't do much more than his present routine before the beginning of April, but I tell you, he'll be pretty fit by then.'

Motivator is tacked up and ready for first lot. It is just four weeks since our last visit, but the change is immediate. Gone are the spots on the colt's now arching neck; what was slack flesh behind the girth feels firm beneath the fingers; there is a glow about the coat that would not disgrace one of Godolphin's sun-kissed contenders out in Dubai. All this on just two canters of a morning.

This is not a human athlete, but an equine one. This is a genetically programmed galloping machine that has been reared from birth to be able to run through a hole in the wind round the Epsom helter-skelter in the summer of his three-year-old season. The job of the Michael Bell team is the one that has challenged Classic trainers down the decades – to help the talent to blossom, not to force it. The task of the rider is to calm and control the buds beneath and, with Featherstonehaugh's left wrist out of stitches but set to keep him out of the saddle for another four weeks, the riding responsibility now falls to 31-year-old Dalibor Torok from the Czech Republic.

Dalibor has only been in Britain for two months and his English is confined to such words as 'strong' (about Motivator) and 'reeding' (meaning 'riding'). But he has been steeped in racing since following his jockey uncle to the track, winning two St Legers back home, and as we follow him and Motivator out towards Rowley Drive and down into Newmarket town, it's clear that Dalibor is utterly fluent in the language of the Thoroughbred.

Motivator likes a conversation. He's not as fresh as last time, but there is a shining energy that marks him out from the rest of the thirty-strong string all on the same diet and same routine. There are no big bucks or kick-boxing blows as in his trotting sessions, but there is the odd jig-jog and quick shuffle that shows the power rippling through.

The clock on St Mary's Church shows at 7.20 a.m. as we wind by. Another ten minutes and Bell's travelling head man Roy 'The Bombardier' Thorpe is politely holding up the traffic as we shrug at exasperated commuters on the Bury Road. Sir Mark Prescott's yard has a defiant 'Fight Prejudice, Fight The Ban' pro-hunting sticker on the gate. We pull up the stirrup leathers from long walking length to a shorter jockey perch for the opening canter up Warren Hill to our left.

The horses begin to tense as they recognise the effort ahead. I am on a so-far docile chestnut called Woodcracker, who delivered a 12-1 touch for the delighted stable in a Class F maiden at Nottingham last May. He does not bother himself as our progress grinds to a halt when James Eustace's string jumps in ahead. For a moment, though, Motivator does.

He whips round to the left in frustration. It is a habit he has had since he started cantering last year. There is no heavy 'nappiness' in it, and Dalibor sits on him as calmly as Shane did last month. Truly difficult horses can plunge and buck at this stage, but Motivator has made his protest and now waits his turn. Eventually the Eustace aces have set off towards the horizon and Joey Smith on the grey Olihider leads off, with Dalibor and Motivator tucked in behind.

This is when it's good to remember that what is termed a 'canter' at Newmarket is something rather quicker than a hack in Rotten Row. Woodcracker is transformed from a weary plodder into the livewire who followed his Nottingham success with a good effort at York and ended his season a touch prematurely by beating one of the Queen's horses a short head at Newmarket's July meeting. We are winging along easily, but Motivator still recedes away from us into the distance.

Walking back down for the second 'canter' is to wonder why, with ten miles of artificial tracks as well as twice that of grass gallops, quite so many of Newmarket's 1,800 horses seem to have chosen this same spot for exercise. But it makes for name-spotting.

The exercise sheets on the string ahead of us have 'LMC.' on the side, and up with the leaders is a big horse with a matching nightcap. It's Luca Cumani's new star recruit from Australia, their Derby champion Starcraft. Cumani's 2003 superstar Falbrav used to wear that nightcap. Both the wool and the trainer have been around a bit.

Beside me is Chris Conway. At a craggy 58 he is in his fifth racing decade, but still plays football keenly enough to be on a tour to Bratislava at Easter. Chris worked with Roy Thorpe and head man Richard Simpson at Jeremy Hindley's, but rode both One Thousand Guineas winner Waterloo and Arlington

No shoe, no horse: farrier Dermot Barry with Motivator.

Million hero Teleprompter when returning to his native Yorkshire to work with Bill Watts at Richmond. 'You know this horse has improved a lot,' he says, indicating Motivator's rippling backside up ahead. 'Last year his back was weak and he didn't have any of that muscle you see now.'

What we see of Motivator on his second canter once again rockets into the distance. This time it is on the grass to the right of the artificial strips and the pace swings along quicker than before. Halfway up, I pull Woodcracker out to avoid the kickback, and for a few thrilling lengths he lets himself stride as if that 12-1 was still on offer at Nottingham.

Walking back by the plantation, there is a suggestion that the horse is blowing less than the jockey. Up front, Motivator's nostrils hardly tremble. Dalibor smiles contentedly and repeats his favourite word with deep Czech emphasis. 'Strong,' he says.

By the time we reach St Mary's, the gold hands of the clock have reached 8.25 a.m., and by the time Motivator gets back in his box, it will have been almost an hour and a half of exercise. He will spend the rest of his day in his box. That's the way it is with racehorses, and when James Cronin comes in to groom him at 4.30 p.m. each evening he finds a very contented piece of horse.

'His coat has come on terrific,' says James, with his native Dublin coming strong in the voice, 'and he has muscled up so much that we have had to get a bigger rug for him. He likes to play and growl at me when I do him over with a curry comb at night. But that's him.

'People can see he's different. He has that swagger about him.'

As hope grew, so did the belief that Motivator would be a good thing not just in the Derby but in everything bar the Boat Race – Two Thousand Guineas very much included.

Like lots of the team, I had juicy bets on both the Guineas and Derby/Guineas double – caution got lost some time ago – but by the time we got to Newmarket's Craven Meeting in the middle of April, those in charge had to decide whether the original plan to start with the Guineas at the end of the month was really the best strategy.

When the news came through that the decision had been made to miss the Guineas, there were some cryptic mutterings amongst the team.

Missing the Guineas – *17 April*

MOTIVATOR gave a buck and a kick as he walked back from his Warren Hill canter on Thursday morning. He didn't know he was out of the Two Thousand Guineas, but the smell of burnt ante-post vouchers still hung in the air. 'The guv'nor has already had hate mail,' chuckled head man Richard Simpson, 'and that's just from the staff!'

Tuesday morning's decision on Guineas withdrawal had at first surprised and dismayed the Michael Bell team even more than it later did the wider racing world. For they had seen Motivator's explosive answer when Johnny Murtagh asked him his first serious question of the year. The Doncaster winner Cool Panic was left six rocking lengths adrift. Fitzroy House thought their bets were safe.

'I ran across to Johnny,' said Motivator's regular work-rider Shane Featherstonehaugh. 'I said, "How about him for the Guineas?", and he seemed to be saying "Great", so I got a leg up and rode the colt back to the yard full of myself. But by the time I was washing him down, one of the boys came round and said, "He doesn't run."'

Shane was talking as he and Motivator wound their way back through school-morning Newmarket, his mind trying to put disappointment behind him. The horse had just motored up the grass bank of Warren Hill smoothly enough to echo last month's verdict that he 'had speed to burn'. Only the irritating pimples on his neck hinted at anything less than perfection on the hoof. But higher powers had spoken. It is the way of things in stables. Decisions of strategy take in wider factors than the power you feel between your knees.

'I suppose it might be for the best in the end,' said Shane as Motivator did one of his characteristic little jig-jogs. 'Win or lose in the Guineas, he would probably have had his arse smacked. The pace they run the Dante should not stretch him until the closing stages. With a bit of luck we could get all the way to the Derby without putting a gun to him. That would help his old head get through the season.'

Such rationalisation after the decision should not detract from the drama of taking it. The final responsibility here belonged not to Shane, Richard Simpson or even the trainer, but to the classy operator Harry Herbert and his astute bloodstock agent brother in-law John Warren, who buy and run the horses under the Royal Ascot Racing Club banner as an adjunct to their famous syndicate scheme Highclere Thoroughbreds.

Herbert and Warren had been talking. On Monday night, they and Bell had stood and gazed at Motivator in his box. 'The more we looked,' said Herbert, 'the more we wondered if the Guineas was the right route. His shoulder, his length, his pedigree all said middle-distance horse.'

No such misgivings were passed to Murtagh next morning. Mick Kinane had ridden Motivator in an undemanding piece of work a week earlier, but now his hawk-faced countryman was being asked to test for real. Murtagh has won the Guineas on Rock Of Gibraltar, the Derby and Arc on Sinndar. He would have an opinion on what was beneath him.

The lead horse, Cool Panic, had landed some hefty bets for fertilizer king Dale Payne when he scooted up on the first Saturday of the turf season over seven furlongs. 'This was the best work we've done,' said Richard Mullen, who was in the irons, as he had been at Doncaster. 'We came a real good clip all the way, but Motivator left me for dead. When we pulled up, Johnny Murtagh turned to me and said, "This could be an Arc horse."'

But what about the Guineas? In Michael Bell's car as it sped away from the gallops, there was temporary silence. Bell was at the wheel, Herbert in the passenger seat, Murtagh in the back, wedged between Warren and eight-year-old Nick Bell, the chunky computer who supervises his father during the holidays.

Then the jockey spoke.

Herbert recalled: 'The first thing Johnny said was, "What an exciting horse. He gives me the feel of something that could be running in the Arc."'

'Johnny feels he has "middle distance" written all over him. He worked brilliant, but could be susceptible to a top horse over a mile, and the hustle and bustle might not be the right route to the Derby. Johnny's view is that the Guineas would not be in the best interests of the horse.' It was an uncanny echo of the reservations Warren, Herbert and Bell had discussed in Motivator's box the night before. Murtagh had to hurry off to ride work for Sir Michael Stoute. The impromptu conference was concluded. The decision was taking itself. York's Dante Stakes on 11 May would leave three and a half weeks to the Derby on 4 June. It was a cooler schedule, but Herbert now had a hotter one. He had to inform the owners before the news blew up on Betfair.

There are 240 fairly impressive movers and shakers in the Royal Ascot Racing Club. But the course's grandstand is currently Britain's most exclusive building site and for a few minutes Herbert feared chief executive Douglas Erskine-Crum might be buried under its rubble. Finally contact was made, emails dispatched, press announcements released, and then there was nothing more than facing the ante-post wrath of the stable.

Herbert has been in deeper than this. Before last year's Melbourne Cup the Australian press descended on this tall, smooth-looking actor-manqué toff confident that he was ripe for the plucking. Half an hour of Harry reciting Banjo Paterson and reminiscing about his great-grandfather Lord Carnarvon and the tomb of Tutankhamen had the hacks precious close to grovelling.

Herbert may actually have trod the West End boards, but his racing views are a bit more serious than drawing-room comedy, and when he got to the races he needed his serious hat on. 'People kept coming up to me saying how sorry they were, what desperately bad luck,' he said.

'Plenty imagined something had gone wrong. I had to keep saying it was nothing of the sort.'

'The key thing,' he concluded, 'is that Johnny Murtagh was very, very excited about the horse. But we are talking about Derbys and Arcs and Irish Champion Stakes. It's a very long season to hold a horse together and if you get the early racing wrong, you can ruin everything.'

It's pretty convincing, even for those of us with torn-up tickets. But, as with all great showmen, Herbert has a final trick up his sleeve.

'Johnny Murtagh is a jockey who works with you,' he adds. 'On Wednesday he rang Michael Bell to say he had been thinking a lot about the horse and how he would like to take him to Epsom, to walk and trot around, to get a good association of the place, and to do it sooner rather than later.'

So on Wednesday morning Motivator, Murtagh, Bell, Featherstonehaugh, Roy 'The Bombardier' Thorpe, Herbert, Warren, the Royal Ascot Racing Club, TV crews and assorted hacks will decamp to where Lord Derby had his great idea more than two centuries ago. Motivator will march around the paddock, hack round Tattenham Corner and we will all click our teeth in appreciation.

With one Classic bound, disappointment will be replaced with a living location of the Derby dream. If you were not close to it, you could suspect that something had been done with smoke and mirrors. But out beyond the promotion you know it actually makes sense. The horse's future is being planned not for this month's fix, but for the whole season. The hate mail might have to stop.

So the Guineas came and went without Motivator, but ironically the ground at Newmarket came up so fast that it's highly unlikely that he would have run anyway. It's true that if he had run, his best form would have meant he would have won it. But in view of what happened to him later on firm going, it's also very possible that he might have ended up like the Aidan O'Brien-trained winner Footstepsinthesand, and never run again.

The race which, uniquely, had two 100-1 outsiders Rebel Rebel and Kandidate in second and third places, saw the O'Brien second string Oratorio finish a close fourth, a short head in front of the 11-8 favourite, Godolphin's hitherto unbeaten Dubawi. As that little colt – one of the single crop of his sire, the magnificent Dubai Millennium – had been Motivator's main rival in the Derby betting, the mood in the Bell camp lifted another notch.

Motivator's trip to Epsom in the week before the Guineas had been a significant success, though one or two hacks crabbed our hero's action as he cantered easily round Tattenham Corner. In the week after the first Classic we could all sense that the countdown had begun. The next Thursday's Dante Stakes at York would be our reality check.

Before the Dante – *8 May*

THE MANTRA from the trainer, like the politicians, had been 'actions not words'. But driving back from watching Motivator gallop on Friday morning, Michael Bell can't help himself. 'It's just so exciting,' he says. There is an image he can't get out of his eyes. Ten minutes earlier, Johnny Murtagh had pulled his whip through from his left hand to his right as he gathered the colt beneath him. It was no more than an elaborate re-threading of the reins, but in an instant Motivator quickened to smother the talented Glen Ida as a class horse should. Less than a week to the Dante, just four weeks to the Derby itself, this is the authentic Classic dream – and with it come the nightmares.

The seven and a half furlongs that Glen Ida and Motivator had travelled was up Newmarket's Watered Gallop, just 100 yards across from the Rowley Mile on which the Dubawi dream so memorably foundered when he finished only fifth in the Two Thousand Guineas last weekend. All that winter sunshine, all those Dubai Millennium genes, all that Godolphin attention to detail availed him nothing when the crunch came, and frailty claimed him. At York on Thursday, it will be Motivator's turn to load into the stalls. In two and a quarter minutes, it could all be over. 'I think it will be a long week,' Roy Thorpe had said earlier as he held Motivator's bridle and legged a sky blue-

Motivator (left) tries out Tattenham Corner with Magic Sting.

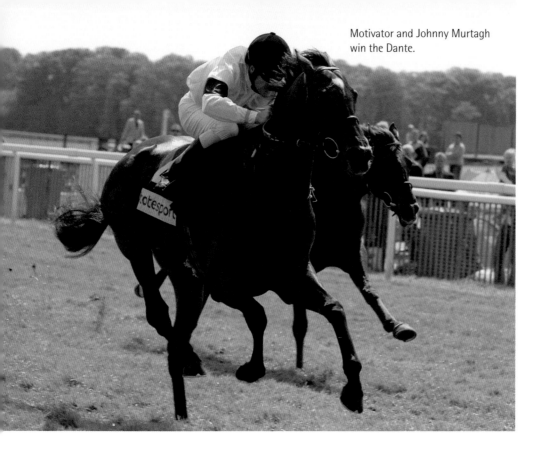

Motivator and Johnny Murtagh win the Dante.

jacketed Murtagh into the saddle. The former bombardier is normally the most fireproof of characters. But he has delayed retirement to his longboat in Ely for the chance to drive Motivator to Epsom. Two weeks earlier, he took him there for a rehearsal, to be the star turn at Epsom's Derby promotion 'Breakfast with the Stars'. The challenge had been there for all of us to see.

We saw Motivator jig-jog in the paddock and whip round before the start. Will he boil over on the big day? We saw him come down the hill on the wrong leg and seem to have a slight knee action. Will he handle Epsom's notorious cambers at racing pace? But we also saw the way he cruised up to the decent handicapper Magic Sting. Why look further for the Derby favourite?

Yet the fact that everything with Motivator has so far progressed so perfectly only increases the pressure on those closest to him. Training is about avoiding avoidable mistakes, but volatile three-year-old colts are always close to the unavoidable. As Motivator and Glen Ida follow Ruby, the big, white-faced stable hack, up the avenue to Newmarket's Rowley Mile racecourse on Friday, one of those 'unavoidables' jumps at us.

It is a tractor-mower, and Motivator takes exception to it. He does his trademark whip round to the left and Glen Ida does likewise. Suddenly a knot of non-cooperation is tightening in his mind. He backs towards the fence posts. Bell has seen it before. He is out of the car and running to prevent contrariness becoming confrontation. He gets to the horse's bridle, but

Motivator tries to push him back into the posts. Murtagh stays quiet as the colt's unwillingness is disentangled. Eventually, Motivator and Glen Ida both consent to join old Ruby in a rather undignified bucking trot, out way past the back of the grandstand and off to the far end of the track.

There is only just time to get the car across to the end of the gallop. It is a brilliant May morning. In the wider world, exhausted post-election politicos are spouting about new beginnings. Here, with the Newmarket stand gleaming in the sunshine, the little historical sporting universe of the racing game does not seem that petty an escape. Two specks on the horizon develop into Glen Ida and Motivator, winging close to the white rail that guides them. Italian Derby hope Glen Ida was a length off the subsequent Dee Stakes winner Hattan last time. Aboard him, Richard Mullen is carrying a good 10lb less than Murtagh, but as Glen Ida quickens, Motivator closes up in an eyecatching flash. It's a lot less than will be required at York, let alone Epsom. But the impression will do.

Returning down the avenue, Motivator is still jogging and snorting as the adrenalin surges through. But by the time the little party reaches the stables, he is back to his normal domestic calm. The saddle is removed to reveal an athlete really lean and ready. He is walked off to crop grass as Murtagh, Mullen and Bell go into conference.

'For me that's the best bit of work he's done,' says Mullen, who has ridden the target horses throughout. 'My fella travels really well and is rated 103, but Motivator was all class. The ground was good and he moved brilliantly on it. Don't anyone tell you he is just a heavy-going horse.'

Murtagh has been through the Derby hoops. He took Sinndar all the way to Epsom and Longchamp in 2000, and came in for the perfect spare ride to win the Derby on High Chaparral two years later. He is too sensible to start giving 'We are the champions' quotes prematurely, confining himself to the facts so far. 'He has done everything right,' he says. 'I am pleased he went to Epsom. He handled the track well. He's in good shape and we are all set for Thursday.' Murtagh is one of the understated heroes of our age. A small bowl of cereal was all he allowed himself at breakfast. After a black coffee, he will limber up for racing with the regular four-mile run, which helps to pare 3lb from his skeletal frame every day.

After the birth of twins two months ago, his wife Orla now has five little Murtaghs at the family home near The Curragh. The youngest twin only came out of hospital on Thursday. Despite his other worries, it was Murtagh who suggested the Epsom reconnaissance trip, he who advised missing the Guineas for which the fast ground would have anyway ruled Motivator a non-runner. Murtagh is a specialist fully wrapped up with the case.

His is the last and most crucial of roles. But the whole team must plan every step to those starting stalls. Before the Dante, Motivator is likely to hack away early from the paddock to avoid any mind-knotting whip-rounds. He will be boxed rather than led over the Knavesmire for fear of his ebullience exploding. He will be driven up to York on Wednesday for what will be his first ever night away from home. He will be plated on Monday afternoon to give the foot time to settle, and farrier Dermot Barry will use six nails rather than the usual four.

While Murtagh goes off for his run, the Bell second lot walk through Newmarket to gallop up the Warren Hill Polytrack. I ride Planet, a big, tall three-year-old for whom the John Warren/Harry Herbert team paid 115,000 guineas as a yearling, 40,000 more than they shelled out for Motivator. Bell remembers being envious when the yearling Planet was sent to Sir Michael Stoute. But promise was not fulfilled. Planet has had his 'satellites' removed and Bell is now undertaking a lesser campaign for the gelding which has already clocked up a little race at Windsor. Planet stretches well enough up the gallop but the racing reality lesson hangs harsh in the air. 'I am beginning to feel rather sick,' says Shane Featherstonehaugh, who has spent so many hours in the Motivator saddle. 'I won't be at York. I am not sure I will be able to make myself watch it on TV. I don't know how I will take it if he just turns out not good enough.' Doubts and then renewed determination; with the Derby closing in, it is ever thus. James Cronin will be holding Motivator's head as his would-be champion bounces into the paddock on Thursday. 'He's taken everything so well so far,' says James. 'He's very fit, but he will be pretty fresh next week. He's just begging for a run.'

As Dante day looms, he won't be the only one begging for the dream to continue.

Motivator duly collected in the Dante, winning easily enough from a horse rejoicing in the name of The Geezer but giving us a little worry by hanging quite sharply right in the final furlong. Three weeks to go to Epsom. Three weeks of worry, and by the time we went back to see him with six days to go we all knew the shape of the opposition.

Dubawi was on a retrieving mission for Godolphin. Oratorio, the Guineas fourth, was doing battle again for Ballydoyle, but Aidan O'Brien's stable jockey Kieren Fallon preferred Gypsy King, winner of the Dee Stakes at Chester. Ireland was also represented by David Wachman's Fracas, unbeaten in three races, most recently in the Derrinstown Stud Derby Trial at Leopardstown. The Chester Vase winner Hattan came from Newmarket and France fielded the massive, free-sweating Walk In The Park, whose narrow Lingfield Derby Trial defeat by Kong, the John Dunlop Derby hope, might have been avoided if he had not pulled like a lunatic in the early stages.

As always there was a lot more hope than proof. But the hour was near. Here is the final pre-Derby report.

Days to the Derby – *29 May*

You could see his ribs. Only from an acute angle from the front and then just an outline against the gleaming flesh along Motivator's flanks, but for the first time in six months of these Newmarket pilgrimages, you could see exactly what everybody had been working for. The Derby favourite is ready.

It is no small achievement. This year, as in the two full centuries before, the long road to Epsom has been littered with horses who didn't make it. But Michael Bell and his Fitzroy House team have got Motivator almost there.

The explosive freshness of the January trotting break moved to the hardening canters in sometimes snow-clad February, to the first work in March, the excitement of the gallop in April, the dilemma of the Guineas to Dante switch, the delivery on the Knavesmire, and now this image of readiness as Shane Featherstonehaugh pulled the sheet off Motivator's back at seven o'clock on Thursday morning.

But Featherstonehaugh, Bell and all the rest already know that pressure heightens as destiny closes in. One false move and even taking part in the Derby dream is over.

On Tuesday afternoon Johnny Murtagh erred, a faulty move in a footling race, a flint-hearted stewards' panel and a minor ban became a massive blow. For unless his appeal worked he would be watching the Derby on television rather than through the ears of Motivator.

Thursday morning's paper had Darryll Holland on standby as Murtagh's replacement, and a host of late news updates from the previous day's successful Epsom breakfast briefing on the Downs. But back in the stable nothing matters compared with the horse.

He is what they can influence. He is what they believe in and worry about. As every hour passes, both the belief and the worry grows.

Seeing him in his box, standing tall and composed under bridle and saddle, was to have relief that Motivator can't read the papers, listen to the news or watch endless replays of Derby trials, or of his own impressive, but not wholly straightforward, performance in the Dante.

He has taken his preparation well. Head man Richard Simpson cannot sleep but Motivator can. Simpson is getting up at 3.30 a.m., feeds Motivator with a bowl and a half of corn at 5.30, another two bowls at lunchtime, and two and a half plus extras in the evening.

'He left a little bit Wednesday morning after that final work on the Al Bahathri,' says Simpson, 'but he's back in today. He's eating really, really well. Run your hand over him. I think he's spot on.' I trace my fingers over the arch of the neck where the pimples used to be, press the palm against the rib-cage behind the girth and take it on to trace the now fully defined lines of muscles along the quarters.

To run your hand over a champion's frame is the most intimate experience athletics has to offer. Motivator may not win the Derby but his physique, like his form, does match a Derby winner's profile. There is enormous power but no excessive weight, slabs of hardened muscle beneath a silky skin, a sense of coiled vitality almost electric to the touch.

That sense of crackle becomes much more evident once the horse comes out and takes his place in the string. Other horses plod or march along, Motivator stalks, the eyes very aware, the neck upright, the hooves placed carefully until a sudden sparking current of wellbeing sends them dancing on the spot.

'He is very, very well,' says Bell in tones that have become well versed as he gives interviews at a rate of about fifteen to the hour.

'He has worked well, run well and is in very good form. If he handles the whole Epsom hoopla, we think we have a winning chance.'

This simple, open strategy is as well considered as it is refreshing. For the trainer is stating, without hyperbole, what the stable believes.

'It seems extraordinary to be saying this,' he offers at the Epsom press conference, 'but the truth is that we will be disappointed if he doesn't win. Of course all sorts of things can go wrong, but we think we are sitting on something exceptional.'

They are also entering a closing countdown where the worries nag like toothache in the mind.

'I didn't like the way he hung right at York,' confides Featherstonehaugh. 'Johnny Murtagh has said that he was going across to some better ground and was a bit green, but I can't really have that.

'Still, he's in great heart. I think he'll stay because he will be coasting in the race. I just hope he gets through all the razzmatazz beforehand. I think he'll fizz a bit in the parade.'

Featherstonehaugh will watch it at home with his partner Louise and her little boy Cole. When Motivator hit the front at York, they made so much noise that poor Cole burst into tears.

At Epsom it will be the brawny arms of James Cronin holding the lead rein with the super-experienced Roy Thorpe on the other side. 'He was fresh when we unboxed him at York,' remembers James in his tough and sunny way. 'He gave a few bucks but calmed down. Epsom will be a bit crowded but yeah, we'll get him through it.'

The horse himself does not give interviews. Pity really, because you think that by now he would be treating the whole hoopla with something close to Roy Keane disdain.

He is a three-year-old colt who has been reared for this moment since the day he was foaled at Deerfield Farm just three miles away in Dullingham.

Running is what he does. On Thursday he did it twice up the Warren Hill Polytrack, but it was after crossing the Bury Road on the way home that he made his statement. As a wobbly trailer rattled by, Motivator suddenly put in two enormous, saddle-shifting bucks. Featherstonehaugh sat tight. Empires have been lost for less.

Walking back through Newmarket, past and present combine. The Godolphin horses are all bright blue jackets and snowy white bandages on the skyline. Somewhere else the Derby-winning Sir Michael Stoute is testing his two possible outsiders and Derby-craving Clive Brittain is getting Hattan primed.

All of them know that what happens at Epsom is more than just a horse race, more than the mere fulfilment of a professional dream. It is their chance of a place in history.

Chris Conway has been almost fifty years in racing, claims to have done more winners than anyone in Newmarket, but has never had a Derby runner.

'Well, I did have when I was at Jeremy Hindley's,' he says as we ride through past St Mary's, 'but I had a broken leg and couldn't go. A little horse called Cocaine. He finished fifth.'

The Vodafone Derby, 2005: Motivator and Murtagh in glorious isolation.

'This horse of ours has lots of class. He might not stay but he should be able to cruise for a long time. It would be great for the yard.' Saddles are off, girth marks are sponged, hooves are hosed as farrier Dermot Barry readies himself for his crucial six-nail-a-shoe plating which he will do on Wednesday.

Motivator poses for final photos. We bask in the simple pleasure of being around an animal on whose handsome but unwitting head so much depends.

Later in the morning, Bill Cowe and his team at Deerfield Farm will proudly hold a cheeky bay yearling which is Motivator's full-brother and therefore may achieve a six-figure increase in value just by cropping grass next Saturday.

The stud staff stand around remembering silly nursery things about what is now a headline horse, rubbing the lamp of memory as they too dream of a golden entry in the record book.

Back at Fitzroy House, Bell goes to do a spot of hedge-trimming to escape the telephone. But Motivator does not know he is Derby favourite. As always he gets down in his box to have a good roll after exercise.

As he gets up he shakes the shavings off and gives a little snort of satisfaction. Life feels extra good. Come Saturday it could feel even better yet.

Johnny Murtagh managed to talk his way out of the stewards' displeasure so that Darryll Holland ended up a spectator rather than a rider in the hottest saddle of all. It was the day everyone had waited for – and I am happy to admit that the tension was getting to me too.

Being a newspaper reporter is in some ways more nerve-wracking than the TV, for in the latter, once started, you are just battling with what is in front of you. Writing a report of the Derby or any other major sporting event is something of a Faustian pact. You have the best seat in the house, but at the back of your mind you know that once the game or race is over you have got to get through the mincer a thousand words which are supposed to be still alive and relevant in the morning.

Motivator's Derby was always going to be one of the most direct of challenges: to try and tell the story without getting between the reader and the real participants. This is what went through the ether to the Sunday Telegraph *a couple of hours after the Derby had been run.*

Epsom glory – *5 June*

HE PROVED even better than they dared to hope. Ever since Motivator bolted home in his first race last August, the Michael Bell team have dreamed of what might happen when he was asked the question in the Epsom straight. A full two furlongs from home Motivator gave his answer. It ranks him amongst the most brilliant of Derby winners.

There were five long lengths back to the French fireball Walk In The Park, a further three to a frustrated Frankie Dettori on gallant little Dubawi. Next came Fracas running past Kieren Fallon's ride Gypsy King, long time leader Hattan was sixth, Unfurled seventh, The Geezer eighth and poor old Kong posted thirteenth and last place after First Row was withdrawn at the start. Those are the facts, but a good Derby deals in magic too.

Somewhere within a champion there is a spark that the others don't possess. Many times you may think you see it in a horse's early days. Sometimes it actually emerges on a racecourse. Very, very occasionally it gathers flame into a raging furnace of a talent that burns down the stockades that guard the gates to greatness. Sixteen years into his training career Michael Bell believed he had found that spark in Motivator. For him and his team these last ten months have been the most testing and fulfilling of their lifetimes. They believed they just might have a superstar. Yesterday was the glorious proof that they were right.

Since January it has been my monthly privilege to log the Derby favourite's progress. It has been the most enjoyable and illuminating experience of my career as a journalist. For the spark in Motivator is fairly close to the surface and in other hands, with another groom, another daily exercise rider, a more rowdy stable, Motivator's highly charged temperament could have boiled over at home, let alone at the racecourse. But from Michael Bell himself, to head man Richard Simpson, to groom James Cronin, to daily rider Shane Featherstonehaugh, to farrier Dermot Barry, to the soon-to-retire travelling supremo Roy Thorpe, there has been a commitment to calmness as well as scrupulous detail that has been a joy to observe.

As the big day got closer, the doubts grew in the mind. Would Motivator cope with the razzmatazz? Would he handle the helter skelter of the track ? Would a horse described by his trainer as 'having speed to burn' really last out this most demanding mile and a half of them all ? At 3.55 p.m. James Cronin and Roy Thorpe marched Motivator out of the stables. The horse held his

After the Derby – with (left to right) John Warren, Michael Bell and Harry Herbert.

head firm and steady. As he walked away you saw the gleam of his skin, the hard muscle lines on his quarters. He might buzz a bit in the next few minutes but you realized that this was a challenger ready for the ring, that 300 years of breeding might not be in vain.

For Motivator is a running machine. He jigged a bit as he left the paddock. As James and Roy led him on the parade you could see some plumes of sweat creaming beneath the saddle cloth and the bulges on James Cronin's brawny right forearm as he prevented his colt indulging in his characteristic left hand pirouette.

The horse was tense but not trembling. In the saddle Johnny Murtagh had his hands forward in a short hold of the reins. Two minutes later he was hacking off up to the start. The first big hurdle was over.

The next two, handling the contours of the course and staying the distance, were tackled even more directly. Knowing Motivator's natural speed, Murtagh jumped him with the leaders, settled his partner in close third behind the pacemaking Almighty and Hattan and sailed round Epsom's contours as if he was one of the rollercoaster cars in the Epsom fun fair. But Almighty was weakening before Tattenham Corner. Motivator was going to turn into the straight in second place with Kieren Fallon already attacking on Gypsy King. Motivator was bound to be in front very early. For a horse with his unproven stamina this would surely be too soon.

Oh we of little faith. Murtagh could sense what was beneath him. He has already ridden Sinndar and High Chapparal to Derby glory. He shortened up the reins and gave Motivator a flick with his whip. Far from flinching, the colt punched clear in glorious answer. We looked back for closing dangers. Pursuers came there none.

Motivator is just a three year old horse who can run faster than the others. But for those close to him, for those who have backed him, for anyone who can thrill to the sight of a star in the making, he was something more. He was the dream that only a Derby can bring.

Even as a mere chronicler the pleasure was overwhelming. I somersaulted over the rails and legged it down the course. James Cronin is a tough guy from Dublin but he was crying like a baby. Chris Conway is the oldest footballer in Newmarket but he like Roy Thorpe and head man Richard Simpson have been with Michael Bell at Newmarket's Fitzroy House almost from the very beginning. Motivator and Johnny Murtagh came back up towards them. They clutched the jockey and the horse and each other. Happiness is a Derby winner.

At that moment they were celebrating their moment in racing history. In the hangover of this morning there will be the challenge of something else. The Bell team and the management of easy-moving Harry Herbert and super-shrewd John Warren have achieved one of the greatest coups racing has to offer. Yet there is still an Irish Derby and an Arc and the whole of next season ahead.

This was an extraordinary day. But for the team landing its first classic, it could be the start of something even bigger yet.

The first something was a proper celebration back home at Newmarket. It's not often in life that you know precisely what you should do next. But the moment the Sunday Telegraph *report was finally checked in back in that paper's offices, my steps went unhesitatingly to the car, which locked itself as unerringly onto its destination as any racing pigeon released from the basket.*

Down into Leatherhead and up onto the eastbound M25 we went, then gunned round to the Dartford Tunnel before finally heading on northwards up the M11, with Stansted Airport a mere place name to be flicked by in our wake. There never would be another year when we had spent all season following the Derby winner.

We needed to share the pleasure too, and this account of the celebrations appeared in the Racing Post *two days after the Derby.*

The morning after – *6 June*

I T WAS after midnight and the last Motivator replay had faded from the screen. 'Time for bed,' said Michael Bell to his three children at Fitzroy House, 'but remember the day, remember the day.' Motivator belonged to them too.

The horse himself had got back to his box at 8.30 p.m., and in the four hours since he crossed the line the sense of ownership had spread way out beyond those now-famous Royal Ascot Racing Club members who had crowded the Epsom victory circle.

But however proprietorial thousands of winning punters and millions of dazzled TV watchers might feel, it was at Newmarket that the event had marked most deeply.

The Bell team were all in the pub just up from the High Street suitably named The Yard. Outside, Roy 'The Bombardier' Thorpe was on his mobile phone with a huge grin on his face. Inside, James Cronin had a drink in his hand and an ear-to-ear smile which would be there for weeks. The pair had looked very different as they marched Motivator out of the racecourse stables and up the hill towards the paddock. Back then, they were ready for a fight.

It was that memory which stuck on Saturday night. In a minute the warm sea of celebration would toss us dizzily around the bar, but the mind flashed back to that Epsom moment as Roy and James set off for the reckoning.

If they dithered and allowed Motivator to become fractious, all that everyone had worked for could be lost. The next thirty minutes belonged to them. Roy had been in the Forces, James had twice climbed into the ring to win the Stable Lads' Boxing Championship. This was their chance of history. They would not let it pass.

Bell had already played an ace by saddling Motivator in the quiet of the racecourse stables, rather than in the teeming tumult of the paddock. The horse who walked up that hill looked as calm and hard and ready as you could want a runner to be.

The colt who stalked in the parade was a coiled-up image of aggressive athlete, but James Cronin's right arm and Roy Thorpe's left held him in a vice. When Johnny Murtagh finally cantered away, all Motivator's extraordinary bubbling energy was still intact.

Down at the start, Bell had a second calming ace in the craggy presence of Chris Conway, complete with towel to wipe away any excess sweat. Not much of it was needed on Motivator, but Alan Munro was happy to accept a wipe down on the lathered-up Walk In The Park. Motivator was locked in the stalls early, but thankfully Murtagh's heart beat a lot slower than those of his horse's supporters in the stand.

Team Motivator.

Back at Newmarket, both head man Richard Simpson and exercise rider Shane Featherstonehaugh could scarcely bear to watch. Over at the winning post, Cronin was walking about in a trance. When the race started and Murtagh parked himself up a close third, the tension got even worse.

The horse was going well but he was bound to be in front very soon. Past Hattan he went, and eyes scanned for weakness and for pursuers. Eyes could not believe what they were seeing. The ultimate dream of all those mornings was bursting right into the very back of the retina. Motivator was not just going to win. He was taking the Derby apart.

After the winning post, the horses disappeared over the horizon. For a few brief moments there was empty grass and various Motivator team-mates running up it. James Cronin was sobbing like a baby. Roy Thorpe came rushing across shouting: 'Jimmy, Jimmy, we did it boy. Wasn't he awesome?' Big Dermot Barry the farrier scooped me up in his massive arms. A little figure hurtled across from the far side. Chris Conway had sprinted back from the start – not bad for a man whose next birthday would be his sixtieth.

Then the actual participants were among us; Motivator blowing but not distressed, Johnny Murtagh smiling and serene, a man who had masterminded this victory from the moment he sat on the colt seven long weeks ago.

There was much rejoicing and pressing of flesh. Michael Bell came up, his face lit with a happiness from deep within – a trainer who had set a shy at greatness and nailed the target in the bull. As Motivator was finally led into

The morning after: Motivator and Michael Bell.

the winner's enclosure, Dermot saw he had lost the plate on his off-fore and the rest of us teased him relentlessly on how good the horse might be if he was ever properly shod.

Dermot was flying by the time we got back to the bar of The Yard. So too were James Cronin's parents, and Richard Simpson, and Chris Conway and Dave Murray and all the others there. Shane Featherstonehaugh had already left, as had Michael Bell, who had family mouths to feed in the local Chinese. Ed Dunlop was at the table and Kev 'The Car' Williams. Darryll Holland was across the room. For a few days he had been part of the Motivator fairytale. Now he has to file it only as one of the great 'might have beens'.

It got late. Going to bed, you still held the happiness in your head. In the morning you needed to get the papers to check it had actually happened. Better still – the ultimate joy on a Derby morning after – walk out of the house, up through the yard, and there in his box was the Derby winner. And with him was a reality check called Dermot Barry.

'He's just a bit sore,' said the farrier, fitting a shoe to the offending hoof, 'and the spots from those midge bites have come up bad on his back. He's a very highly tuned athlete and that makes him very sensitive too.'

On Motivator's near-side flank great blobs swelled up like a heat rash where the saddle had been and a vein stood out against the skin. As he walked rather feelingly out on to the tarmac, the Derby winner looked something of a wreck.

But the moment passed. Amy Weaver took him over to crop grass in the meadow. With a shoe on he felt easier. The vet came to give him the cortisone injection he was unable to administer for the midge bites before racing. The horse cropped some more. He, like his supporters, was just tired and content.

A team photo was agreed for 10.30 and we could return to debating with Barry whether the shoe was lost in mid-race or, as all farriers insist, only after the race was won.

After breakfast the sun came out and the phone and the fax began to flood. Johnny Murtagh rang to ask about the horse and his handlers. Hughie Morrison faxed with prices on where Bell should relocate following his statement that Motivator was 'a horse who could change your address'.

Photographer 'By Appointment' Edward Whitaker arrived from the Cotswolds. The team gathered for the photo, and eight-year-old Lucy Simpson stuck her specially painted tribute to Motivator on his door.

They put the red sheet inscribed 'Vodafone Derby Winner 2005' on his back. Two dogs raced and fought and little Tom Simpson played with a hosepipe. Two years ago he had weighed just 3lb when poor Debbie was confined prematurely. Now he looks set to follow thirteen-year-old Ross Simpson, just voted player of the season for the mighty Moulton Panthers.

The sun came out. It was a family affair. Michael and George had Alex and Amy and Nick with them, just as they had on Saturday. There were group photos, single photos, at one stage there was even a 'hack's photo' when I got my own slot for the album.

Phrases like 'He's just unbelievable', 'What's going to beat him now?' and 'The guv'nor seems keen on the Eclipse' floated around. We took turns to give Motivator a pat of thanks.

Which brings us back to gratitude. Michael Bell, in his direct but unpompous way, had said how 'bloody lucky' they all were to have a horse like Motivator in their lives. It is not confined to him and his team. When racing gets it right it links directly into personal, professional and national heritage. The horse stands in the centre of it and you wonder how so simple and yet so marvellous a creature can link so many strands together.

All of those around him know that they have climbed to the top of the racing mountain – that whatever else happens they will always have been part of a Derby winner. Whose horse is he? Thanks to them, he now belongs to all of us.

Then we came to the headiest time of all: the high summer of 2005 between the Derby and Motivator's next target, the Eclipse Stakes at Sandown Park at the beginning of July. Our horse had gone from an unbeaten contender to an awesome unchallenged champion. It was almost too good to be true – or, in hindsight, to last.

But there's no apology in relating this. Just for once, there was a song in every tree.

Eclipse preparation – *26 June*

H E IS fresh again. So fresh that earlier in the week he had caused a turning, bucking commotion just on the walk from his box to the circling ring where he is now stalking stablemate Skidrow like some predatory panther. It is 6.15 a.m. on Friday 24 June. Motivator is not just ready for work – he needs it.

Three weeks on from his Epsom heroics, Motivator is a very different creature from the tired, shoeless, spotty-skinned animal who had posed for the team photos on the lawn behind us. A fortnight of mere regular canters up Warren Hill has restored him to the rudest of health. Skidrow and rider Hayley Turner have to put up with alarming snorts and jumps behind them every time Motivator has an excuse to move.

The plan is to box the two horses over to the Al Bahathri gallop on the other side of town to re-enact the same one-mile piece of work that preceded the Derby. Johnny Murtagh is over in Ireland, so work-rider Shane Featherstonehaugh's long-legged cool does duty in the saddle. It has been the hottest night of the year. Michael Bell is in shorts, and so is Duggie Honeywell.

The latter is taking on the role of Bell's long-serving head man Richard Simpson, who was trapped into a Spanish holiday last week after what was billed as 'a barbecue in Bishop's Stortford' turned out to be a diversion off the M11 to Stansted.

Despite his posturings, Motivator is calm and dry-coated as he is loaded up, but by the time he is unboxed and Featherstonehaugh is back in the saddle, the adrenalin is beginning to pump and the sweat is rushing through. As the horse is led past to the start of the canter, Roy Thorpe's right arm braced hard

Motivator and Johnny Murtagh return from exercise.

against his bridle, there is something ferocious in the pent-up power behind the bit. This is the sweat not of fear, but of readiness.

For our car there is a gate to open and a bumpy avenue to navigate before we mount the wooden viewing stand six furlongs up the Al Bahathri. Suddenly we are back into the rural, hay-sweet peace of a summer morning. A motor beats the other side of the railway line, larksong is almost loudly obtrusive, and just half a dozen of us gather for the two dots to thicken on the horizon.

Skidrow is a decent three-year-old who finished a good fifth in the Britannia Handicap at Royal Ascot at York last week. He also did this same task with the same rider in the pre-Derby workout. For a while the two-horse Indian file seems to be closing rather slowly, but as they near and Featherstonehaugh moves Motivator out, you are hit by the moment every racing person always dreams of – the sight of a true Thoroughbred on the stretch.

But Motivator isn't anywhere near all out – the stretching is in Shane's arms. He has the reins on the same long hold Johnny Murtagh used in the Dante, a great daub of sweat flecks the neck, and Motivator's whole being exudes an urge to run a hole in the horizon. One of the oldest and wisest sayings in racing is that 'all horses go fast past trees', but Skidrow in receipt of two stone is not exactly a tree, and Epsom has already shown us what Motivator can leave in his wake. As he rockets away from us towards the awakening town, we know that Motivator is back.

There is a strange, quietly spoken euphoria after an exciting piece of work. The actual athlete cannot talk, so all other participants are quizzed and re-quizzed.

'Skidrow actually went keener than last time,' says Hayley Turner. 'I wasn't hard on him, but when Motivator came upsides, he made a huge impression.'

Featherstonehaugh has one of those faces that does not readily crease into a smile, but the frown now is one of awe, not worry. 'He was really tremendous,' he says of his now-relaxed partner whose nostrils, quite literally, would not blow a candle out. 'When I moved him out he gave a terrific feel. I honestly think he is better and stronger than ever before.'

Such delicacies are passed from mouth to mouth. Georgina Bell is there, and Master Bell ready with a new streamline haircut to defend his title in the under-nines 50 metres later in the morning. Our local scribes consign the golden words to the notebook. 'Very satisfactory,' says the trainer with a chime

The Coral-Eclipse: Oratorio beats Motivator.

in keeping with his 'Jingle Bell' nickname. But when we have got into the car and are tracking the two horses on the way home, he lets the emotion out. 'Just look at him,' he says as Motivator follows Skidrow beside the Bury Road. 'That's the only bit of work he has had in three weeks and he is not blowing at all. He's just a fantastic natural athlete.'

Back in the yard with the horses stripped down, hosed off and cropping grass as contentedly as cows in a field, the debrief and the rekindling continues. Yet there is already a very different tone than was pervaded on the same spot before the Derby. Then, there was a yearning that the greatness they dreamed they were nurturing would actually emerge as reality across the Epsom turf. Now, they are getting used to being the guardians of a super talent, confident of the challenges ahead.

First up is Shamardal in the Eclipse on Saturday. 'It could get trappy,' says Michael Bell. 'Frankie will try to slow it down from the front. But I doubt he, or anyone, has the acceleration to match this horse. He has really thrived since the Derby. He has still had only four races. He is growing up. He is getting better.'

Our hands are on him. Before the Derby the skin was almost tight along Motivator's rib-cage; now there is just a hint more elasticity in the texture and an even deeper glow of wellbeing in the bay shine of his coat.

This is a three-year-old Thoroughbred on his way to prime. But the indulgence of patting him like a pony cannot conceal the pressure he must face. The skin rash that so disfigured his withers after the Derby is growing over, and down on his feet, Dermot Barry has not just nailed the shoe back on, he has glued it. Next Saturday he has to run.

To be serious, Barry has had to resort to the American resin Equilox to ensure no repetition of the off-fore shoe loss, not only during the closing stages of the Derby but again at the end of his Warren Hill exercise ten days ago.

'The trouble is that he doesn't grow any hoof,' says Barry, who also tended Motivator's feet as a foal and yearling in his nursery days at Deerfield Farm. 'He was fine as a two-year-old, but since December the feet have hardly grown any horn at all. You could pare them off with a nail file. Other farriers tell me they have had this with champion horses. They seem to be that more refined a machine than the others.'

Barry's answer to the conundrum will be to fix both front racing plates with the Equilox resin on Thursday. 'It takes a bit of time and you have to be very careful, but once it has been done you are as certain as can be that the shoe will stay on. We used it on a good sprinter Red Carpet a couple of years back, so we do know it works.'

Motivator consents amenably as we prod away at the offending off-fore hoof with its orangey brown coat of resin above the shoe. In his switched-off mode, he remains the relaxed creature who so memorably lay down and went to sleep when some of his celebrated owners were admitted to his box a couple of months ago. You give him a friendly pat on the neck as you do any horse. Then you remember that you are patting a Derby winner and feel almost cheeky doing it.

For next week, he will once again be very far from the cuddly pony. Roy Thorpe and James Cronin will march him manfully into the paddock. Johnny Murtagh will stroke those long, calming fingers on the neck, and back in Newmarket the Fitzroy House team will look on in both anticipation and wonder.

'It's extraordinary,' says Sarah Nicholson, a long-standing member of the Bell team, as we trek back down from Warren Hill later on Friday. 'I rode him a year ago and he seemed so weak, yet now he has emerged into this mighty being. I guess it's what we dream of.'

The Eclipse at Sandown was the day we came back down to earth. With Shamardal a late withdrawal through injury and the giant Starcraft all but jumping out of the paddock, Motivator was 5-2 on in a seven-runner field. He looked a certainty too, as he swept to the front at the quarter-mile pole with only the Guineas fourth and Derby failure Oratorio and a hard-at-work Kieren Fallon in shouting distance. But it was not to be.

Who knows if it was the firm ground that brought his head up and his stride short in the last hundred yards? Maybe it was the odd pace which saw the too-keen Motivator stranded in front or without cover for the whole ten furlongs? Or was it the hidden effects of the Derby which, not unusually, saw not one of the first seven home win another race all season?

Oratorio was only tenth at Epsom but he found himself at Sandown all right. At the line he had swept past to win by half a length, and the Motivator bubble, or at least that aura of invincibility, was irredeemably burst.

It took a bit of getting used to. But as in life, you have to pick yourself up and find another target. Motivator had a well deserved break for the rest of July, but once into August he began to be prepared for the Irish Champion Stakes at the beginning of September.

The horse was great, but no one could deny that a little of the magic had gone out of the whole saga. That was all the more reason for hanging in there, but it meant there was a slight edge to the mornings. Those close to the horse still believed, but we got decidedly scratchy when people started querying Motivator's status – and in particular, as you will read, when someone like Frankie Dettori defected from his back.

Before Leopardstown – *8 September*

IN THE last month, a lively sprig of completely white hair has mysteriously grown at the end of Motivator's mane. No one knows why it has come, but on Tuesday morning it is the training team, not the Derby winner, who are getting the grey hair treatment.

The greying may be a bit premature – by the following morning there is rain forecast for Leopardstown, and the Derby hero is odds-on to make the Irish Champion Stakes line-up – but on Tuesday the concern and frustration are palpable.

'It seems so bloody silly to only start watering on Monday,' grumbles Michael Bell as he sips his tea in the kitchen at 6.45 a.m. 'Without a lot of rain forecast, I don't see how it can be good ground, can't see us running. And the horse is so, so well.'

The frustration is equally rough in the fug of the tack room. 'It looks like a bullocks to me,' says Motivator's groom James Cronin. 'All my family have booked tickets to come to Leopardstown. So have Shane's and Dermot the blacksmith. The horse is in great shape. He has come on real good since his break. And now it looks as if we are scuppered.' It's a sultry morning in Newmarket and all our moods seem to match.

All, that is, except Motivator's. Five weeks ago he had looked almost sleek after spending most of July on an easy routine following that first defeat in the Eclipse.

Now, the muscle definition is hard along the line of his neck and across his quarters. The month back on full exercise has sharpened him mentally as well as physically. Last week, he chased James Cronin across the box. Motivator doesn't read the papers. He just feels ready to rumble.

'Yes, he's absolutely crying out for a run,' says exercise rider Shane Featherstonehaugh as we make our way out of the Fitzroy House yard and set off through the town. 'He has done three pieces of work, the last one with Frankie Dettori on Friday. He shows so much speed that I think Leopardstown would suit him.

'But not if it doesn't rain. I looked at the Eclipse video again yesterday and it's obvious that the ground was the problem – his head came up and he just wouldn't stretch.'

Threading our way through the four-wheeled and four-legged early morning traffic was to sense how quickly the slippery soap of fame escapes. Back in June, Motivator was a superstar; now he is merely another horse in the string: nobody points and says, 'There's the Derby winner'. The Irish Champion and other big races could go by without him. Next year he will probably be at stud. Was that golden Epsom memory just a passing joy?

Such gloomy thoughts are suddenly overtaken by more important matters. As we walk towards the Bury Road, in the distance we can see two figures galloping up Warren Hill. The large one is trainer Bell on Ruby, the heavy-footed stable hack; the little one is eight-year-old Nick Bell on nineteen-year-old It's A Secret, an old pony entrusted to give him the thrill of playing the jockey game up the gallops before going to a new school on Thursday. Nick's chunky smile afterwards tells of mission accomplished.

Back with the string, lead horse Glen Ida suddenly declines to do his duty as we file along the railed walkway before the start point. Motivator backs sideways in huffy disapproval, and it is left to me and the admirable Woodcracker to step past and ease the knot. The moment before launch-off always carries the potential for bucking, kicking chaos. But as Glen Ida pulls himself together and shoots off with Motivator in tow, order is restored, and from behind you can admire the most valuable backside in racing as the hooves flick up divots on the designated strip between the white markers.

To be sneakily truthful, he doesn't always go between the discs. A lot of other horses had already been up the gallop and as the early part is quite chewed up, Featherstonehaugh takes something of a Derby winner's prerogative and puts Motivator on the clean turn outside the markers.

'Just my luck,' he says as we pull up. 'The better ground was too good to resist, but halfway along there was the gallops man watching. I suppose he is entitled to his moan.'

That irritation cannot dim the moments that have gone before.

Wooodcracker is a perfectly decent horse and the stable hope for the Cambridgeshire. At pace he sets his chestnut neck good and straight enough to give me a uniquely privileged close-up of what makes Motivator tick. The stride is not long and floating as, say, Nashwan's was. It is quick, super-efficient, the hocks flipping back as the muscles bunch on the hind quarters above. It speaks of tactical speed, and that could be crucial come Saturday.

'I think Azamour is a cracking horse,' says Shane as he yearns for Leopardstown to have something different from the sizzling sun that is now hot enough to have the admittedly sweaty Temple Place in a lather as he readies for his pacemaking duties this weekend. 'But I think the course would suit us better than him. Azamour looks like a horse who takes time to get going. Mick Kinane has had to really stoke him up. It will be a difficult job for Soumillon.'

At that stage, we don't know about the defection of Dettori, who after riding work on Motivator cried off to ride the favourite Scorpion for Coolmore in the St Leger. But walking across past Sir Mark Prescott's to do a second canter up the Polytrack gives time to visualise the opportunity that awaits Kevin Darley. Azamour is a full size bigger than Motivator. At this moment, he represents the absolute beau ideal of the mature, powerful

Motivator and Frankie Dettori.

Thoroughbred. But his awesome finishing punch needs quite a swing to make it effective. With Motivator, Darley should have the more manoeuvrable fighter.

That's the theory. On Tuesday morning it still looks unlikely that there would be the chance of practice, which means more grumbles as we pull up at the end of four and a half winging furlongs on the Polytrack.

'That horse is really ready now,' says head groom Richard Simpson looking at Motivator from his seat aboard the white-foamed Temple Place. 'And to think that they have leased this guy specially to be a pacemaker. They are booked to fly on Friday.'

We loose girths, lower leathers and file back down the walkway beside the road. Up the Polytrack, the Godolphin horses are a long, swinging battalion of royal blue. Among the spectators are a Newmarket Tours group, who don't recognise Motivator, and Michael 'Whispering Death' Holding, who does.

The great fast bowler is, of course, a Bajan countryman of Sir Michael Stoute, who is now busying around his string as he rearranges them for their second canter just ahead of us. Down the other side of the road, the regulation beige shirts of the Cumani string include one aboard the Aussie star Starcraft, who came good so impressively on Sunday when making all the running to beat France's best in the Prix du Moulin at Longchamp. Big stars, but the brightest could still be the light-footed bay in front of us. On cue, Motivator skitters sharply left. 'All dressed up,' Bell had said mournfully, 'and nowhere to go.' Not so.

It seems an age since we began these stable visits back in the January chill. In those nine months Motivator, still only three years old, God help us, has fulfilled his promise and has matured mentally. But now he has to do more. And when we finally reach home, strip off saddles and have a hose-down, you can inspect the reasons for believing that possible.

When he was wound up for the Derby, you could detect just a hint of ribbiness. Now, although he is hard and fit, he has kept a bit more substance behind the saddle. At 16 hands, he is not a huge horse. But when you run your hands over him, you can feel that every piece of him works.

Even his feet. The loss of an off-fore shoe in the Derby had been repeated at exercise. The time off after the Eclipse has given the foot a chance to mend and farrier Dermot Barry picks it up to show the 'new balance' system he has adopted, the shoe tacked slightly inside the edge of the hoof, to avoid overreach. 'I'm happier with him now,' says Barry. 'I'd be even happier if I knew he was definitely running and my tickets weren't going to waste.'

Time to move on. Bell is in the office and there is a slight change to his tone. 'They now say there is the possibility of some quite heavy rain in Ireland,' he says as he comes off the phone. 'Maybe it's too late, but you never know. I have always said that this was the race I thought he could win.'

Meanwhile, the bookmakers remain disbelievers. Some don't offer Motivator at all, some at as much as 4-1 or 5-1.

The King's Theatre is on the road down from the Bell stable to St Mary's Church. Their next attraction is called Never Judge A Bookie. This time, though, the bookies could be wrong.

Dermot Barry's tickets did not go to waste, as the rains came and Motivator and pacemaking Temple Place duly showed up on what was perfect ground at Leopardstown. It was not a perfect result – another half-length defeat by Oratorio – but there was plenty for us to take forward for his closing target, the Prix de l'Arc de Triomphe at Longchamp on the first Sunday in October.

With Hazarista in as a pacemaker for Azamour, the two front-runners rather cut their own throats, so that by the beginning of the uphill Leopardstown straight Motivator and Kevin Darley were left in front – with little option but to make the best of their way home and vainly hope that the avenging angel that was Kieren Fallon on Oratorio would not cut them down at the finish.

The papers headlined it 'Another defeat for Motivator', but we felt better about him. And upset though we all were ten days later to read that the Derby winner would be retired to the Royal Stud at the end of the season, it meant that there was a renewed sense of 'We'll show 'em' determination about the yard.

And as always, the stable was the best place to be.

Approaching the Arc – *29 September*

ABSENT friends at Newmarket, but a still-resident hero. Motivator was limbering up yesterday morning but Michael Bell was away at the sales, box-driver Roy Thorpe was under the weather, farrier Dermot Barry was under the table celebrating the birth of Hugo Barry, and the media – well, most of us hacks seem to have forgotten about Motivator.

'That's the way I like it,' said head groom Richard Simpson as I rode beside him on Ruby, the colossal hack who last week caused his trainer a quick trip to Newmarket 'nick' by knocking over a disgruntled ex-owner in what is splendidly described as 'an altercation'.

'The press don't know what good shape Motivator is in,' adds Simpson. 'He never leaves an oat, and from the way he goes about his work, I promise you he is better than ever. I am going over for the Arc. I have never seen him run in the flesh and this will be my last chance. Pity – what a four-year-old he could have been.'

This slightly harsher mood, of resentment at credit not given and of future chances now denied, adds an edge to a glorious autumn morning with the leaves changing in the plantations on Warren Hill.

'Frankie Dettori was quite crabby after he rode him before Leopardstown,' reveals Shane Featherstonehaugh, as we trekked back down from the first canter. 'He said: "This is not the horse that ran away from me and Dubawi in the Derby. I don't think he is right." But that's just the way Motivator is now. He doesn't really stretch except on the racecourse.'

The second canter up the steeper Polytrack gives a clue as to Dettori's reasoning. Motivator walks down far more relaxed than the dancing dervish of the early spring, and once he swings up to lead horse Magic Sting in the gallop, his slightly round action freewheels in hardly impressive fashion.

'He just goes up to them and that's all,' says Shane. 'But all year we have been training him to relax, so we aren't complaining. He moved good enough at Leopardstown and, best of all, he put his head down when the others came to him.'

So rose the truth that had dared not speak its name. The thing about the Eclipse defeat at Sandown that had most upset Shane and several other members of the team was not merely the loss of Motivator's unbeaten record, but the colt's apparent lack of fight when Oratorio tackled him.

'At Leopardstown he had his head up a bit as the others came to him,' says veteran Chris Conway. 'I said to myself, "Put your head down and fight, you little bastard!", and he did. He ran all the way to the line. He should get a longer lead at Longchamp. He will really get the trip. I think he will take all the beating.'

Amy Weaver, at 24, is almost four decades Conway's junior, and only took on her present role as Fitzroy House assistant in January. But like the others she has had Motivator's season indelibly imprinted into her life and is in a unique position to pay tribute to the absent trainer.

'I like the way he set out Motivator's routine and stuck to it,' she says. 'The boss was always open about what the horse was doing, how little work he needed, and I think it has paid off. Look at him now.'

We are walking back towards the town. Autumn is coming, gloves are needed, no more glimpses of trainer John Berry riding out in shorts and gumboots. If the stallion syndication deal goes through, and if a surely much-needed rethink is not taken after the Arc, there will be few more glimpses of Motivator before his final shot across the Atlantic in the Breeders' Cup.

'It's a pity,' says Amy, whose brief career has already spanned spells at Cheltenham, Beckhampton and Mill Hill, north London, where she used to ride out each morning after working nights as a dealer in the Clermont Club, 'but I suppose that's racing.'

The business part of it, no doubt – but not the thing that will grab the throat this Sunday. That's about a small group of people using their collective knowledge, judgement, sweat and long-term application to get an athlete to the track to do things that can change their and our lives for ever.

It's an opportunity that comes to very few. It's come to Team Fitzroy, and out of it they and we have had Motivator's Derby dream. But now there are only two chances left, and you look hard again at the white-starred bay as he turns home into the yard. He joined history at Epsom, but Longchamp is where legends are made.

Back in the box, Shane takes the saddle from Motivator and starts to sponge out the girth mark while the colt makes mock-threatening lunges with his teeth. Over the years, I have been lucky enough to also stand beside Arc heroes Dalakhani, Motivator's sire Montjeu, that horse's stablemate Suave Dancer, the superstar Dancing Brave, the great mare Allez France and the little marvel that was Mill Reef back in 1971. It's a roll-call that's worth repeating, because you have to believe that the horse snarling in front of you ranks among that company.

He has many of the attributes – fine tactical speed, fully proven stamina, and a good Derby on his shield. He will also have as committed a support group as ever crossed the Channel. Roy Thorpe and James Cronin will fly with the horse from Cambridge on Saturday morning. Shane and his lady Louise will go on the ferry in the afternoon – 'I have never been to Longchamp, may never have another chance.' Richard Simpson is going, and Dave Murray and Dermot Barry, despite the appearance not only of Hugo Dermot Barry born on Monday, but of a hospital visit for heart treatment a week earlier. Sounds like kill or cure.

The Bell family will be out from school in force. Amy Weaver will have to mind the shop. At 3.30 a.m. on Sunday morning, an hour when some Paris roisterers will at last be considering shut-eye, she will be in the yard supervising the departure of eight Sheikh Rashid horses to Heathrow and Dubai.

Amy had to watch the Derby from Doncaster and the Irish Champion Stakes from Goodwood, where the death of Motivator's lead horse Glen Ida underlined the fragility of it all. 'But this is my job,' she says, 'and this has already been a year beyond believing.'

Getting to Longchamp for Arc weekend can often be a logistical nightmare: airlines strike, ferries stop, tunnels shut. Instead of arriving at the Bois de Boulogne in a the frame of mind to appreciate this most gorgeous of big-race settings, you arrive in a frazzled state of nerves eager to inflict your Travel Bore-of-the-Year story on any unlucky acquaintance.

For me 2005 was different. It was the chance to fly unfussed to Longchamp with a real Arc contender – and not a jockey but a horse. It was also a way of filing a Prix de l'Arc de Triomphe preview which did something more than talk about weights and tips and what should be. You can even say, quite correctly, that this report for the Sunday Telegraph *came from dangerously close to the horse's mouth.*

In the air – *1 October*

IN 1971, when Mill Reef left Kingsclere in Hampshire to become the first British-trained winner of the Prix de l'Arc de Triomphe in 23 years, it took special clearance from the Pentagon to have a Boeing ship him from the American Airbase at nearby Greenham Common. Thirty-four years on Motivator only had to pop down from Newmarket to Cambridge to catch yesterday's charter.

But if flying now sounds familiar, the close-up sight of a horse, and in this case a £6 million-valued Derby winner, braced against the power on take-off is still a daunting one. The clock showed ten past two as the BAE 146 opened its four-engine throttle. Motivator ducked his head slightly and a huge tremor ran through him. James Cronin, his long-time groom, ran a reassuring hand

The 2005 Arc: Hurricane Run goes clear of Motivator, who is about to be passed by Westerner.

over his neck. There were three other horses on the plane. Suddenly it seemed rather small.

Motivator was standing looking back at us in his stall on the right hand side of the aircraft. Behind him to the left was the Michael Stoute-trained filly Red Bloom; further up the plane facing forward was the fellow Prix de l'Opera runner Kinnaird; and ahead of her was the sprinter Majestic Missile. All horses were braced, watching humans braced too. No seat belts for equines: if they fly the balance has to be up to them.

Even the most travelled among us still get their odd moments on take-off. This was only the third flight of Motivator's life, the first two having been to Leopardstown and back just three weeks ago. As the engines roared and Cronin's hand kept patting the neck, this was merely a nervous three-year-old, not a multi-million-pound blue-blood set to carve his name in the history of the Arc. Motivator shook but he didn't panic. The engines levelled off. The horse began to pick at his hay net. 'He's got it now,' said James Cronin: 'Last time he got quite worried for a while. He's a quick learner.'

Quite how fast a flat racer has to mature is emphasized by the Arc, just the seventh start of Motivator's career, being his final race in Europe. But rather than railing against the business ethic that produces that great incongruity, a racehorse too valuable to race, yesterday was a time to marvel at quite how organized a high-class runner from a skilled stable can become.

For some of us the morning had been a time of agitated calls about changes of schedule. At 11.30 Motivator himself was so nervous that there seemed no sign of him in his box at Michael Bell's Fitzroy House stables. Closer inspection found him. He was lying flat out on the floor – fast asleep.

'That's the way I want him,' said the trainer. 'I don't know why some people are crabbing this horse,' he said. 'He ran a great race last time at Leopardstown. It's been raining in France which means he will have his favoured softer ground for the first time this season, and also for the first time he should get a good lead into the straight. Believe me, he is going to run a big, big race.'

First he had to get there. At 12.40, the seasoned Roy Thorpe began wrapping blue protective bandages around Motivator's feet while assistant Amy Weaver fitted padded boots around his legs. At 12.50 the box pulled out of Newmarket onto the Cambridge road. At 1.10 it joined the three other wagons circling round the ramp-lowered plane. At 1.15 the fun began.

Majestic Missile is an impressively muscled sprinter. He walked up the ramp well enough but soon afterwards a succession of wall-battering blows suggested those muscles were being put to mischievous use. Five minutes later he was led down the ramp in disgrace while worried air staff went to inspect the damage. He and they took their time but eventually Majestic Missile was reloaded and we were airborne, and but for one moment in mid-flight when we hit an air pocket and Cronin and Thorpe jumped to either side of Motivator's head, the one-hour miracle of air passage went without incident.

It was sunny at Le Bourget. So too was Motivator's gleaming coat as he walked from the plane into the waiting horsebox. He had literally not turned a hair on the flight, and neither did he in the fifty-minute journey through the suburbs and along the Seine to the edge of the Bois de Boulogne and to the departing crowds at Longchamp.

It was 4.30 when he walked into his box, less than two and a half hours since take-off, less than four hours since he left his stable. Nearly two centuries have passed since Lord George Bentinck won £60,000 (six million in today's money) by building the first horse box and shipping the presumed non-runner Elis north from Goodwood to Doncaster to win the St Leger. It is 55 years since Wilwyn flew from England to win the Washington International and stopped at Shannon for an Irish coffee refuel. But however the travel, the treasured ambition remains the same.

As James Cronin led Motivator round the ring within the stable complex, sounds of jubilation came from the small man leading round a washed-down horse ahead of him. It soon became clear it was the winner of the last race. 'Il a gagné. C'est fantastique,' the little wizened figure shouted into his phone.

There are reasons, as well as wishful thinking, to suppose that Cronin might be breaking into something similar this afternoon.

James and I were not alone in our hopes. Indeed, there was weight enough of overseas money to see Motivator start as 5-2 favourite by the time the fifteen set off from the stalls and Longchamp's famous old windmill that showery October afternoon.

The thought was that Motivator's pace might be too much for the Irish Derby winner Hurricane Run, who had made a winning comeback in the Prix Niel three weeks before. If that were so he would surely be too fast for France's great stayer Westerner and for the St Leger winner Scorpion. If he was also too good for last year's Arc hero Bago, the talented German Derby victor Shirocco and the Aga Khan's progressive Prix Vermeille winner Shawanda, our season and our story would have a crowning beyond compare.

Motivator had his moments. With just over three hundred metres to run he took over from Shawanda, and for a few giddy seconds he was in front with the whole Arc field in desperate pursuit. Your heart longed for him to sustain it but your eye told you he would not. His head was a little up, his stride tightened a fraction, and launching up the inside was yet again the nemesis that was Fallon, this time aboard Hurricane Run.

The Irish Derby winner was past Motivator, but as the post loomed ever closer a place still looked certain. Even when Westerner thrust by, third was still there for the taking, only for both Bago and Shirocco to nail him right on the line. It was a fine run – maybe he had hit the front a touch early – but there was some disappointment in the air.

Back in January everyone would have been delighted to have got as far as this. But after the ultimate heights at Epsom, fifth – albeit a highly commendable fifth – still felt a tiny bit of a letdown. It looked liked the season was ending in anticlimax.

Then out of the blue came the surprise announcement that he would have one more race – a tilt at the Breeders' Cup Turf at Belmont Park at the end of the month.

Suddenly all the fizz was back. At the thirteenth hour our hero could snatch back his glory. Visiting Newmarket a fortnight after the Arc was to find a place and a team full of hope for what could happen across the Atlantic two weeks later. But it took only a week more before I got the call.

Here's how it ended.

Breakdown – *25 October*

O N SATURDAY at Doncaster, the name 'M Bell' flashed up on my mobile phone. Exactly a year before it had been on the winners' board after the Racing Post Trophy and in that same room our idea of following a Derby favourite through his winter and spring preparation had begun. Now Motivator's trainer had news of a final brilliant gallop but also of a career-ending lameness once back in the yard. For all of us it was over.

For all of us it has also been quite a journey. To follow a Classic favourite and what his training meant to those closest to him had been a personal ambition ever since we made that film about Mill Reef back in 1972. For, by the time of the film, Mill Reef was already a Derby and Arc winner from the season before.

Last October, Motivator was just a hyped-up hopeful. Yet for Michael Bell and his Fitzroy House team he was the best horse they had ever handled, their first Group 1 winner. Now he was the stuff of Derby dreams. We would need to tread softly.

What was at stake for the Bell team was a place in racing legend. They knew, as we all know, that most horses either go wrong, don't match expectations or – and this happens very often – get messed up by the training team. From late last summer, they had been convinced they were dealing with something exceptional. The Racing Post Trophy confirmed it. Now they had to get him to the Classics. And they accepted us in.

It was the most enjoyable long-term assignment of my career. With an article a month there was space for all the characters to emerge. Richard Simpson, the head man with the 4.30 a.m. start; James Cronin, Motivator's groom of the bulging forearms and the boxing medals; Shane Featherstonehaugh, the exercise rider who could sit calm in a whirlwind – as Motivator was on fresh occasions; 'Bombardier' Roy Thorpe, box driver, traffic stopper and Motivator's right-hand man in the big race lead-up; Hayley Turner, the stable apprentice blessed with a superabundance of talent; Chris Conway, the craggy veteran still playing classy football at 59.

The list goes on, as it does with all stables, to embrace everyone from office to saddle, from entry to exit. What was special about 2005 is that, from the beginning, everyone at Fitzroy House knew they had the chance of living out the ultimate racing dream, and that all were a part of delivering it. In time they will all, even eight-year-old Nick Bell, grow old. But even in their dotage, there will be the shaking of an aged head and the phrase, 'I was with Motivator.'

That's what a Derby winner can do for you and, as the horse recovers from his injury, the memories come tumbling through. There was the explosive moment when the lorry hit its airbrakes on the Bury Road and Motivator did an instant 360; galloping through the snow with Czech rider Dalibor Torok replacing a broken-wristed Featherstonehaugh; the first piece of work with a sunlit Newmarket grandstand emerging out of the mist; the decision to miss the Guineas – 'The guv'nor's getting hate mail,' said Richard Simpson, 'and that's just from the staff.'

When Motivator won the Dante, we had to confront the dream becoming reality. And no image better illustrated how much it meant than the sight of Cronin and Thorpe leading the colt out of the Epsom stables and up towards the parade ring. They were breathing deep, faces set, the horse saddled. Getting through the next twenty minutes was their responsibility.

Everyone who has ever had a runner knows the tension, anyone lucky enough to have a winner knows the elation. But to have a Derby winner is something else.

I was only a passing scribbler who had occasionally galloped up Warren Hill in vain pursuit of Motivator's muscled backside. Yet when he went clear in the Derby it was my most thrilling moment on a racecourse since Mill Reef went clear in the Ganay and the film, on which my future depended, was safe. As Motivator swept past, I somersaulted over the Epsom rails and sprinted up the track to dance around with James and Roy and Dermot Barry the farrier. It was as silly and as stupendous as that.

In your gut you sensed it couldn't get better, and it didn't. Not that Motivator ran badly – indeed, his fifth in the Arc remains his highest Racing Post Rating. But after Epsom, after that wonderful night in Newmarket and that hungover morning with the horse spotty and sore-footed from his exertions, a touch of reality only reinforced how special Derby Day had been.

While the Eclipse was being run, I was covering the ladies' final from Centre Court at Wimbledon. A text beeped on my phone. It was from Clement Freud, 'Disgruntled' of the Royal Ascot Racing Club, who had thought membership had conferred money as well as honour. 'The horse I don't own,' it said, 'did not win the Eclipse.'

The worry then was whether Motivator had shirked a fight. At Leopardstown he proved that wrong, but was stuck in front and still got beaten. At Longchamp he got the break too soon and didn't quite last home. Returning on the plane, James Cronin had cradled the horse's head in his arms and said dolefully: 'I suppose that might be it. But I know one thing. I will never do another like him.'

At the Bell yard there was a dampened feeling, as if everyone was still soaked from the pre-Arc downpour at Longchamp. The two-year-olds, normally the stable's strong suit, were proving useless. The star was off to stud.

Then came the decision to run in the States, in the Breeders' Cup Turf at Belmont Park. Roy, James and Shane all got visas in excitement. Hadn't the great Sir Ivor's career ended in triumph across the Atlantic? And he didn't run as a four-year-old either.

Belmont, with the help of both bute and Lasix, could be the answer. At Newmarket on Champions' Day, Featherstonehaugh came up with a smile as warm as the sunshine. 'I tell you what,' he said in his quiet Irish way, 'he worked really brilliant this morning.'

Motivator leads the way – a memory of the best of times.

It was not to be – a cracked pelvis on the gallops ruled out the Belmont trip – but in the grand scheme of things it does not matter. In terms of pure merit, Motivator was not the best Classic winner we have ever seen, nor actually even the best of his generation. But he was the one we were closest to. That mattered. May the memories never fade.

Motivator sure had to pay the price of his summer of good fortune. When he had recovered from his cracked pelvis, his first season at the Royal Stud was cut short when he injured himself slipping up at exercise. But now he is back at the fathering again, and in 2009 we will see his first two-year-olds on the racetrack.
For me his offspring will always bring back memories – of the best of times.

Great Impressions

*G*REAT IMPRESSIONS – *that's what you want people to make. No amount of statistics or tributes or photos can match that opening truth. So I want to share a dozen people who have made a huge impression on both me and on racing.*

Picking just twelve from six decades of racing life is an invidious task, for it involves the reverse of choosing the passengers for Peter Walwyn's famous bus. The criterion for that renowned fantasy vehicle was that the individuals should be of such low merit that they would be hoicked aboard the double-decker (Big Pete was never short of names) and driven over Beachy Head. My bus is on a less fatal route, probably to some celestial York on a sunny August day, or to Cheltenham with the daffodils in bloom. My people will have drinks rather than death on the rocks.

But this first conveyance is far too small to accommodate all those who have impressed me down the years, and the only way I can limit it to twelve is to assume that a couple of them have gone ahead. Which, in the case of my father and my first mentor Frenchie Nicholson is not difficult, because they would certainly both be at Cheltenham ahead of me. Maybe there will be time to get a second bus out soon – and to try and confine that Walwyn one to the garage.

You will know these people – some better than others. I will not attempt to re-hash all their achievements but I do want to introduce you to the still unforgettable moments when they made those impressions on me. That might just begin to repay the unfathomable good fortune that an interest in racing has brought to me. I have presented and written about the game all over the world and, even more important, all around Britain. We live, nationally and internationally, in disunited times. How good it has been to find racing as a unifying factor.

On my desk is one of my proudest possessions – a block of coal from Stubbin Colliery in Yorkshire, commemorating the occasion when ITV's John Rickman and I spent an afternoon underground at the coal face and an evening under the influence at the Miners' Club. In my mind also is another rather different place, but one where the racing interest was just as strong. It is where we will meet the first of these Great Impressions.

It was Buckingham Palace.

Previous spread: Lester Piggott, Vincent O'Brien, Robert Sangster.

THE QUEEN

THIS WAS not practised charm, although the lady in the centre of the room must have had more practice than anyone in history. It was a party to celebrate the Oaks and St Leger winning heroics of Dunfermline in the Jubilee year of 1977. Dick Hern and Willie Carson were there, but so too were all the West Ilsley team – head lad Geordie Campbell, travelling head lad Buster Haslam, work rider Brian Proctor and box-driver Peter West, who would end up driving four Derby winners to Epsom. Wives and girlfriends too, although it was thirty merciful years before the word 'wags' was invented. The Queen was not just in her palace; this was her element, too.

She moved from one leathery handshake, from one Sunday best to another. Wary weather-beaten faces soon creased into smiles as they relived the golden moments that had brought them all together. There could be no tension because they knew that she knew those memories had been theirs

Royal Ascot, 1958.

as much as hers. They knew, too, that she enjoyed the private moments at the stables every bit as much as the public triumphs at the racetrack. This was the most gracious of thankyous, but it was deserved.

Quite how someone like me got in I can't remember, as this was most definitely not a press occasion. Indeed I was extremely hopeful that the Queen would not remember the first time she had been forced to lay eyes, quite literally, on her lowly subject – for he had been lying at her feet. It was at Relko's Derby in 1963. In a filthy student coat with a half-drunk bottle of wine in one pocket and a packet of peanuts in the other, I had tried to push through the throng, only to trip and fall right in front of the royal party processing down to the paddock. And they say Her Majesty never forgets a face.

I should not have worried. She was bubbling with enthusiasm at what a year it had been and how good it was to see all those familiar faces around the room. She was small but only in stature, friendly but not over-familiar. She talked of the future in that fingers-crossed way that only owner-breeders can. 'I am not sure Dick thinks that much of the two-year-olds,' she said before adding with a terrific smile, 'but you know what he is like.' She did not know that I had long been hooked by her racing past.

In these far less deferential if not exactly republican days, it might be hard to imagine quite what a central shadow the royal family cast across the country in general, and racing in particular, in the war and immediate post-war era. The shared struggle off the track meant that King George VI was in RAF uniform when he led in Sun Chariot after the 1942 Oaks; that the then Princess Elizabeth was in her ATS kit when she accompanied her father to the 1944 Derby, which was run, like all wartime Classics, at Newmarket.

The gleam of those purple silks with the scarlet sleeves and the gold braid were a symbol of hope of better times in the grey, rationed world of the late 1940s. In October 1950 they even delivered a coup. Above Board was a runaway winner of the Cesarewitch, having been backed from 40s to 18-1.

Admittedly the handicapper had taken quite a chance allotting just 7st 10lb to the winner of that year's Yorkshire Oaks, but King George was sufficiently concerned to carpet Cecil Boyd-Rochfort, who explained that the filly had not been right when she was beaten in her Cesarewitch prep. Of course all this passed me by, but at nine years old I was already memorising the names and pedigrees of the horses in my dad's racing magazines. I remember Above Board being a bit of a stir. My dad probably backed it.

To follow the royal horses was a bit like being a football fan with the breeding thrown in. By that comparison, Manchester United would by now have sons and grandsons of Law, Best and Charlton, not to mention lots of wayward Eric Cantonas. Imagine the thrill, therefore, when on the Saturday of Coronation week in 1953 my parents took me to Tattenham Corner to watch the young Queen's Aureole spin round the turn in a scarlet and purple flash before running on to be second to Pinza and the newly knighted Sir Gordon Richards.

Imagine the impact today. The radiant 26-year-old Queen honouring the man inevitably dubbed 'The World's Shortest Knight'; her high-fettled

Aureole who was that year to run second in the King George and third in the St Leger before taking both the Hardwicke Stakes and the King George in 1954, to make the Queen the nation's leading owner. At Royal Ascot she would be photographed galloping up the straight mile in the early morning. After the King George, a small figure came racing past Bill Curling of the *Daily Telegraph* as he made his way to the unsaddling enclosure. It was the only recorded sighting of the Queen running in public. Looking back, it was beyond a marketing man's wildest fantasy.

The running may have stopped but the interest never has, despite its full share of disasters. She was champion owner again in 1957 and Highclere had won both the 1,000 Guineas and Prix de Diane three years before Dunfermline put the Queen once more at the top of the list in 1977. But in between she lost one top colt, Doutelle, when he bled to death after tearing his rack chain, and another, Magna Carta, when he broke his jaw strung up on his haynet.

Then in the 1980s events conspired to produce not just an *annus horribilis*, but a whole decade of travail.

Every private stud yearns for one great mare from which champions will spring. In 1981 the Royal Studs had found it when the big, leggy Height Of Fashion strode away with the May Hill Stakes and the Hoover Fillies' Mile. When she broke the Newmarket mile-and-a-half track record in the Princess of Wales's Stakes the next season, she was so impressive that Sheikh Hamdan offered a then unthinkable £1.2 million. 'What ifs' don't make history, but this sale did.

Everyone knows the unhappy saga. The money was used to buy West Ilsley as a private stable. So when Dick Hern was first crippled in a hunting accident in 1984 and then had a heart attack in 1988, his future lay at the royal decree. When a decision was leaked in early 1989 that Dick was to be effectively sacked, it caused an outrage inflamed into near rebellion by Height Of Fashion's Sheikh Hamdan-owned son Nashwan as Horse of the Year.

When the big chestnut was led back to Hern's wheelchair in that Newmarket unsaddling enclosure after the Two Thousand Guineas, it was racing's equivalent of the no-flag moment outside Buckingham Palace before Princess Diana's funeral. Asked by me what should be written, a leading member of the establishment said: 'Go for the jugular.' When I reported this verbatim in the *Sunday Times*, some royal insiders did a neat closing of the aristocratic ranks and claimed the words were my own incitement. I never felt my head was in danger, but for a while I didn't go too close to the Tower of London.

As in the Princess Diana tragedy, the Queen's popularity suffered from her unswerving avoidance of public comment. In racing, this was exacerbated by the contrast with the Queen Mother's merry march to the 100 mark. The crowd would give raucous cheers for 'The Queen Mum', but merely respectful applause for their monarch as she quietly made her way, almost security free, through the paddock.

It is a poignant truth that only now, with her mother laid to rest in St George's, Windsor, do both the racing and the wider world truly appreciate what Elizabeth II has given them these last 56 years.

What they are coming to realise is what hit me so instantly at that party back in 1977. That at our head there is a lady not just of charm, but of wit, wisdom and a real commitment to others. For racing, there is the most impossibly lucky extra. It is that this game, with all its glory, exasperations, triumphs, absurdities and disasters, remains her historic abiding passion. Above all else, the Queen, still riding in her eighties, is intrigued and fascinated by the horses at the heart of it all; the families she has nurtured, the foals she has seen. One day in the 1980s I was at Wolferton when one of the royal mares foaled down. Within minutes there was one of those phone calls which in stricter days saw the recipient standing to attention. Few owners could have mothered more.

The royal complement of some twenty broodmares and a similar number of horses in training is roughly the same as when they were the big players of my youth. Today these numbers are but a tenth of the big battalions, but while this makes top-race competition difficult, certain new factors make it not impossible. For years the royal breed was limited not just by its parsimony in avoiding big money on American stallions, but by the political imperative that made Irish visits impossible.

The situation is now very different. Look down the new list and you see colts and fillies by Montjeu, Danehill Dancer, Galileo and 'Big Daddy' Sadler's Wells himself. In the summer of 2008 one royal insider was even moved to echo that headiest of racing refrains: 'This is the best set of two-year-olds anyone can remember.' We may not all be invited to the next Classic-winning party at the Palace, but everyone in racing should pray that it will happen.

Access to icons is a privilege which becomes more pleasurable the more unlikely they may originally have seemed. For the ten-year-old boy who waved a little Union Jack from a scaffolding seat in a rainy corner of the Mall as the Coronation Coach rolled by, even to meet the Queen would have been beyond his wildest imaginings.

But no more so than the idea that one day he might share time and work with the strange silent youth who was already casting a unique spell across the racetrack.

Lester Piggott was royalty too.

LESTER PIGGOTT

JUST AFTER 10.30 a.m. on Thursday 4 June 1970 I was in the most coveted place on the racing globe – Lester Piggott's car as he drove to Epsom the day after Nijinsky's Derby. He was 34. The famous face was lean but healthy behind those dark blue wrap-around glasses. It had been his fifth Derby success. He was at the height of his power. There was a very real sense that the fingers on the wheel had the world by the reins.

He was a mystery, but a highly organised one. 'Be outside Harrods at 10.30,' was the terse answer to the telephone request for a lift from London to a Jockeys' Association meeting at Epsom next day. A couple of months earlier I had got my leg snapped in a fall at Worcester, and so it was a figure on crutches that Lester would have seen leaning against the Harrods front window. He did not hesitate. The big black Mercedes mounted the Brompton Road pavement in a stealthy move that was half ambulance, half mafia car, and in a trice Lester was helping me into the passenger seat. 'The leg's taken a bit of time,' he said.

For quite a while, that's all he said. But it was a satisfactory silence. Lester had his cigar, a bright day and a clear run on his special traffic-dodging route to the course that he had made his own. I had an extremely superior taxi ride and a unique chance to treasure the moment when a legend comes to life. For in my racing memory, Lester had been there from the very beginning.

Lester and Petite Etoile.

Lester and The Minstrel.

At first the child: he was twelve when he won that first race on The Chase in August 1948 and, at three and a half years old, I can't say I remember the fuss about the chubby-cheeked pre-teenager who made all the headlines. But I clearly recall the 'Boy Wonder' drama when he rode the blinkered Zucchero (who wouldn't start) in the Derby three years later when still only fifteen. Not surprising really, because by then Lester was already champion apprentice, had a deserved reputation for attempting and often achieving the impossible, and caused Peter O'Sullevan to dub him 'a potential genius with the look of a wilful cherub'.

Today's racefans are encouraged to laud jockeys in their late teens and early twenties as exciting new hopefuls, but Frankie Dettori was nineteen when he first rode in the Derby, Ryan Moore 21. Just think what it was like when the wilful cherub was second in 1952, won the race for the first time on Never Say Die at the ripe old age of eighteen, and promptly got suspended for three months (probably unfairly) for a barging match on the same horse in the King Edward VII at Royal Ascot.

There was a naked, dangerous challenge about him. Back in the 1950s a lot of the senior jockeys were in their forties and horrified at the inspired impetuosity of Keith Piggott's precocious young son. Such disapproval and the official sanctions from the authorities only increased Lester's attraction. He may have been ruthless, but we could sense he was brave as well as brilliant. He won the Triumph Hurdle at eighteen, always thought he would get too heavy and go jumping like his father and grandfather, and so was as idolised, if not feared, by us jumping pilots just as much as he was by his Flat racing peers. No one but the hardest of the hard could have won the One Thousand Guineas in 1981 on Fairy Footsteps the week after being trapped in the stalls at Epsom and having half an ear torn off, or raced again after the 1992 Breeders' Cup crash on Mr Brooks when he was already 56 years old.

He was a one-off as a person, too. The idea of anyone trying to organise his rides for him like today's agents is literally laughable. There was the big red book in that immaculate trophy and portrait-lined living room which stood as a temple to his talent. He would sit with it and plot his way through the racing calendar – telling people where they should run as much as asking for rides. As the world knows, it got him into a double-booking scrape or two, but in the midst of one of these hiatuses he looked up, pulled on his cigar and muttered: 'Something will turn up, it usually does.' Believe me, he was loving it.

That was something his rather dour public demeanour – Jack Leach's great line of 'a face like a well-kept grave' – always kept hidden. Lester had iron discipline and drive. He beat his weight problems by straight mental control. He often beat opponents not so much by sweat as by strategy. 'I wanted to settle him,' he finally said about Nijinsky on that never-to-be-forgotten Epsom journey, 'but I overdid it a bit and when we turned in, he had gone to sleep on me. I had to give him a couple to wake him up. Then he was good.' There was nothing more to say. Piggott and Nijinsky sweeping past Gyr to win that Derby remains one of the defining images of man and horse at the gallop. The genius had spoken.

It's a big, big word, but in Lester's case I believe it is the right one. He qualifies on the premise that talent is doing what other people aspire to, genius is what other people can't even dream of. At his peak he could achieve things with the Thoroughbred racehorse beneath and the rivals around him that no one else could contemplate. His short-stirruped style occasionally did not give enough leverage – have a look at Alleged's St Leger defeat in 1977 – but he had an unmatched mix of equine understanding, athletic balance and competitive nerve, and the range of his talent was unique. No one was better at finessing a volatile filly like Petite Etoile or Park Top; yet at the same time, no one could outpower him. Think The Minstrel's Derby, Athens Wood's St Leger, or, a personal favourite, the utterly implacable ride he gave the grey Saritamer to win the July Cup in 1974. I can see him coming past me now, head down, whip cracking, his whole body coiled into a raw, compulsive effort of mind and muscle. Defeat was not an option.

When he came back after retirement and jail, he had lost a bit of that power and the protective aura it gives. Yet it meant that the roots of his genius were more apparent. It was in the saddle and behind the ears that he found fulfilment. He was Yehudi Menuhin reunited with the violin. Even then no one could roll a horse as instinctively beneath him as he did with little chestnut Rodrigo de Triano in the Guineas and the Champion Stakes. Lester was a force, a fixer, a man of finesse, and a Centaur too.

A couple of summers after that Nijinsky car trip my own inadequate riding career came to an abrupt end and for about three years I became a rather chaotic Boswell to Lester's unlikely Dr Johnson. Getting an article a week was sometimes blood out of a stone, but overall he was very kind. He liked to correct the spelling of French horses' names with his silver pen, would say

'Thank you' very quickly if you offered to pay the lunch bill, and travelling with him all over and as far as Singapore was an extraordinary insight into the man. As Aristotle said: 'There is no great genius without a touch of madness.'

One day he was riding at Dieppe and I had hired a huge car to drive us on to Ostend. After some good smoked salmon for lunch, he slid home a horse called Ramilles in the Grand Prix as slyly as a conjurer's card and we hammered off northwards for Ostend. After a long, tedious haul we reached a set of canals and corners. 'Stop the car,' said Lester, and took the wheel. For half an hour he gave the big Chevrolet the sort of treatment Saritamer remembered to his grave. Then, just as suddenly, he stopped the car, padded round to the passenger seat, lit his cigar and muttered: 'That's better.'

He was a man who had mastered his own universe but it was his and our tragedy that he crashed so horribly to earth when applying his own interpretations to the rules of the Inland Revenue. Whatever the justice, there was real poignancy in what he said as we walked a final time down the Rowley Mile a week before his trial. It was: 'I can't see the point of locking me up.'

That is why his eventual return to the saddle was so therapeutic for us all; and why 28 October 1990 will always remain the favourite memory.

That was Breeders' Cup Day at Belmont, and what had become an afternoon of horrors – three horses killed and Dayjur's victory lost by shadow jumping – was saved by Lester Piggott and Royal Academy, the greatest comeback in history.

Even now it is almost impossible to chronicle it. He was 54 and just twelve days in from a five-year layoff, over a year of which had been spent in prison. He had dropped his horse in last along the rail and then swung out in the straight to gun the leader down in the final fifty yards, just as he had on Sir Ivor in his pomp. The whole choreography had a poetic inevitability about it, and when he flashed past to win with whip-cracking certainty, it is the absolute truth that the hairs stood up on the back of my neck.

It could not have happened but it had. The ghost of all those adventures past had come back from Hades to land the richest race of his career. As he was led back, only the feet out of the stirrups betrayed the strain; and as he came over to do the interview, something much stronger than the TV arclights lit his face from deep within. There was Belmont mud in his smile, but there was something immortal in his answer to the impossibility of it.

'Ah no,' said Lester Piggott, 'you never forget.'

Neither should we.

It is easy but entirely wrong to describe Lester Piggott as one of the great actors of the racing stage. He is not an act. Neither is Peter O'Sullevan.

He really is as elegant and eloquent as that legendary voice has always suggested. But he is also rather more than that.

PETER O'SULLEVAN

W E ASSOCIATE Peter O'Sullevan with the great occasions, but part of his greatness was being just as at ease with the small ones. They didn't come much smaller than the nine-race Southwell meeting in December 1963.

The prize for the Burgage Selling Handicap Hurdle was a princely £181. But for me, the reward for winning on a kind, white-nosed old horse called Blue Peak was infinitely larger. I got to meet Peter O'Sullevan.

The weighing room was a long, stilted, wooden hut with a smelly loo and two wash basins at one end and a tea urn and sandwiches at the other (though better than at Wye, where they were all in the same corner – ugh!). The message came through that there was a press man outside.

That's heady stuff if you have ridden only three winners. When it's Peter O'Sullevan, complete with trilby hat and that trademark wool-lapelled raincoat, it's knockout time.

Yet the clear, abiding memory is not of any crowd-hogging celebrity but of a quiet, supportive, rather solitary studiousness. He had seen everything. He knew the horse, was a friend of the owner and had almost certainly not missed the comic little cameo in the unsaddling enclosure.

As the heavily bandaged Blue Peak was led in, the trainer had come over and in a loud voice said: 'Looks like he has broken down again.'

As I began to protest that it was just the lad twisting the wretched beast's head to make it limp and deter interest at the auction, he shut me up with a brutal smile and hard blow on the ankle. There was no bid.

POS with his horse Attivo.

O'Sullevan had probably backed it. He was already 'The Voice' that guided us through the drama and the glory of Aintree, Cheltenham, Epsom, Goodwood and Ascot, but his greatest attraction to racefans was that he, too, was a punter. In those days – you have got to believe this – he would be more famous for his column in the *Daily Express* than for broadcasting on the BBC, where betting was still taboo.

A sense of news from the inside has always been addictive stuff. O'Sullevan, with his unfeigned friendships with everyone from Aly Khan to his ubiquitous 'Bert at the Garage', with his travels to the strange distant racing land that was France, with his ante-post coups and genuine scoops, was the most addictive there ever was or ever will be.

Of course the voice was, too. For me it had been there almost from the cradle. At the very start there had been the frenetic radio mastery of Raymond Glendenning, but once the arrival of TV had revealed old Raymond as half a furlong behind the action, it was O'Sullevan behind the pictures. That honeyed verbal mix, somewhere between Noel Coward and Michael O'Hehir, became a central part of the great occasions. It was racing's ultimate good fortune that it was the most skilled and passionate and eloquent of any voice in any sport.

In 1952, I had the good luck to be ill and at home during the Cheltenham Festival. It was the first time I had seen racing on TV. The flashy young chestnut Mont Tremblant won the Gold Cup, the super-professional Sir Ken took the Champion Hurdle. The set was black and white. Sir Peter put the colour in.

But it was only half of O'Sullevan. He was no 'look-at-me' TV host, and you hardly ever saw him in vision. Away from the screen he was a reserved figure who steered clear of the press pack, a wolf who liked to walk alone, but also a gourmet who valued good friendship as much as fine wine. He was a perfectionist with an art-lined flat in Chelsea but was never afraid of the hard miles on the open road. That day at Southwell he would have driven himself there in one of those famous Jaguars in which, in later times, he is once supposed to have watched The Morning Line on a portable TV set whilst steering the wagon to Haydock.

He liked details, he liked a story and he was meticulous in his gratitude. In December 1967, after a group of us had taken horses to Cagnes-sur-Mer to beat the foot-and-mouth outbreak, he sent us all a Christmas card and for years would keep thanking me for suggesting he try the food at Le Cagnard. If you ever got stuck with O'Sullevan, you had only to ask about recent meals he had eaten. One freezing day at Sandown, we were shivering to death waiting for some TV shoot, only for him to warm us up with some super succulent memory from France – 'with the peas persillées as they do in Provence'.

His reporter's voice was careful, friendly, but usually right on the money. If the phone rang and you heard that slightly drawling 'It's Peter here' introduction, you knew he had spied a story to take the game on.

In March 1971, he even found one to take me out. I was lying with a back injury in a cottage hospital near Warwick which clearly doubled as an abortion clinic. 'The Voice' came on the line understanding that he was now talking to an ex-jockey with one injury too many. It was a scoop – one of O'Sullevan's all-time smallest – in the *Daily Express* next morning.

It had been with Peter on the BBC that I had made my first ever broadcast at Newbury the previous summer. As my throat tightened in terror, Peter gave out the most generous and gentle of verbal baton passes and somehow there was my voice saying something fairly unintelligible about how Joe

With Jenny Pitman.

Mercer rode horses to the start. In the years that followed, he remained the staunchest of supporters, no matter for whom I was working, no matter where we were – even on the hairy occasion at the 1987 Irish Derby when he, I and Michael O'Hehir were left isolated on the grandstand roof while the crowds were evacuated onto The Curragh because of a bomb scare. 'What price,' said O'Sullevan in the driest of tones, 'they know something we don't?'

You will imagine the irony when we found ourselves under the same circumstances at Aintree ten years later. I was there not to broadcast, but to write an article about his fiftieth and final Grand National. We had climbed the 107 steps to the tin hutch of a commentary box for the earlier races. But when the evacuation order came, we were down at the weighing room for one more jockey colours check for that giant, personalised racecard that was always his Grand National lifeline.

O'Sullevan was insistent that we should climb the stairs again. 'The captain should be on the bridge,' he grumbled, 'to tell everyone what is happening to the ship.' It took about three police inspectors to stop him.

In the closing years the commentary had sometimes become a trifle frail, but with the winning post in sight he took on an extraordinary burst of resurgent energy and humour. 'An even £100 it's a hoax,' he said as we shuffled out of Aintree. 'If we live, you pay. If we get blown to bits, I owe you a century.' And with that he repaired to the hotel with Tony O'Hehir to yarn the night away with stories as magnificent as they were well-lubricated.

At 80, as he was then, it would be reasonable to assume that is all he would do. But not a bit of it. The establishment of the Sir Peter O'Sullevan Charitable Trust and the millions it has already raised for horse and human welfare charities has at first sight been one of his most astonishing achievements. Yet then you remember the real anger in his voice when he talked of those who sold stallions (not to mention food horses) into terrible conditions abroad. You recall the firm but relentless way, starting with a column he wrote on a muddy day at Fontwell, in which he persuaded non-believers (including me) that we needed to do something about the whip.

It was the perfectionist in him that could not bear to leave things uncared for and would drive others to follow suit. When he agreed to recreate the race commentaries for the film we made about Mill Reef – the fee was 'a monkey [£500] for me and a monkey for the stable lads' – he strove tirelessly to get his part right, enjoyed working with Hugh McIlvanney and Albert Finney, but castigated me for the choice of music.

Back in 2003 we took him to lunch at La Poule au Pot in Pimlico and persuaded him to do a book on his horseracing heroes. The idea was for it to be a happy, mostly ghosted, nostalgic tour of one of the greatest careers in history. Not for Peter. He gathered together more books than you would find in a medium-sized library, found a man to restore his antique electric typewriter and, at 85, set out to type as detailed and moving and elegant and accurate a memoir as you will ever read.

Well, we thought it was accurate. After about ten sets of proofs we finally went to print with what turned out to be three faulty captions in a total of 216 illustrations. 'Riddled with errors – *c'est un catastrophe*,' he said, lapsing into French as he does for special emphasis. 'It's just inconceivable how all of you could be so totally incompetent.' The book has been a critically acclaimed bestseller but he hasn't really forgiven me yet.

One of the joys of being a friend of Peter O'Sullevan is the private audio delight that is an answerphone message from the great man himself. In it, the voice is as eloquent and mellifluously evocative as ever it was. One Tuesday in February 2008 there was a beauty. It was an invitation to a lunch for his ninetieth birthday in March – at which occasion the joy, rightly, was unconfined.

Monday 3 March 2008 was a brilliant, bright sunny day across London, and the party, in the stylish cellars of Berry Bros in St James, was one to match. I could attest the weather some time before the company, because a delayed flight from Athens was then stacked, circling above the capital, and with increasing frustration I could look down clearly enough almost to see Sir Peter himself.

Fred Winter was not granted ninety years. But he too, is a legend that will never die.

FRED WINTER

HE WAS smaller than most but above us all. He seemed about a hundred years old and had a bit of a belly on him. But when we were looking down, we were looking up. It was in the Cheltenham weighing room on 9 April 1963.

It was the first time I saw Fred Winter naked.

He was actually only 36 at the time, but that would be twenty years since he started out on his war-interrupted career as a jockey and, mentally as well as physically, there was a bulk of experience about him. He had won everything, the Gold Cup, the Champion Hurdle, the Grand National, the jockeys' championship, and a race the day before at Cheltenham. For a skinny amateur having his first ride at jumping's greatest temple, Fred Winter was not just respected – he was revered.

As sporting pleasures go, this is the ultimate case of dream becoming reality. Everybody who has ever followed any sport has had the fantasy of getting kitted up alongside their heroes. Their hitherto unsung talent has suddenly been recognised to put them in the company of Jack Nicklaus, Bobby Moore or Gareth Edwards. This was my St Andrews, Wembley, Twickenham dressing room moment. I was getting changed next to Fred Winter.

Well not exactly 'next to'. By unwritten but long-established practice, the pegs in jockeys' changing rooms are allocated by the valets in order of eminence, and the heroes' monographed kit laid out immaculately to await their arrival.

Fred was in the place of honour; next to him would be Tim Brookshaw, Stan Mellor, Bobby Beasley, David Nicholson and Terry Biddlecombe. Mr B. Scott (7) would be in a corner with make-do saddle, boots and breeches. But he had arrived in heaven.

It still hardly seems possible. First flaky memories of the Isle of Wight point-to-point. The pictures of one of Manifesto's Grand Nationals on the wall. The jockey mime flapping of legs and arms on gnarled and uncomprehending old ponies. The addictive challenge of riding out with the Frenchie Nicholson string. The mentioning of the great ones as if on Fred and Tim first-name terms. Now, fanatically keen but utterly wet behind the ears, here I was opposite Fred Winter.

The actual race, the fourteen-runner Painswick Hurdle, run at 5.10, is a bit of a blur. I was on an old, dodgy, but very talented charge called Arcticeelagh who would not go until we began to run down the hill.

When he did I had never been so fast in my life and he took me right on to the front stage of fantasy land – he landed with a chance on the run-in at Cheltenham.

That's when a figure emerged from the blur. It was clamped around a horse called Brocade Slipper and as the crowd roared he swept away to the winning post he had made his own. It was Fred under full power.

Watching a great jockey in a close finish is to sense an almost tangible inevitability about the outcome. His rival may appear to have the advantage, but that champion's blend of mind and stride and matter would somehow snatch victory at the line.

Fred had this quality more than any rider before or since. For the crowd in the stand could recognise what I was feeling on the track. Fred did it differently from the others.

He drove with his body. There was no flapping of legs or flailing of whip. He seemed to sink into a horse, his powerful, hunched body becoming a moulded extension of its effort.

The oldest, least-heeded truth in horse racing is that the only way a jockey can actually physically ensure a horse goes faster is by thrusting his own body weight down the lever of the hind leg as the animal powers itself forwards. All the rest – the whipping, kicking, shouting – is just an attempt to goad extra effort, and when done out of stride amounts to actual impediment.

Fred Winter was the ultimate personification of that original thrusting truth.

It was clear to the growing national audience on TV; it was evident to racegoers round Britain; above all it was obvious to those of us trying to do the same thing.

The images of Fred lifting home the likes of Mandarin, Saffron Tartan, Kilmore and Clair Soleil were seared into our consciousness. They were our equivalent

Fred Winter
and bit-less
Mandarin, Grand
Steeplechase de
Paris at Auteuil,
1962.

of the Botham six, the Bobby Charlton pile-driver, the Rory Underwood try. They hurt us, but we treasured them. That's why after Fred's fourth winner of that Cheltenham meeting we all stood up and cheered.

But Fred's greatness came from a lot more than what he could do in the saddle.

He set himself standards off a horse as well as on it. He enjoyed life. Before his marriage, he and Dave Dick would go down to the south of France in the summer break and party until the money ran out. But he had an unswerving code of honour, from which he never faltered. Fred showed you could win in racing without monkey business. He did more than adorn his game. He gave it credibility.

Indeed he became pretty grand. The first time I had actually met him, he was wearing a top hat, a cutaway black coat and that slit-eyed faraway look, out hunting with the Heythrop, near Stow-on-the-Wold.

In those days, the Heythrop field would have contained some of the biggest names in the City, as well as the odd duke or two. But there was no doubt who was the most important figure in the gathering. At some moment our paths crossed and I was introduced to him. He nodded politely. I nearly fell off in terror.

There was a much-told tale about the royal trainer Peter Cazalet trying to contact Fred on a Sunday morning, only to be dismissed by some manservant with the magnificent phrase, 'Mr Winter is at Divine Services'.

However apocryphal, the story was relished because there was some truth at its core. Fred may have started out as a trainer's son, and indeed been seriously injured in only his second ride over jumps, but he had made himself anyone's equal and had done it without losing a sense of belief. The cheering in that first meeting at Cheltenham was because they knew their hero was a good man as well as a brave one.

We may even have sensed that life had been a lot more difficult than he might make it seem.

He had not wanted to be a jockey and he did not wish, at that Cheltenham time, to become a trainer. His hope was to be a starter, but one of history's unnamed numbskulls in the Jockey Club said an ex-jockey might favour his friends. So, to put it very mildly, he made the best of what he had got. Indeed, when he started out as a trainer a year later all he had was a dozen horses and Richard Pitman. Mind you, one of the horses was Jay Trump, with whom he would win the Grand National.

Some of the strain showed in his face. The eyes, when you could see them through the gun-slits of the morning, were very direct and the lines in his cheeks would add thunder to his frown.

It made you wary, almost fearful, of him, but that only made his approbation more eagerly sought. He was very tactile. He would take your arm, put a hand round your shoulder. He had an awareness of the effect he had and used it almost as if he was putting heat into you.

One night, well into his training career, I was driving him back from London. He was weary and had a couple of drinks in him. But he was aware of my own frailty and some difficulties I was having. 'Look,' he said, turning in his seat and holding my elbow, 'you can only do the best you can do. It is the same for all of us.'

That inspirational voice, with its almost affected Burgundy drawl, rings on down the decades, and brought added poignancy to Fred's closing years.

Fred, the colossus, the great communicator, could not speak.

He could start to say something, but then the effects of the stroke that ended his training career would cut him off. The man who had stood above us all was now imprisoned by his own infirmity.

He used to come to our Injured Jockeys' Fund holidays in Tenerife. He would love to play backgammon and was not above taking an edge. Those who had known him as the absolute master of our game would see him more afflicted than any of them, yet keeping a smile on his face. It was as cruel and undeserved a twist as fate could play. Yet to see him struck down only enhanced his status in our eyes.

Fortune had turned on him but he did not flinch. Being with him made you realise how much we owed him. For he had given us a direction, a meaning, a justification of our lives. It was a gift beyond price.

Fred Winter changed the way people thought about jump racing and it was his and our incredible good fortune that his exploits and influence could be extolled by someone equally unusual. John Oaksey always said that the first time he met him, Fred was walking round the room on his hands. The admiration, rightly, was mutual. For John Oaksey was the best writer and one of the greatest figures that the game has ever seen.

JOHN OAKSEY

H E WAS not nearly so cuddly back then. He was friendly but tough, with a very direct intelligence. He had a lawyer's voice but a boxer's handshake, and there was a sense of challenge about him. John Oaksey was one of us, but a man apart.

He could not help it. When I first rode against him, in Epsom's Moet & Chandon Silver Magnum which he won on Thames Trader in August 1963, he was already a unique figure not just in racing but in sport. For he was both a big-time player – he had won the Whitbread and Hennessy on Taxidermist on 1958 – and the finest chronicler his game had ever had. Earlier in 1963, he and Carrickbeg had become one of the epic losers in Grand National history.

By then, I would have read every word he ever wrote. Three or four times a week he would file pieces, often deprecating his own exploits, in the *Daily Telegraph*. Every weekend he would pen a 3,000-word essay ranging over all the issues of the day in *Horse and Hound*.

There has been nothing like it before or since. It was elegant, informed, clear, humorous, forceful, and unbelievably evocative. For me, who knew John only from afar, it was in every sense an inspiration.

The 1963 Grand National was its apogee. From the page we knew all about John taking a half-share in Carrickbeg; of their being third in the Leopardstown Chase and then hitting the deck at Cheltenham; of his own and the stable's excitement as Aintree closed in. But what happened on the screen was as bitter-sweet a masterpiece as broadcasting has ever produced. Beforehand the BBC took us on a low-level helicopter circuit of the course over which John did a brilliantly eloquent, oratorical commentary, ending with the lines: 'The final dregs of stamina are draining fast for horse and man alike, 100 yards to go and perhaps another's head appears at his knee.'

In the race the words came true and within minutes of the finish they were being brilliantly reassembled for the *Sunday Telegraph*.

'It still seemed possible,' wrote John about Carrickbeg fifty yards from the winning post in the greatest 'live' participatory report filed from a major event, 'but then, like Nemesis, the worst sight I ever expect to see on a racecourse. Ayala's head appeared at my knee.'

Those words still chime. Imagine how they rang for an awestruck young amateur as he changed opposite this short, hairy-chested but bald-headed figure.

The head always struck you. It was almost over-large, like the Mekon in the Dan Dare comic strip. It had been bald from his early twenties, and I remember the surprise when Mr J. Lawrence appeared hairless as well as hatless to receive his trophy for winning the Whitbread Gold Cup in April 1958 only a month after his 29th birthday. It made him seem older and more solemn than he was. Anyway, you don't cuddle a competitor.

In fact, his success in the saddle was more down to competitiveness than class. There were many more stylish riders than him; smoother through a race, stronger in a finish. But he was calculating, unhealthily brave, and he was a winner.

Somewhere I have a picture of us jumping the last fence together in the 1966 Horse and Hound Cup at Stratford. There is no question that I look the sharper, tidier, more professional of the pair. But he won it – and has been reminding me of it ever since.

It was his limitations as a rider that made him such a wondrous ambassador for the game. Not for him the seemingly effortless, stylish mastery of a Mould or a Francome. John had to work at it and no one treasured his moments in the saddle more. He became very good at it but remained an amateur in its original, Latin *amo* – 'I love' – meaning. He adored the game and all that was in it and, being John, never lost a sense of gratitude for his good fortune in being there.

He was like that in life. He may have been brought up to country house life and Eton, Oxford and Yale, but he and his family had a conscience. He rightly takes great pride in creating the Injured Jockeys' Fund, but he also found it the absolutely natural thing to do. Tim Brookshaw and Paddy Farrell had been paralysed. There was no proper insurance or support system. Something had to be done. He may have been as busy as any media person, but for 25 years he found time every month to sit on the bench at Malmesbury Magistrates' Court. Why not? He was his father's son.

Of all the conversations I have had with John, the most fascinating was the first time he told me the full story of the 1946 summer holidays he spent watching his father carry out the most important judicial role in history – presiding judge at the first Nuremberg Trial. We were running round Battersea Park in preparation for doing the London Marathon together. As we jogged, the middle-aged broadcaster melded back into the seventeen-year-old schoolboy watching in awe as his father looked over the dock at Goering, Dönitz, Hess, Speer and the rest of the Nazi High Command. To say this put our own efforts into perspective would be something of an understatement.

But a realisation of duty should never detract from a sense of fun. As a companion John Oaksey was Classic class. As riders we knocked around together quite a bit, and even had a trip to ride in Milan which included disgruntled punters trying to burn down the weighing room and the diminutive Frankie Durr stealing the tallest and sexiest bird from right under our noses in the night club.

As part of the ITV and then Channel 4 team we were at times almost joined at the hip, and long journeys north would be lightened by his fund of stories and great chunks of Shakespeare, Tennyson and P.G. Wodehouse.

Boredom and inactivity were never allowed. In case the delights of televising Redcar might begin to pall, John arranged for us to do the Lyke Wake Walk, 44 miles across the North Yorkshire moors, the day before. Our party on that first occasion was a typically eclectic Oaksey mix: Tim Richards and me from the hack pack, television director Rick Stroud from London, and the Andrew Devonshire from Chatsworth. Two years later we did it overnight between broadcasts. Next day, the credits closed with a famous shot of John's dog Jacko giving an enormous yawn. It was not the only one.

He didn't enjoy doing television that much, finding it a strain to haggle through the details of form, and preferring public speaking to the false intimacy of the screen. He tolerated our leg-pulling but probably stayed on a bit too long, sometimes allowing himself to be patronised as an old buffer by people unworthy of cleaning his boots in his prime.

Yet then, as now, it was a measure of the man that he would not stand on ceremony. On our Injured Jockeys' Fund trips to Tenerife he has been at his happiest sitting in the midst of our assorted battered old heroes. Not many of them had been to Yale but they were part of his racing family and would always remain so.

The 78-year-old with the shepherd's crook and the shuffling gait was a fair way removed from the achieving superstar of that first day at Epsom. But no one has contributed so much in between.

Mind you, the 'black dog' of depression has tried to get through the door once or twice. John had a feeling that his very evident gifts were being wasted on trivia, that his speech-making ability might be harnessed to a greater cause,

With high-class hurdler Carruthers, whom he bred and co-owns.

that his love and mastery of words might be challenged in wider fields. The break-up of his first marriage was a very painful time, as was his battle with his recent memory loss. When he began to feel it slipping, he was very much into 'rage against the dying of the light'. But his family's forbearance and his sense of the absurd has won through to where he can again look on and laugh.

He has, of course, been sorely tested by a few of us. One spring day in the 1980s he rang up and said we should go to Ireland to watch some Classic trial. It seemed a good enough wheeze and we duly flew to Dublin, hired a car at the airport and hared off to The Curragh. So far, so good. It was on the return journey that things began to worsen.

John's complexion has always been on the yellow side since he lost his spleen in a terrible fall at Folkestone. But soon after Newbridge he began to go green. 'Brougho,' he croaked (no one else called me that), 'you had better stop the car'. Hopes that the serious puking session which followed would be the end of things were dashed when he began to thrash around on his seat, and by the time we had rerouted to a hospital in Dublin he was writhing about on the floor.

It was the agony of a kidney stone which was soon relieved by the surgeons, only for John to face a humiliation of another kind. He had a very nice if rabidly anti-foxhunting nurse who later in the afternoon allowed me to push my head through the curtains. 'Lord Oaksey' she said, 'your son is here'.

John harrumphed with horror at this insult to his age and family. I could wish for no greater compliment.

Ireland was a lot further away in the 1950s. So when Vincent O'Brien trained the Grand National winner three years running it was as if he had come down from Mars. Even in the dizzy black-and-white clips of the newsreel you could detect something mysterious in the dapper young figure in the double-breasted overcoat animatedly overseeing the victory moments.

The voiceover would duly ladle out the hyperbole, but over the years it became obvious that both that and the mystery was true. Vincent was special. And to be with him was special too.

VINCENT O'BRIEN

H E WAS in a silent mood and it had been a tense morning at Ballydoyle. It was late May in 1984 and three weeks earlier El Gran Senor had won the Two Thousand Guineas with an élan to match all the greats that had gone before. Now the Derby – what would be a seventh Derby and a seventeenth English classic – beckoned. But Vincent O'Brien did not want to talk.

It was as if something was hurting him, as if all the worries of forty years of training were closing in. The sun shone, the birds sang and El Gran Senor posed perfectly. It was an idyllic Tipperary May-time scene with the slopes of Slievenamon as a gleaming backdrop. But the man who had created this most wondrous of all academies of the racehorse was deep in his own thoughts. This was not arrogance, it was pretty close to anguish. It seemed ill mannered to intrude.

This reticence and sensitivity was absolutely central to O'Brien's genius. No one had shouted that morning at Ballydoyle. No one ever had. In a world of action, Vincent stood out for his stillness. In a discipline where people spent a lifetime discussing physique, the thing that struck you about O'Brien was his head. It was a head that was studious, fastidious, well-groomed and at race meetings always stylishly well-hatted. In it, you felt, were so many secrets of the racing universe that it was no surprise that Vincent often mumbled and paused to prevent too many falling out.

The sensation, that morning, was of the pressure inside: of all the thoughts and ideas and options cramming into the skull; of what it must have taken to transform this sleepy, rural corner of 1950s Munster into the most disciplined, state-of-the-art centre on the globe. But Vincent was a human being too. At the end of the morning, with the photographer gone and the notebook still empty, his face eased. 'Come in,' he said.

The kitchen was big but it was the fridge that was important. Out of it Vincent took a bottle of champagne and a large slab of smoked salmon. With characteristic tidiness he then gathered plates and brown bread and butter and we settled down to an afternoon of talk. In the pantheon of blessings the game could bestow, there was nothing to match this. For Vincent O'Brien had been the ultimate, magical, mysterious racing legend all my conscious life. There never had been, never would be anyone to compare.

Early Mist winning the 1953 Grand National was the first time I registered that something special was happening out there in Tipperary. The breezy pukka tones of the Pathé Newsreel would have told us that the neat little figure in the slightly tilted trilby was trainer Vincent O'Brien, and that he had already won both the Gold Cup and the Champion Hurdle three years

running, with Knock Hard adding a fourth Gold Cup only three weeks earlier. There were pictures in the paper of the horses being loaded into planes at Limerick. That, in 1953, seemed a long way away indeed.

When Vincent then saddled Royal Tan and Quare Times to make it three consecutive Grand Nationals, the fascination for a racing-addicted youth was complete. Imagine the thrill when, after winning ten divisions of the Gloucestershire Hurdle (today's Supreme Novices) in eight years, he had switched to the Flat in 1959. The previous year he had saddled those two super champions Gladness and Ballymoss. The mare Gladness won the Gold Cup and Goodwood Cup before winning the Ebor under 9st 7lb, while Ballymoss won the Coronation Cup, Eclipse, King George and Arc de Triomphe. They were heady days and they were to get better.

For Gladness was the first O'Brien horse to be ridden by Lester Piggott, and when in 1966 Lester jumped ship from Noel Murless to win the Oaks on Valoris for Vincent, we had the one of the most exciting, if least communicative, partnerships in racing history. The aura they generated was unique and the fact that in public Lester said virtually nothing and Vincent very little only added to their attraction. For it meant that the horses had to do the talking and often, as in the zenith of Sir Ivor and Nijinsky, that didn't leave many superlatives left unsaid.

When Vincent did speak the words were quiet, careful and very respectful of the talents he trained. When I began to interview him on TV in the 1970s, it was like talking to a shy professor about a subject a bit too complicated for general explanation. He had a disarmingly modest smile but was not quite as bashful as he would have us maintain. One very reluctant day at Newmarket, I

sent word that if it was too much trouble we would be happy
to go on without him. In five minutes he was round. He
didn't say much. But you could see he was Vincent O'Brien.
The public should be aware of that too.

In an earlier visit of mine to Ballydoyle he had also been
keen to state who wore the trousers in the Piggott/O'Brien
partnership, at least as far as preparation was concerned.
'I think Lester is a great jockey,' he conceded but, and he
was happy to have this quoted, 'I would like him to ride in
all the big races but none of the gallops. All he does is mess
them up trying to find out things for himself.'

When he talked like that you realised the innovative
grip that he had on his metier. He had a cool, questioning
intelligence, tilting his head to one side as he hoovered up
any unlikely information you might be able to give him. He
had a logical, perfectionist approach which put him light
years ahead of his time – not just flying horses, but weighing
them, testing them, ensuring the best of everything as he
made a science of an often haphazard profession.

In private he was much warmer and more relaxed and
had time for fishing and family and friends. On a train trip
to York with his daughter Elizabeth in the summer of 1973
or 1974, he was even talking of scaling his whole operation
and 'doing it just for fun'. But we were within three years of the great The
Minstrel/Alleged season which was to put the John Magnier/Robert Sangster
Coolmore operation on the map, and with it more need than ever for the
O'Brien name on the ticket.

There were occasions when you felt that this commercialisation was
compromising him, that the younger generation was in danger of prostituting
his talent, as in the Classic Thoroughbreds fiasco when the O'Brien-picked
yearlings turned out to be a costly embarrassment to all concerned. But
training the racehorse was where he got his fulfilment, was something he
did better than anyone who had gone before. When asked around this time
whether he was tired by the thought of having to win everything all over again,
he paused, watched another couple of horses go up the gallop and then said
quietly, 'Is there anything wrong with winning everything all over again?'

He had certainly looked tired that El Gran Senor morning, but he
brightened up once we got the champagne going. He didn't particularly want
to talk about his current great horse beyond saying what a thrill it was to have
one who ranked with the mighty. He wanted to tell about the early days : of
the fun he had himself jumping horses around the farm; of Cottage Rake and
Early Mist and Hatton's Grace; of Bryan Marshall schooling at Ballydoyle; of

thinking ahead, trying new things, of weighing horses like he did his greyhounds before his training began, of the gambles he had because 'the money had to be won.'

As he spoke a wonderful truth began to dawn. That this superhero was actually as much in thrall to all the wonders and absurdities of the game as the rest of us, that at heart the professor was a player too. How could we have ever doubted it? Look at those old black-and-white photos. There is Vincent on a donkey, Vincent in hunting gear, Vincent leading in the winner of the 1939 Irish Cambridgeshire on the wettest, soggiest of days at The Curragh, but Vincent's trilby and elegant overcoat as immaculate as if it were a passing shower in Piccadilly. He was already a diamond in the dross.

Then there are the images of the Grand National parties, of the team in the early days at Ballydoyle, but also of Vincent shooting, fishing and skiing, most of all of Jacqueline and the children in all the stages of family life. You begin to develop the picture that 'the professor' was also a very complete man. He had a soft, chuckling laugh with a glorious sense of the ridiculous. The abiding memory of that Ballydoyle kitchen is of Vincent O'Brien laughing at all the fun that had been had, of him shaking his head with the crinkly smile at just how silly some people had been.

But there was more than just good company. The one thing that stood out in the conversation was the way he talked about the horses and the people closest to him. It was with lucidity and humour but also – and let's be very careful about this word – also with love. Not for nothing does the Bible call it the greatest quality of all, and it's not too strong an image to explain the very roots of the O'Brien phenomenon.

Nineteen years after El Gran Senor, the readers of the *Racing Post* voted Vincent O'Brien 'Racing's Greatest', and there was a small lunch in London to celebrate. Lester was there, and Scobie Breasley, Peter O'Sullevan, Will Farrish the American ambassador, and John Gosden, who as Vincent's assistant had put the cotton wool in The Minstrel's ears before the Derby.

Vincent had slowed a touch and needed the lift to get down the stairs. But he got the message. That all of us loved him too.

Live a little. That's what racing offers. That's what Robert Sangster did quite a lot. But he was important – and not just for bailing us out as Australia played. Robert Sangster changed the face of the racing world.

ROBERT SANGSTER

T HE JOURNEY to that 1980 Melbourne Cup had good news, bad news and best news. The good news was that our 'space available' tickets began by sweeping us first-class over the Atlantic and across the US. The bad news was that in Los Angeles we were banished to the back beside a screaming Filipino baby for the overnight flight to Honolulu, and then were decamped indefinitely. The best news was Robert Sangster.

For by the time photographer Gerry Cranham and I finally reached Melbourne, we were without credentials on the very eve of the Cup, our plans were in ruins, and our only chance was the phone number we had scribbled down a month before. Every life needs an introduction. At that perilous moment Robert Sangster was more than that. He was salvation.

'Come on over,' he said, and within minutes we were sipping champagne in his hotel suite and everything was possible. He was 44, and within five years had turned himself from the Repton-educated youngest member of the Jockey Club, set for a jolly career in the British racing establishment, into the biggest tycoon that the racing globe had ever seen. A month earlier, three days after Detroit had followed Alleged to win the Arc in the green and blue Sangster silks, I had been in the shining new office of The Nunnery, his not entirely appropriately named home in the Isle of Man. At 279 I had given up the count. That was the number, over six countries and 36 trainers, of his racehorses in training.

Even in these globetrotting Godolphin days, it is hard to comprehend such a spread. Back then it was impossible. Robert Sangster, the friendly but slightly shy, trilby-hatted steward who had got the giggles when I tried to explain how I had missed my ride in the first at Haydock through being stuck in the sauna, had become an international revolutionary. He was treating racehorse owning as a business and, from the memory of that office board (there were another 400-odd mares, foals, stallions and yearlings) and the look of the Melbourne hotel suite, he was making it pay.

At this point in any Sangster discussion, you have to deal with the issue of Vernons Pools. For it is, of course, true that Robert was bankrolled by the millions his father Vernon Sangster had made on his eponymous football pools, and indeed that Sangster junior was cleared of some £60 million of debt when he finally sold the organisation for £90 million in 1987.

But plenty of other fun-loving – and Robert most certainly loved fun – tyros have made a small fortune at the races by the old gag of starting with a large one. Robert, for all his public diffidence, was something of a wolf in middle-sized, rather well-cut, sheep's clothing. He was looking for a deal.

Of course, he wasn't as establishment as he might appear, and was very proud of running a cigarette racket in Berlin while doing his Cheshire

Regiment National Service in the ranks rather than in the officer corps. While there, he also knocked out the Army light-heavyweight champion in the boxing ring, and would love to tell how as a teenager he had been taken to a gym in Soho to spar with the legendary Freddie Mills. Robert lived in a gilded world but had an edge of ordinariness about him. It meant he was prepared to experiment and to listen – especially to the Irish.

Back in England we were a bit suspicious of them – and of him. We thought there was something not quite right about cashing in on racehorses as stallions. It meant that their public appearances were all about getting a reputation. Once achieved, once stud value established, any idea of running a horse for their own – let alone public – amusement would vanish.

The Minstrel had been a $200,000 part of the original Sangster/Magnier/ O'Brien shopping spree at the Keeneland yearling sales in 1975. After blowing out in the English and Irish Guineas he came good in the Derby, the Irish Derby and the King George at Ascot, and was promptly syndicated for $9 million, perfectly healthy but never to appear again.

As the stud valuations soared, so the scepticism rose. The Minstrel had at least won the Derby to earn his price tag. Try My Best and Storm Bird had merely won a Dewhurst, to be cashed in for five times more. This led to some quite difficult public confrontations. With Vincent O'Brien playing the preoccupied training genius and John Magnier, then as now, opting for the non-speaking Svengali role, Sangster, reticent by nature and wary by custom, had to step forward as an unlikely front man.

He used to start it at Chester in May. He would have had a good lunch with the course chairman, Bobby McAlpine, and watched some Barry Hills three-year-old run home in a Classic trial before being wheeled before us to state how all was well in the Sangster empire.

Richard Phillips developed a best-selling routine mimicking the 'ums' and 'ers' as Robert tried to explain why some highly touted O'Brien hopeful was temporarily indisposed but still a great prospect for the future. About halfway through he would produce a piece of paper from his pocket to try to ease the punishment. It would chronicle the stunning successes of his Swettenham Stud horses down under. I never believed it. Until I got to Melbourne.

Bart Cummings was in that hotel suite – Bart, the iconic 'Cups King' with the lived-in face that had given a victory smile to the race that stops a nation four times already, and who thought that anything Sangster did in Oz was a good idea as long as the man didn't get fancy ideas of flying in a pansy Pommy horse to run off the plane.

Bob Charley was also in attendance. In later life he was to become a major force as a lucid and forceful administrator on the international scene. Back then Bob was just an upwardly mobile hustler with a dazzling wife, an Australian version of Timeform, and control of a sand-baked, dust-flyer of a track called Hawkesbury some fifty miles west of Sydney, where a row of ten farriers stood ready to put shoes on the runners when they arrived from the bush.

Two days after the Melbourne Cup I was driven out there by a young, very bright, sharp-shirted, blue-tied young bookmaker called Robbie Waterhouse, whose wife Gai had just come back from a turn as an actress in England to assist her trainer father Tommy Smith. Wonder what happened to them …

But best of all, Robert introduced us to Colin Hayes, trainer of his next day's Melbourne Cup winner Beldale Ball. At 5.30 the next morning we drove from the hotel car park to the Flemington track. The experience of accompanying Colin on this day of life fulfilment equals anything I have ever done before or since.

Anyone who seeks an understanding of the racing madness needs to sample Flemington on the first Tuesday in November. If you were fortunate enough to go through the whole process with a national legend winning it for the first time, and end up in Maxim's where the then Mrs Robert Sangster were to dance on the table with Cup aloft, you would think it time to die lucky. For me it was better than that. A week later I was flying west from Melbourne to Lindsay Park.

Colin Hayes was a visionary, and as the small plane came in towards Angaston, some 100 miles north of Adelaide, you could see that he was in a land where a vision had already landed. The conifers of Victoria had given way to the big gum trees of South Australia, before revealing the terraced vineyards of the Lutheran refugees who had trekked up with their vine plants some 130 years before.

Colin had started his stud and training operation at Lindsay Park more recently, but his determination was just as strong. As you drove through the entrance gates the overhanging sign spelled out his watchword: 'The future belongs to those who plan for it'. Everything inside – artificial tracks, short uphill gallops, swimming pools, weighing machines and full technical back-up – showed the future made flesh.

Not all Robert's ideas were successful. The experiment of bringing the untried Michael Dickinson to untested Manton was a disaster for all concerned, and his post-Coolmore persona had a touch of sad boredom about it. Yet he was the man who brought over Steve Cauthen as the greatest gift British race-riding ever had. And, while David Robinson had earlier made a good crack at rationalising racehorse ownership, Sangster was the man who took it worldwide.

Robert did not have Hayes's silver tongue, O'Brien's genius or Magnier's unrivalled strategic touch. But in two short decades he was the catalyst that took the game forward. Back in the 1970s there was a sense of hopelessness about European, and particularly British, Flat racing. Robert Sangster showed that it could be both big business and fun, even if he then attracted his own demise.

One day at Newmarket, late in the 1980s, he took me to one side. 'I am just a small player now,' he said. 'Sheikh Mohammed and his team can outbid me any time they want. But John and the Coolmore team might regroup, and at least I might have begun something.'

The globalisation of our game has increased immeasurably since 1980. An Irish horse, Vintage Crop, has even travelled down to win the Melbourne Cup. But it needed someone with wealth, energy, vision and appetite to kick-start the process. I was not the only one that Robert Sangster introduced to international racing.

Robert Sangster died in 2004 at the age of 67. His legacy stretched over many things, but ask any racing fan, any racing commentator, what personally touched them the most, and there can only be one answer. The truly extraordinary thing is that it was done partly as an act of 'giving a fresh start' generosity. And Robert Sangster never did anything better than bringing us Steve Cauthen.

STEVE CAUTHEN

T
HE FINISH was tight, the back was flat, the two big guns were driving on either side, but the green and black stripes of 20-1 shot Tap On Wood ran home straight and true to clinch the 1979 Two Thousand Guineas at the line. It was our first sight of Steve Cauthen in a big-race success. I couldn't believe our luck. Still can't.

He was the greatest import British racing ever had. Both as a jockey and – as the wider world began to realise when he came over for the TV interview – as a man. For he had a voice and a personality to die for. A deep, musical, Kentucky voice but one without any redneck aggression; a pointed, almost feminine face, but one without fear; a manner full of charm but not of syrup; a mind self-confidently lucid but without conceit. He had turned nineteen on 1 May, just four days before that Two Thousand Guineas. But he had lived one complete life already.

Exactly a year earlier he had sat, rose-garlanded, aboard Affirmed after winning the Kentucky Derby on his way to landing the Triple Crown and to going on the cover of Time magazine. Five months earlier he had become the only jockey ever to grace the front of *Sports Illustrated* as their Sportsman of the Year. Chris Evert had been there in 1976, Jack Nicklaus didn't make it until 1978. Seventeen-year-old Cauthen's 1977 total of 487 winners had not just put him top of the US national rankings but made him the first rider to top $6 million in prize money and brought him three Eclipse Awards and the type of awestruck adulation that culminated in Affirmed's trainer Laz Barrera saying: 'He must have come to earth from outer space on a flying sausage.'

It could not last. In the California winter of 1978-79, the pursuing press became not cooing doves but circling vultures as they chronicled the downward spiral of a losing run that extended to 110 defeats and even saw him jocked off Affirmed by the sky-gazing Barrera. Eight months on from the climactic moment when Affirmed inched out Alydar to seal the greatest three-race duel in Triple Crown history and the media hailed Cauthen as the second coming, it was obituary time.

Step forward Robert Sangster. The move to bring Steve to England was as brilliant for him as it was for us. It enabled the teenager to live and breathe and, quite literally, to grow. The little baby-faced figure they had called 'The Kid' had become a willowy five-foot-six-incher who ranked among the tallest in the weighing room. The pounds would always be an issue, eventually an insoluble one, but in England the 8st 7lb to 8st 10lb range was tolerable. So was the media attention. There wasn't any.

Well, not compared to America. Sure, there was a recycling of all the Triple Crown stories when he first arrived. And there was great excitement, not to mention amusement, when he scored on his very first ride at a Salisbury so rain-sodden that proceedings were delayed when the stewards' car got stuck in the mud. But even after his Tap On Wood triumph there didn't seem much more to say. He was left alone to become a fun-loving part of the Lambourn racing family. Back home he could not date a girl or have a drink without it becoming a magazine event. Now he could do a fair bit of both. He had his life back.

For once, there was something healthy about our chauvinistic English refusal to be over-impressed. Punters would remain sceptical until the results became unanswerable, and professionals didn't expect him to crack it straight away. At the York May meeting, Harry Wragg booked him for a horse normally the ride of Lester Piggott. 'Well, he's good,' said Harry in response to the maestro's disgruntlement. 'Yes,' Lester conceded, 'good, but not that good.'

He was later. Accustomed to uniform flat, left-handed ovals, it took Cauthen two or three years to get the hang of different directions, cambers and gradients. He won friends in and out of the weighing room by the way he applied himself to the task, and it was only when it was all over that he admitted how difficult he had found things. 'Goodwood, Epsom, Brighton and "Salls-berry",' he remembered when he came back over in 2002, 'when I first rode there I seemed to be sliding all over the place.'

He laughed at the memory, a warm, deep laugh which was a feature of

The 1985 Derby: Slip Anchor and Steve Cauthen round Tattenham Corner.

those early years. He loved to play golf and tennis, to go shooting in well-cut plus-fours with the highest in the land. He was quite the dandy. 'Hey,' he said one morning when we walked down from Tattersalls, with the burly master of the Sangster revels that was Charles Benson, 'we have got good horses, good friends and a good suit. Life's a beach!' He was sunshine and we liked it.

He was first champion in 1984 but it was 1985 that is most packed with golden memories. That was the year of the link-up with Henry Cecil to take four of the five Classics. Slip Anchor rocketed home in the Derby and Oh So Sharp took the fillies' Triple Crown, beginning with that still unbelievable late, late run up the outside to clinch the One Thousand Guineas right on the post.

Cauthen had developed his own style now, the perfect blending of American toe-in-the-iron poise with English drive and control, albeit retaining an element of the acey-deucey (deeper left leather) style of his formative years. To balance British horses on British courses, he rode more upright than he had across the water, but the clock still worked in his head and, with the natural boldness of the Cecil horses, he took the art of front-running to a height never seen here before or since. Its apogee was Reference Point's Derby in 1987.

His rivals knew that to get the lazy but front-running Reference Point beat, they had to jump out fast and get him shuffled back down through the pack. When the stalls opened, they had their chance because the favourite, drawn in the middle, missed his kick. But in a dozen furious strides, Cauthen punched Reference Point up to the head of things to clock an astonishing 24.6 seconds for that first uphill quarter (some five seconds quicker than the two previous Derbys). Once there, Cauthen steadied down to a 28-second quarter, ready to roll his big horse down the hill.

If you want to see what Cauthen was about, have a look at the video of that Derby finish. Reference Point was continually switching leads as he tried to cope with the Epsom camber. Steve's whip was up fully two furlongs out, but three times he put both hands down on the reins to rebalance his partner before one final change of legs at the furlong pole and the colt was into a rhythm no rival could match.

As with all great riders, there was an inevitability about him. When the *Sunday Times* deadline for the report on Reference Point's St Leger was set before the TV show finished, I wrote 800 words in advance about the timing in Cauthen's head as he made the running. The only changes needed were the positions of the third and fourth. More memorably, there was a sweet, unhurried haste about his elbow-pumping finish, like the slow swing of a great golfer. Just one glimpse and you knew it was him.

But it was not all sunshine. Cauthen's weight rose as his interests widened. To begin with, he used the binge and purge (not to mention 'heave') method so many Americans continue to this day. But by the end of 1985 he was in a clinic to try to re-focus his mind, and from then on there was often a touch of melancholy about him as he looked out from the prison cell of privation that was needed to keep the weight in check.

In September 1988 he broke his neck in a horrible fall at Goodwood. He didn't ride again until the next April and time spent with him then revealed a fitter, harder but in some ways more lonely young man than ever. 'The dieting is simple,' he said rather mournfully in the tiny lodge gate cottage on the Stetchworth Park Stud, 'but it is never easy. The grass is always greener on the other side.

'Sometimes you fly to Rome on a Sunday and look at other people and think that their life is much more carefree. But the guy who has the corner store has his problems. I work with a team to get the horses ready. My part I can only do by myself, and I have to motivate myself.'

It was a baring of the soul that suggested, rightly, that we were on borrowed time, even if there were still some golden moments ahead. If you put 'YouTube – Steve Cauthen' into the Google search engine, you will come up with those slow-flicking Cauthen elbows powering Old Vic home at Chantilly and The Curragh.

He was a family man. When the phone rang one day in that little cottage, it was his mother Myra back home in the States. He wanted a family of his own. When he and Amy married in 1991, he didn't need the racetrack for happiness.

He was with us for little more than a decade, but his legacy was not confined to the inspiration he gave to a little Italian apprentice at Luca Cumani's called Frankie Dettori. He brought us achievement, and class and accessibility. He also gave us perspective. 'Hi Buddy,' that deep voice sang out in the paddock at Lone Star Park in October 2004. He was 44, fuller-faced and balding. He was over from Kentucky to help with a racetrack chaplaincy programme. He had pictures of his two girls in his wallet. He was a happy man. And a great one.

Just occasionally in life you live out scenes which even at the time you try and treasure in the memory. You are with someone so unusual, so utterly at ease with their unlikely circumstances, that you desperately hope the film and sound recorder in your head will not let you down.

It was like that early one summer morning in Chicago. Mind you, there has never been anyone quite like Charlie Whittingham.

CHARLIE WHITTINGHAM

T HE 4.30 a.m. start time was not a shock. During his 50 years of training, others had long set their clocks by Charlie Whittingham. Neither was the early morning taciturnity unexpected from the tall, trim, shaven-headed World War II veteran who could still drink his juniors under the table. It was the gun that was a trifle unnerving.

It was August 1986 and we were in the Hilton car park at Arlington Heights, Chicago, en route to the racecourse backstretch where he was readying the six-year-old mare Estrapade to win the Arlington Million.

Three months earlier Charlie Whittingham had been the toast of America, not to mention every septuagenarian in the universe, when he had saddled Ferdinand to win the Kentucky Derby, and next morning said to the waiting press: 'Sleep's overrated. You get all the sleep you need after you die. I had three hours last night, usually have five. Never had a headache in 73 years.'

So back to Chicago, an audience with the master, and a conversation to treasure.

BS (in piping public school accent after a large automatic has been placed firmly on the dashboard): 'Charlie, you, er, always have a gun?'

CW grunts affirmative.

BS: 'Er, have you used it lately?'

CW: 'Not for two weeks.'

BS: 'Where was that?'

CW: 'In the parking lot at Hollywood.'

BS: 'What happened?'

CW: 'Big guy tried to rob me.'

BS (voice now more piping than ever): 'Did you, er, shoot him?'

CW (73 years old and entirely unimpressed with the whole conversation): 'No, I just pistol-whipped the sonofabitch.'

There are a thousand Whittingham stories like this, a lot of them harking back to his scuffling days in the Damon Runyon 1930s and none better than the one about him walking into the bar run by the redoubtable 'Big Tits Judy' near Bay Meadows racetrack. As Charlie came through the door a big bloke thumped him in the mouth, surveyed the reeling handiwork, and said: 'Sorry, I thought you were someone else.' Charlie picked himself up, went and had his meal, and downed a few drinks. But just as he left he turned, flattened the original guy with a mighty right-hander and said – you've guessed it – 'Sorry, I thought you were someone else.'

But much as we may revel in such tales (and if you haven't you should treat yourself to Jay Hovdey's thoughtful and beautifully written biography *Whittingham: A Thoroughbred Racing Legend*, published by The Blood Horse),

they only testify to Charlie's roistering side. It was a part of him that no doubt helped him get through personal tragedy, the Great Depression, two years with the Marines in the Pacific, and the endless ups and down of the racetrack.

But it was only the outer part of the pineapple, and of much more significance on that Arlington dawn patrol was the next conversation. And it was even shorter than the first.

Estrapade was looking out of her stall when we got to her. Charlie ran his hand up and down her neck, tweaked her ears and sat himself down on a straw bale with her head at his shoulder. Back at Santa Anita she was used to going out at 5.30; as a big-race visitor she would have to wait an hour. I asked Charlie what he would do now. This time it was not an uninterested reply. He looked at her, looked at me with a hint of kindness in those very penetrating, deep blue, Marine Sergeant's eyes, and there was a whole lifetime of reflective wisdom as he gently said: 'Just watch her.' He thought about it some more and then repeated: 'Just watch her.'

It was as if he was imparting his secret and I came to realise that he was. There are only two complete physical fulfilments in horse racing (betting counts as 'financial'). They are either the big-race jockey's moment when he digs deep into the horse beneath and the winning post flashes by, or the trainer's almost post-coital satisfaction as he sees his charge cantering back as a sweating but victorious tribute to the decisions made and hours spent.

My earlier life in the saddle had given a tiny taste of the former. The latter, if not a mystery, often seemed slightly lessened back home by the wider achievement of the 'academy' system that most European stables run, with the horses coming up through the classes and the trainer taking only the crucial daily decisions to get their scholarship pupil through his exams. Make no mistake, the great ones – the Herns, Cecils, Stoutes and Fabres – have the most astonishing grasp and judgement of the Thoroughbred psyche. But even at big-race time they have to delegate quite a lot. With Whittingham you could see the hands were completely on.

By 1986 he would have been 52 years with his training licence and long into legend, first for his pre- and post-war association with Horatio Luro, then for his own first champion, the two-year-old Porterhouse in 1953, for the big races across the West in the 1950s and 1960s, and then all across the nation in the 1970s, when he five times topped the earnings charts, as he did again in 1981 and 1982. Even in inward-looking, we-invented-the-game Britain, we had heard of Ack Ack, Cougar and Perrault. Even we had heard the stories of how, unlike so many of his rivals, Whittingham used patience as a watchword, saying of his horses: 'Either you wait for them, or they make you wait.'

These were indeed very different circumstances to the depression days in Tijuana, when his only horse died of a snake bite, or the opening of Bing

Crosby's Del Mar racetrack in 1937, when Charlie showed up with two useless runners and a cross-eyed coyote to guard them.

By Arlington time he would have some 150 horses under his care, split between the on-track stables at Hollywood Park or Santa Anita and his training base out at San Luis Rey. Both the horses and the owners would be handpicked and the latter would soon know that Charlie brooked no interference. 'Have you tested him for worms?' asked Burt Bacharach after one of his horses ran badly. 'Hey Burt,' came the withering reply, 'I hear that piano of yours has not produced many hits lately. Tested it for worms?'

There was something mesmerising, almost melancholy in his concentration. It was not a great surprise to later learn of bleak moments in his past – his father Ned committed suicide when Charlie was just a year old, his teenage brother was killed in a shooting accident and, bleakest of all, his son Taylor shot himself at a drug-fuelled party aged 22.

Sunday Silence beats Easy Goer, 1989 Breeders' Cup Classic.

Charlie had pared his life down so that the horses, and those magical hours around daybreak, came first. Watching him watching Estrapade that morning, in the barn, on the track, as she was washed down, confirmed what the results suggested. That Charlie Whittingham got closer to his horses than any other. They were his weapons, and it would be he himself who loaded the gun.

He knew how dangerous it all could be so he would not run horses until he was sure they were ready. It could be frustrating for owners and press alike, but it brought us some of the greatest moments in racing history.

The year after that first Arlington morning we had one of the best of them – Ferdinand beating Alysheba in the Breeders' Cup Classic at Hollywood; two Kentucky Derby winners head to head and 56-year-old Bill Shoemaker getting first run on Chris McCarron.

Working for NBC, I had been at the start, and I can see them now duelling off the final turn in the fading evening light. Shoemaker, a tiny, ancient gnome dwarfed by the massive chestnut beneath but exerting a clamped-on compulsion to fire the mighty bullet that his old ally had readied for him.

It was one of those images that you expect never to be bettered. But a year on McCarron and Alysheba had their own Breeders' Cup triumph in the near dark of Churchill Downs, and then in 1989 Chris linked up with Charlie

Whittingham on Sunday Silence to win the epic duel with Easy Goer at Gulfstream Park, when just about the only light you could see was reflections off the water on the Everglades.

Charlie was 76 by now, but the dawn routine and the hands-on concentration had never wavered that summer as he took Sunday Silence through the Kentucky Derby and the Preakness, only to be run over by Easy Goer in the Belmont. The re-match in the 1989 Breeders' Cup Classic was one of the most awaited and longest delayed broadcasts that Channel 4 Racing had ever done. Peak time on Saturday night and the horses were almost ten minutes just walking to the stalls. It meant that when Sunday Silence finally outsprinted Easy Goer we had to scramble off air without suitable tribute to the training triumph. A month later came the chance to do it in person.

The photographer Chris Smith and I had been in Las Vegas covering the deeply futile third battle between a world-weary Sugar Ray Leonard and a little motivated Roberto Duran. After five days with the phoneys there was an overwhelming desire to visit someone who had no intention of going over the hill. So we hired a car and sped south across the desert and Death Valley to be at Hollywood Park next morning. There, in barn 59, out alone on the right with its sing-song mixture of Spanish and southern voices and chattering, leather-chapped riding girls, we found him. The old blue eyes were as clear and watchful as ever. At £7 million, Whittingham's horses had earned three times those of Michael Stoute, our champion, that season, but what he wanted to talk about was the future.

Sunday Silence was walking round the shed row, on recuperation drill after two little chips had been taken from his right knee. Whittingham looked at him. Whole chapters had been written of how his latest champion nearly died as a foal, was too unattractive to get sold as a yearling and needed a miracle to survive his van turning over on the way back from sale.

Charlie didn't believe in miracles. 'Sure he looked a bit weak and sickle-hocked,' he said. 'But I don't mind that. I liked the way he moved. He was like a cat – when I first saw him gallop I will never forget it. We are taking him easy. We will build him up. And we will take anyone on.'

Charlie Whittingham died, still with his licence, on 20 April 1999, aged 86. Even he could not beat the century. But he sure could handle a gun.

If John Francome had been in the Wild West, he would have soon had every gunslinger, not to mention every saloon girl, eating out of his hand. That's the trouble with him: there is no scenario in history that you can't think would not have been improved by the entry of the rollicking voice, the tutored hands and the lightning wit. He would be Blackadder without the bungles, and a fair bit of bedtime added. Good Queen Bess would never have felt the like of it.

It would make a great TV series, but for racing it has been for real. It would be something of an understatement to say that we have been lucky to have him amongst us.

JOHN FRANCOME

IN NOVEMBER 1975 John Francome had the most glittering prospects of any jump rider in history. Supremely gifted, dazzlingly funny, disgracefully daring, the former British junior show-jumping champion was a month short of his 23rd birthday and heading the list as stable jockey to Fred Winter en route to the first of his seven championships.

'But listen,' he said after finishing some deplorable story involving a nurse and an Alsatian, 'if something came along which could earn us more money, I would stop tomorrow.'

Without the wit you could be almost frightened by the harshness of the sentiment or the sheer relentlessness of the achievements. That summer, high above Lambourn, he and his father Norman had themselves built an immaculate Cotswold stone stable block, to be followed a couple of years later by a mansion eventually sold at a hundred times the £8,000 cost of the place's original tin shack with its loo in the kitchen. It was a draughty first step on the Francome property ladder, which was soon to include chip shops, caravan sites and a bankload of investments. John knew the value as well as the price of everything. 'Okay,' he said when his 5p offer for a 6p bag of chips was declined, 'have a chip back.'

Norman's two watchwords were 'Make work a pleasure' and 'If all else fails, read the instructions.' John never bothered with instructions but the pleasure he has found and the laughter he has spread in everything he has done cloaks the teetotal discipline and tireless ingenuity behind the joker's mask. The sight of the mop-haired smiler blocking the traffic while he finished his story all those years back in Lambourn could suggest an easy, seamless link between that and the fresh-faced seventeen-year-old sliding down the Hickstead Bank with a Union Jack on his saddle-cloth. The truth had been much more difficult.

From early on (and the first winner had come in December 1970) you could see he was a rider but wondered whether he would make a jockey – and so did he. He was beautifully balanced and controlled crossing an obstacle, but his arms and feet looked too big and his frame lacked power as he tried to drive a horse forward. 'I'm so weak in a finish,' he would say with alarming candour. 'I don't seem to have enough strength. Perhaps it's all that weight I had to knock off when I started.'

Winning the 1978 Gold
Cup on Midnight Court.

He broke his wrist on his second ride and his right arm twice in the next three years. You worried that he might be a bit fragile for the game.

But he was never fragile as a person. The line about doing something else if the money was right was a long-running refrain which continues to this day. It freed him from the sense of subservience which often limits the horizons of those in racing, and its origins were based more on the need for self-support than simple selfishness. He never forgot how much his working-class parents had scrimped and saved to see their dimple-chinned son serve it up to all the Henrys and Charlottes in the Pony Club, how much it had stretched their resources to finally buy the Grade A-class Red Paul who even flew the flag in Europe. Go to Francome's latest empire on the hill today, and Norman will always be around – 'finding something useful to do'.

But it was John's mother Lilian who was the making of him. Without her, most of us, and he, dread to think what might have happened. Sure, he had the balance, the energy, the bravery and the wit: 'What has been your lightest weight?' Fred Winter asked at the first interview, to receive the deadpan '7 pounds, 10 ounces' in volleyed return. But Lilian added a sense of values and of people to the charm. She was a diminutive docker's daughter from Cardiff who brought music and laughter and a special sort of serenity to everything she did. 'He was actually very polite,' Jonathan Powell and I told her about her then tousle-haired, rebellious-looking offspring's behaviour at some early public function. 'I should think so,' she replied, 'he's my son.'

In 40 years of watching the long-armed youth become the rampant jockey, the master craftsman, the side-splitting speaker, the unfazeable pundit, there has never been a time when his emotions have been so open to the raw as when he stepped into the nave of St Michael and All Angels at Lambourn after his mother's funeral in November 1990. That familiar deep, unchanging Wiltshire drawl would pipe upwards as he choked in grief. But he wanted to stand in front of us to show how important she was. There was even half a joke as he said how Lil tried to keep them on the straight and narrow – 'not an easy job with the Francome family'. It was the bravest, most difficult, most necessary thing he ever did.

It also laid bare the hidden compassion, unsolicited visits, unprompted phone calls which are always in danger of getting him a good name. A long time back one of our paraplegic Injured Jockeys' Fund beneficiaries had achieved the unlikely feat of being thrown out of the house by his wife for two-timing from his wheelchair.

Our almoner was visiting the god-forsaken Portakabin that was our man's temporary home when there was a knock on the door. John had heard on the grapevine and so had driven a hundred miles to help. John Oaksey has always said that the best thing for any hospital would be to put Francome on the ward once a week – and that's not just for the nurses.

But good deeds are only the underside of being bothered. More than anyone else you will meet, John Francome has harnessed a low boredom threshold to a need to do things well. 'Otherwise what's the point,' he will say. 'I would rather go and play golf.' He puts his talents in the ledger, thinks up the plan, and then sets them to work. The race-riding was just the start, the beam from which everything else could hang.

Mind you, he brought some pretty precious assets to the saddle: balance, brains, will, temperament and eyesight. The last was the quality to which he used to airily ascribe his unique ability to assess a stride and ease a horse over a fence without hassle. But in truth all the other attributes were used as he adapted the clamped-in, show-jumping push for take-off which took him low and close to the horse over the leap. It re-set the standard for all who followed. 'He was,' said Fred Winter, 'the best man at presenting a horse to a fence that there has ever been.'

That wasn't enough. John wanted to do a lot more than just look pretty. Despite his titles, it took him until about 1981 to develop a finish to match his finesse, but it then became a formidable enough package. Not as neat as Dunwoody, nor as implacable as McCoy, but blessed with the match-winning quality of being able to think at full gallop and having the nerve to carry it through. Everyone correctly cites Sea Pigeon's 1981 Champion Hurdle as the ultimate example of Francome cool. But I guard the memory of a hitherto unreliable brute called The Burghermeister in a selling chase at Fontwell one January day in 1983. Two from home the iron fist came out of the velvet glove and the horse was swept into and over the last in an effort it would never repeat.

Most of all, John had daring. This is something more than mere bravery. It requires an awareness, a nerve and a cheek that few possess. John had it in spades. It took him very close to, and sometimes over, the line on a horse and off it. As when he had to skip round a fence in the fog and got rumbled only because another jockey grassed and the offending hoofprints were found in the turf. Or when he put a bundle of bras and panties in Richard Pitman's arms directly under the security camera of a store in Brackley with the happy rustic rejoinder – 'Oh no, I haven't bought them, Richard, I've just stolen them.'

Daring made him a wonderful, irreverent public speaker. It meant that he had a gorgeous, unfeigned charm that could appeal to every type of person and, at the sad cost of his marriage to Miriam, to any sort of lady. It gave him the ability to be the most magnificent, wide-eyed bluffer you would ever meet. It made stewards' lives a misery and sometimes left punters scratching their heads. And it finally gave us a TV blessing, a unique blend of informed analysis and entertainment.

Courting him for Channel 4 was a tricky business. We had to be very casual, almost take-it-or-leave-it about using him. It was absolutely obvious that he would be sensationally good if only he could be interested, if we could somehow creep in below that boredom threshold.

We trod very carefully through the jumps season, trying to encourage without crawling. Then one day producer Andrew Franklin rang after a Kempton meeting. 'He says he's very interested in Flat racing,' said Andrew. Oh, was he? We were on our way.

He doesn't like presenting, preferring to depend on his lightning reactions to what he sees on the screen or hears from his colleagues. It took just a little while for him to relax enough and for the audience to be cute enough to catch the speed or the innuendo of his repartee. I once made the mistake of reading out a viewer's brain-teaser asking for racecourses with a part of the body in their title. The answers were meant to be Yarmouth, Chester, and Musselburgh. Francome blinked for a millisecond and drawled: 'Has there ever been a track at Scunthorpe?' For a moment I didn't get it. Then it was definitely 'Time for a Break'.

No one ever wore their trappings more lightly. After John won a BAFTA award a couple of years back, the *Independent*'s Stan Hey asked a touch earnestly what was the mainspring of the great man's broadcasting career. Francome gave one of his trademark shrugs and said: 'It gets me out of the house.'

In many ways horse-racing is the narrowest of disciplines, the most confined of parishes. Mill Reef's owner Paul Mellon told of the damning verdict of his father Andrew W. Mellon, Secretary of State of the US Treasury. 'All that fuss,' said Mellon senior, 'about whether one horse can run faster than another.'

In that sense it is indeed a 'trivial pursuit'. On the other hand, it involves hope, effort, excitement, scholarship, muscle, Mammon, glory, hurt and disappointment – and that's just on an ordinary day.

It also now involves extraordinary people on a global scale – and they don't get much more extraordinary, nor more global, than Sheikh Mohammed bin Rashid Al Maktoum.

SHEIKH MOHAMMED

SHEIKH MOHAMMED swept into the room. It takes training as well as purpose to sweep in like he did.

By that Dubai morning in February 1985 he had already spent fifteen of his 35 years as minister of defence, a point emphasised by the two black-dish-dashed bodyguards with submachine guns across their chests. But it remains a positive rather than a political memory. For in the next ten minutes he was about to conceive the *Racing Post*.

It was not the expected outcome of our meeting. We were supposed to be talking about his imminent purchase of *Pacemaker* magazine. But almost immediately he said: 'No, my brothers and I have discussed this. *Pacemaker* belongs to Mr Sangster. It would be like buying someone else's wife.' He then pushed aside my protests with the statement, 'But we would like to have something that would help British racing.'

At that time, the *Sporting Life* was in strike-ridden threat of closure, so, as a reply, I said: 'The best thing you could do for all of us would be to guarantee a new daily racing paper'. It was an unplanned challenge. But he took it.

Like most unintended conceptions, there proved to be plenty of problems up ahead, but working with Sheikh Mohammed was not among them. Because, for the twelve years that he owned the paper outright, he was enormously supportive in what, for a man who always liked complete hands-on involvement, was an inherently untenable position.

Right at the beginning I said to him, with what seemed wishful optimism, that the credibility of the paper would not survive if he interfered with editorial policy. And he didn't. Sure, there were moments when he was uncomfortable, but never once did we change a headline or pull or insert an article on his direct orders. Can you say that about any other billionaire who has ever owned a newspaper?

The best times were during those first frenetic two years before and after the *Racing Post* actually launched in April 1986. For me it was an unfamiliar and hazardous project which I took on against my better judgement. Once committed, Sheikh Mohammed called conferences, backed appointments, listened to worries – and it was he, finally, who came up with the title of *Racing Post*. There were some difficulties, particularly early on, but I remember him putting his arm around me and saying: 'You have to do what you have to do. We are in this together. We will win.'

And we did win. By June 1998 we were outselling the *Sporting Life* 60-40. But both papers were still losing money, Sheikh Mohammed had far bigger things to worry about, and a deal was done with Trinity Mirror to install us at Canary Wharf as the sole racing paper.

They were not altogether happy years but the paper continued to grow, and because Sheikh Mohammed had kept ownership of the actual title he was able to enact a £10 million payment to charities as part of the sale to our new, independent owners. To say that we, like the charities, are grateful to him would be an understatement.

What you learned, being close to him, was how physical he is. When engaged, he likes to look at you very directly, to almost smell what you are made of and how you are thinking. 'When I was young,' he once told me, 'my father taught me how to understand people, how to listen, how to judge them.'

The English, honed at Cambridge's Bell School of Languages, from which he and Sheikh Hamdan skived off to watch Royal Palace win the 1967 Two Thousand Guineas, has always been very good. But in the early days the almost prophetic simplicity of some of the imagery made you wonder – and this is an extraordinary admission in view of subsequent events – if the mind was not into make-believe.

For on my first visit to Dubai in early 1983, the dual carriageway to Abu Dhabi stopped at a half-finished roundabout by the now defunct Hilton Hotel, with little but desert beyond. Six months later the roundabout was still the same. There was a touch of those failed developments in the Costa Del Sol about it.

This charismatic young man and his brothers may, in the six years since the filly Hatta had opened things in a little race at Brighton, have already amassed three studs, sixty broodmares and 238 horses in training, but most people just thought it a piece of astounding good luck thanks to the oil money.

There was an undoubted element of patronising amongst his early guests. Sheikh Mohammed would fly them all out, take them around his palaces, his horses, his camels, his falcons and his wildlife reserve, and sketch out his vision as to how Dubai was going to be a centre of tourism, business and racing – and heads would nod in agreeable scepticism and put their snouts back in the trough.

'Have you heard his latest idea?' we would ask disbelievingly. In 1987 it was the golf course. Sheikh Mohammed was going to install desalination plants, water the sand and turn the desert green. Everyone laughed. A year later General Zia drove off down the first fairway. Today there are seven other courses and Tiger Woods is an annual visitor. Wonder when the laughing stopped …

In racing, some people still have trouble coming to terms with the Sheikh Mohammed phenomenon, veering between relish when his huge battalions seem to underperform and jealousy if they hit a purple patch. In many ways they should thank their lucky stars that the progress of Godolphin, which takes up some 2 per cent of the sheikh's time, does not match that of Dubai Inc., with which his other 98 per cent of commitment has overseen a more than fivefold improvement in GDP in the last ten years. If the horses had acted like the economy, no one else would have got a look in.

As it is, racing has received an investment in bloodstock, infrastructure, research and employment beyond anyone's wildest imaginings. On the face of it there sometimes seems to be profligacy on a major scale, but whenever you pick holes in the micro picture you have to look across at the macro one.

Sheikh Mohammed (second left) endurance riding in the Dubai desert in 2005.

Right from the very start, Sheikh Mohammed was insistent that his main task was to put Dubai on the map. The horses may have only been a minor, albeit instinctive, part of that, but it is hard to think of how he could have got quicker into our nation's good books than by investing in the Sport of Kings (or, in this case, Queens). And while the Godolphin operation was formed by the wish to have his horses under his own hands and eyes during the winter, the consequent development of the first truly global stable has been yet another way of waving the Dubai flag around the world.

The scale of things is now truly amazing to behold and Sheikh Mohammed's ambitions get ever wider, the investments larger, the buildings taller, and his responsibilities ever heavier, to the point of being one of the crucial power brokers in the Middle East. He is now not mere defence minister, but ruler of Dubai as well as vice-president and prime minister of the Emirates, and with the political savvy that needs to go with it.

In an interview to coincide with President Bush's visit in January 2008 (which included the line, 'I like everything about America except its foreign policy'), he said: 'The Emirates plans do not come from mere ambition, they are a necessity. It doesn't take the visit of an American president for this region to freshly understand that it needs to accelerate economic progress.'

That's all good grown-up politics, but at heart you return to the physicality of a man who loves horses and who in 2003 himself led the Emirates team to the European Endurance Championships over 100 miles at Punchestown. Frankie Dettori does not know how lucky he is that Sheikh Mohammed could never make nine stone.

'Horses are in my blood,' he explained at a very early meeting. 'They used to be the attack weapons tethered at the back of the desert convoys. I have always liked not just to ride them but to understand them. Some trainers think I am just another owner, but I care about the food, the training, the mind, the everything.'

This doesn't always lead to comfortable companionship. Back in January 1993, the latest Sheikh Mohammed idea was to solve the ancient desert riddle of whether a horse would beat a camel over a distance. So 402 of the humpbacks were matched up against 28 horses with 25 miles of sand and scrub ahead of them. 'You want to ride?' he said to me as I twiddled my thumbs a touch superciliously on the sidelines: 'Ride that one.'

They made a video of that first race. Blockbuster scenes of the great camel/horse stampede beneath huge clouds of dust raised by the accompanying 4x4s, and swirled by the helicopters filming overhead.

After a while there were little knots of riders working their way through the dunes, camels loping relentlessly in a desert version of the tortoise and the hare, and finally Sheikh Mohammed and his daughter thundering towards the finishing line. Somewhere towards the end of it there is a shot of me leading my horse back exhausted. It always raises a laugh.

Sheikh Mohammed still sweeps into the room. Early in 2008 it was in Dubai to authorise an astonishing $10 billion foundation to promote education across the Middle East. Before that it was into Berlin University to receive a medal for his overall educational contribution. As in 1985, he did not hesitate to get to the point.

'Those who neglect the new will remain at the back of the line,' he said, unscripted, to the assembled worthies. 'Those who wait for luck to make things happen will be disappointed. Those who let time manage their affairs will find that time is a friend to those who work and take initiative, but an enemy to those who depend on others and grow lazy. Others promise, we deliver.'

It was a message which should be heeded, not just by students and by racing, but by all of us.

One to go in my selection of a dozen people who have made Great Impressions down the years. The choice has been much more reflective than selective. How could it not be when the list does not include Bill Shoemaker or Yves Saint-Martin or Henry Cecil or Jonjo O'Neill or Julie Krone? We started way back in the 1950s with Fred Winter's gunslit eyes, Vincent O'Brien's mastery of Cheltenham and Aintree, Peter O'Sullevan's voice calling us to worship and the young Queen galloping up the Ascot straight on the mornings of the Royal Meeting. We end in very different times but with exceptional people still coming through. And you may agree that the latest is not the least of them.

TONY MCCOY

S CEPTICISM can be a good thing in life – and especially in racing. It is not to be confused with cynicism, which can corrode the psyche. Scepticism is unimpressed with practically anything short of earth-shattering achievement. Then and now, there have always been a few sceptics around the subject of A.P. McCoy. The key to his record-breaking, thirteen-championship greatness is that chief amongst them is A.P. himself.

Twelve years ago this January we were winging down to Wincanton via a schooling session with Paul Nicholls – remember the fuss when Tony later left that connection for Martin Pipe? A week earlier he had passed a hundred winners for the season for what was to be the first of thirteen times. Only sixteen months before he had arrived at Toby Balding's yard as an unsung ex-Flat-race apprentice with just thirteen winners to his name in Ireland and not one ride in a steeplechase. 'I am just very lucky to have the chances,' he said as places like Amesbury and Mere flashed by. 'But people will soon rubbish me if I don't take them.'

He was 21, tall and a bit spotty. He had grown an inch and put on 7lb in the last year, and most of us were only beginning to think that perhaps 'Toby's conditional' might be more than just another driven kid riding the crest of the wave.

Two days earlier a reluctant-looking beast called North Bannister had been compelled and cajoled home at Folkestone. 'I looked at the way the horse got up,' said super-agent Dave Roberts, 'and had to ask myself, could Adrian [Maguire] or Norman [Williamson] have done any better? Tony knows he has a bit to learn but he listens and is learning very quick.'

Then as now, the jockey appeared to take no satisfaction in being told of such praise. He was neither dismissive of the compliments nor greedy for more. Indeed, the overwhelming impression at dinner with Toby and the late Caro Balding the night before was of a very correct politeness and an emerging sense of humour about the absurdity of those in the racing pond, very much including himself. But the central credo that drives him, and which today he can expound upon at deliberately gory length, was already there. 'Winning,' he said quietly at one stage the next morning, 'is the only thing that counts. That's the whole fun, the whole point of it.'

Almost all top jockeys have made that judgement, and those who haven't usually self-destruct. But no one, in my experience, has made it as completely as McCoy, and the reason for its strength comes not in what he was doing a dozen years ago, but in the dozen that went before.

When confronted with champions it pays to examine not so much the famous days in the spotlight, but the long cold mornings from where the greatness sprang. You don't have to be much of an amateur McCoy psychiatrist to see that, mentally as well as physically, there was something very special there from the very beginning.

'When Anthony [Tony is an English application] first came to me,' said the late Willie Rock about the tiny figure who would pedal a dozen miles from his parents' post office at Moneyglass next to Lough Neagh in Northern Ireland, 'he was twelve years old, about five stone nothing, and yet straight away you could put him on great big horses that grown lads could not hold one side of.'

Gifts in the saddle alone would never be enough, and it was the sequel to Willie Rock's testimony that is even more significant. For at fifteen, by which time he was skipping school to take responsibility for the whole yard at Cullybackey, Rock passed him on to Jim Bolger, whose County Carlow base is probably the most demanding academy in the universe and already housed a young man called Aidan O'Brien. 'He did not set the world on fire as an apprentice,' said Bolger of his new recruit. 'He got a bit heavy and he broke his leg quite badly. Not yet a star on the track but already a star in attitude. He had been very well brought up.'

That summary speeds over what, in hindsight, remains the crucial moment of McCoy's riding life, the dreadful fall one freezing Kilcullen morning in January that left the bone sticking out of his leg and gave him long months of recovery to burn a need for success deep into the brain. You can hear everything he now stands for in his reaction.

'I never once thought,' he has said, 'not even for one second, that I wasn't cut out for the job. That fall showed me the dangers in being a jockey but they didn't scare me. I was determined to come back and work hard.' He had the desire. What was wanted was lift-off, and that came in Bolger's wish to keep him away from the risks of jumping. In all the books, films and interviews Tony has given, nothing has better encompassed the resulting nuclear fission than an *Observer* piece in 2006.

Tony told Lee Honeyball: 'Jim said to me, "I heard you at the bottom of the gallops screaming like a baby that morning. That happens to jump jockeys every day. You'll never make it." I admire Jim as much as anyone in racing –

Winning at Aintree on Refinement, 2006.

my time there was the making of me – but he definitely gave me the incentive. I had to prove him wrong.'

Right to this day a conversation with McCoy is likely to be punctuated with his now stylised version of the original incident with him writhing in agony, and hard-man Bolger saying: 'Get up, you're just being soft.' It is gallows humour and it is used subtly to exaggerate the situation to the point of self-parody. 'It's bad,' he said at the end of the first unsuccessful day at the 2008 Cheltenham Festival, his long pale face utterly deadpan and apparently despondent, 'and it will only get worse.'

It is at Cheltenham, of course, where he has flirted most closely with madness and despair.

He literally went demented for a few moments after boiling himself right down to 10st 1lb to win the Tripleprint Gold Cup on Northern Starlight in 1998. He was utterly disconsolate when Gloria Victis was killed in the Gold Cup, and when Valiramix suffered the same fate in the Champion Hurdle it took quite a serious weekend charm offensive to allay the harm that two days of public sulking had begun.

But fearless drive, even one as on the rack as McCoy's, is for nothing with a top jockey if it is not combined with athletic balance and mid-race judgement. Right from the beginning Tony had very good levers, his long limbs fitted around a horse so that he exerted deep, all-round balance with tight, short-leathered purchase. He had the balance as well as the belief to make them jump and he had the ultimate champion's hunger for the winning post.

It was a method that was unbelievably successful, but at times he asked questions of horses almost as alarming as the demands he made on himself. One day at Warwick, Ruby Walsh and I stood at the second hurdle as Tony came up on a free-running favourite of Christian von der Recke's. Instead of letting the horse flip the obstacle in its stride, McCoy pumped it in and up like some desperate, front-legs-stretching, equine long-jumper. Ruby shut his eyes and winced.

Another day at Worcester, Tony was battering around in front on a reluctant, blinkered Pipe favourite, and on the final turn, even he had to give it best. Within a furlong the wretched beast came back on the bridle. 'There are,' said Richard Dunwoody relating this incident, 'many different ways of skinning a cat.'

For McCoy watchers, the delight, towards the end of the Pipe years, was the addition of a cooler calculation to the frequent front-running fire of the greatest winning machine the game has ever seen. This was most perfectly symbolised by the stalking, last-to-first strategy and then ruthless finish on Polar Red to win the Imperial Cup in that record 289-winner season of 2001-02. Today, McCoy is as thoughtful as any jockey and will cut quietly through a field as smoothly as Dunwoody, his original idol, used to do.

The connection with Dunwoody is on the cryptic side. Endless admiration for his skills in the saddle, head-shaking sympathy at Richard's search for something to match the buzz of kicking a horse past the post.

At Belgravia's Motcomb Gallery in February 2008, there was a reception to celebrate Dunwoody's unbelievable 48-day, 660-mile, -30°C, sled-pulling trek of the South Pole. At the back there was the smiling figure of McCoy, fresh out of some ludicrous fridge to speed up the healing of his back. 'He is,' said Tony, raising his eyes towards Dunwoody in amusement, 'absolutely crackers.'

Does it take one to know one? McCoy will acknowledge the question and give the reasoned answer that his whole system cannot function if he lets a shred of doubt through the battened-down hatches of his mind. Only this month he said: 'On the track I think I am unbreakable. I think that however hard I fall I am going to get up.' Sometime, somewhere one of those hatches will be dented. It is what happens next that will be crucial.

It could still all end badly. Tony could yet – as Hugh McIlvanney so sadly and prophetically wrote about Muhammad Ali's second comeback – 'be on the downward path to where the bad times are'. But sceptics are not stupid. They know there has to be a closure. It is only when that comes that history can judge if A.P. McCoy has, indeed, been the greatest hero of them all.

New Hopes

*H*INDSIGHT *too often paints the rosy view. Horses were better, faster, bolder, braver than they are now. It ain't necessarily so, and it's worth recalling one of Lester Piggott's most fabled utterances: 'Every year they say that the three-year-olds are no good, and every year they are wrong.'*

We are not yet a full decade into the new millennium and we have already had a number of horses who have threatened the highest bar, both on the Flat and over jumps. It was in November 2000 that I first went to see what was to become the first superstar of the age. As the world now knows, Best Mate's story ended in tragedy on the track. But in the five years between the writing of the first piece below and his collapse at Exeter on his comeback in November 2005, he lit up the jumping world as no other had, short of Desert Orchid, Arkle and Red Rum.

He won three Gold Cups, eleven of his sixteen chases and, crucially, never looked like falling. What follows first is the thrill of all the hope he engendered. It is great to know that this time it was not all in vain. At the stage of our visit he had run just the once over fences. But it was what he promised that mattered.

Previous spread: Denman (left) seconds from winning the 2008 Gold Cup.

BEST MATE

A HORSE for Cheltenham. Best Mate runs today [12 November 2000]. He was second there last March at the Festival. He has collected in all but one of his other races. He may not make it. The statistics as well as the dangers are uncompromisingly brutal. But at five years old he is the type of lithe young steeplechaser who could be anything: 16 hands 2 inches (5ft 6in) at the shoulder, 1,200 lbs of dark bay muscle on the weighbridge, proud of eye, deep of lung, and quick of feet. He is 'The Dream'.

There is nothing in the whole world of equine or human athletics that measures up to what his sort can do. To gallop and jump round two miles and twelve four-and-a-half-foot fences in under four minutes carrying up to twelve stone of man and saddle. Done well, it requires a mixture of power and courage, speed and agility which makes the spirit soar. Best Mate was soaring last week. And that was just practice.

A stable companion rejoicing in the name of Catfish Keith led him up the five-fence examination in trainer Henrietta Knight's remarkably well drained schooling paddock on the way to the Downs near Wantage. As Best Mate passed us, ears cocked, head bold, neck set, back arching, you could see the power surging through to jockey Jim Culloty's hands on the rein. As he put in a huge long leap at the final open ditch, that power exploded into two squealing great bucks of sheer well being. 'F*** me, that horse is fresh,' said the voice beside us.

It is a voice as redolent of authority as it is of rustic grammar-shattering earthiness. It is a voice which once roared with laughing, big-hearted challenge as it stormed horses fencewards and three times took the champion's crown . It's a voice which ten years ago had, through misfortune, drink, and unhappiness got right to the very edge of the everlasting bonfire. It's a voice which has now found a triumphant and entirely uncensored renewal in its loving partnership with Henrietta, whose fastidious, former school-mistress tones are the ultimate contrast to his own. Terry Biddlecombe is sixty in February. He is in every sense reliving The Dream.

He was the Prince Hal of our generation. A tall, strong farmer's boy from Gloucester with an appetite and a half for everything on offer. It made him an unmatched 'Blond Bomber' in the saddle, but eventually it broke him in body and then in mind. But the demons are long buried, even if enough physical frailty remains for an automatic blood-pressure device on his arm to have been triggered into a strange inflating tourniquet as we had driven across the Downs that morning. 'Just watch him,' he says as Jim Culloty turns Best Mate in for a final run over two bigger fences: 'This is just f***ing poetry in motion.'

After the first Gold Cup, 2002.

Catfish Keith is ridden by Terry's eighteen-year-old son Robert, of whom his father is inordinately proud, albeit not enough to take his eyes off the four-legged star which followed. At the first fence Best Mate's stride takes him close in to the obstacle. The ignorant or incapable jumper would plough forwards with birch-busting risk. With a flick of the forelegs Best Mate is over clean.

'That's it,' mutters Terry, almost drooling to himself as the horse bears down on the fence right in front of us. 'Go at it. Look for the stride. One, two, three.' Best Mate and Jim Culloty fly spring-heeled over and Biddlecombe gives a canine growl of satisfaction from the old days. 'Yeah. That's good,' he says.

'What I look for,' says Biddlecombe, suddenly and necessarily serious, 'is the way a horse presents himself, the way he walks, his mental attitude, his balance, his action of racing. This horse is bold but intelligent. All a jockey has to do,' he adds as Jim Culloty looks across at his mentor, 'is to get hold of his head and not fire him. He will come up on a long stride but he is very clever with his feet. Just negotiate the two open ditches at Cheltenham and keep him balanced down the hill.'

It was not at Cheltenham that Terry first saw Best Mate but at the boggy and higgledy-piggledy Irish delights of the West Waterford point-to-point at Lisnaree in February 1999. For the last four years Terry and Henrietta have spent almost every Sunday in the west of Ireland scouting so successfully for young talent that they now have nothing over nine years old in their seventy-horse string. They are the Leeds United of the training teams [i.e. Leeds in 2000, before they fell from grace]. With Edredon Bleu and Lord Noelie last March, they have already taken trophies in the Cup Final atmosphere of the National Hunt Festival. With Best Mate, aimed this year for the Arkle Trophy, they could go higher yet. 'He could win the Gold Cup in two years,' says Terry.

'We were over looking at another horse, but I saw Best Mate in the paddock and was knocked out by him. It was his first ever run, the ground was dreadful and they pulled him up before the third last. But the way he galloped and jumped. I went to Hen and said, "This is the one we have got to have."'

But investors are needed. Step forward 66-year-old Jim Lewis, a silver-haired retired furniture dealer from Birmingham who fifty years ago stood on the hill looking down on the now defunct Bromford Bridge racecourse holding the hand of his future wife Valerie and said: 'One day I will give you three things. A house, a Jaguar car, and a racehorse.' The first house, a £2,500 bungalow, came four years later. The Jag had to wait a little longer, and if the foray into racehorse ownership did not start until fifteen years ago it has, with Cheltenham victories for Nakir and current two-mile champion Edredon Bleu, been successful enough for Lewis to term himself 'Lucky Jim.'

So after Best Mate duly hacked up in his next point-to-point, it was to Jim Lewis that Henrietta despatched a fax which read: 'I have seen the horse of my dreams. He is so good I would train him for nothing.' A trip to Tom Costello's astonishing young horse academy in Limerick clinched the deal, and if the 'no fees' promise seems to have been forgotten, the fact that Jim was happy to fork out £150,000 for a French horse called Impek at the Paris sales in September suggests that the wolf has not yet vaulted the Lewis's smart new gate. In Best Mate he has the promise of what we are always longing for.

Weather-battered Cheltenham will be reached just one week after Kalanisi and Giant's Causeway's heroics at the Breeders' Cup in Kentucky. But for all their splendour, those two colts are in actual racing sense little more than brilliant one-season wonders. Both will now retire to the harem life at stud where reputations are taken from what their offspring do. But Best Mate and his rivals bring something else. The challenge of a string of winters where the fences beckon yet to the daring. And The Dream lives on.

You will remember that while Best Mate won with soaring authority that Sunday, his tilt at the Arkle Trophy in March was scuppered when Cheltenham 2001 fell victim to the foot-and-mouth outbreak. But you will also remember how he fulfilled all hopes and more by landing the Gold Cup in 2002 and then doing it again a year later.

By then he and Jim Culloty, owner Jim Lewis, rider Jackie Jenner, and of course 'Terry and Hen' had become household names outside the normal racing village. Henrietta even wrote a splendid book about Best Mate. She was signing on Gold Cup day 2004. She would soon have to add a fresh chapter.

Dig deep for victory. Best Mate came towards us with just the final fence between him and triple Gold Cup immortality. He led Harbour Pilot by a length after that soaring leap at the second last. But the flowing stride was now a grinding struggle. The Cheltenham run-in is the most brutal of closures. Best Mate would have to fight every yard of it.

There was wonder in the rawness. The whole world had come to know the Best Mate fairy story. The Irish childhood; the 'Hen and Terry', Henrietta Knight and Terry Biddlecombe, training partnership; the Aston Villa scarves and dreadful songs of silver haired owner Jim Lewis; above all the power and excellence of the equine athlete himself. But that now belonged to another, easier existence. The truth was out here in the drizzle. Jim Culloty reefing his reins as he tried to get the champion to assert. Paul Carberry driving Harbour Pilot back at him on the inside, Andrew Thornton working his long legs on Sir Rembrandt on the outer. Best Mate had some steep history to climb.

It was much, much tougher than we had expected, and the better for it. The preliminaries had been in danger of swamping us in adulation. Sure Best Mate outshone all his rivals in the paddock, his gleaming coat and swaggering walk putting all bar the massive, jig-jogging Sir Rembrandt and the shining, short-tailed chestnut Beef Or Salmon into the shade. The blinkered Harbour Pilot had the sweat of tension on his neck, Therealbandit looked lean and light, and Keen Leader plonked round like an old cab horse with his tongue sticking out. But as they came on to the track and you looked up at the record crowds in the grandstand, expectation tightened on the chest. Three and a quarter miles and 22 fences, not to mention nine implacably opposed horses and jockeys, do not a formality make.

The Frenchman First Gold was the first to show it. Thierry Doumen set him off at the sort of searching gallop that had ripped opponents apart last spring and recalled what a budding superstar the Chantilly horse had seemed three seasons back at Kempton. Down towards us at what was to be the second, twelfth and final fence they drummed. First Gold flew it, the error-prone Harbour Pilot clouted it, and as Best Mate skipped easily over behind him, Jim Culloty's mind got its first test behind the goggles.

The plan had been to stay close to the inside for the best ground, but what if Harbour Pilot capsized in front of him? 'What ifs' can spread doubts through the psyche. Culloty kept his cool. The 'inside' had been the plan. He would stick to it, and all down the back straight Best Mate's jumping was a joy to watch.

It is his balance, the set of his neck, the arc of his leap, that makes him exceptional. Henrietta Knight, who herself rode at Badminton, says he would have gone to the top in dressage, show jumping or three-day event, and there is no reason to doubt her. For the whole first circuit and more, Best Mate and Culloty bowled smoothly in the leaders' wake, the jockey's hand light on the rein, the horse measuring the fences to perfection as they came to him. First Gold and Harbour Pilot might hustle, but it was the others who would hurt. As they swept towards the top of the hill for the final time there seemed no departure from the expected script.

Keen Leader and Irish Hussar had been dropped, Therealbandit was weakening, Beef Or Salmon was working his way back, but only four really counted. And when Sir Rembrandt missed his stride and thumped the eighteenth, we thought there were three, leaving just First Gold and Harbour Pilot to be taken. Down the hill they came, the pace stretching, Sir Rembrandt coming back into the argument but Best Mate now looking awesome on the inside.

Yet just how awesome? Crossing the third last he wasn't going strong enough to take First Gold on the inner, and as he tried to tack out on the turn, Paul Carberry legitimately closed the door with little short of a shoulder charge. For twenty fraught strides the favourite was trapped, but as they straightened out for the second last he had the legs to come outside Harbour Pilot and the power to get room off Sir Rembrandt and a clear run at the fence ahead.

With four sweet strides Best Mate quickened in and over with the jump of the meeting. He was in front; First Gold was finished, Harbour Pilot and Sir Rembrandt were hard on the collar. The coveted third Gold Cup, the much-debated Arkle comparisons, were Best Mate's for the taking. But look closely. Relentless gallops hurt champions and contenders alike. Best Mate was in extremis too.

At the fence he had no rhythm to his stride. Wise-headed Culloty let him 'pop' it, and then reached and reeled at the reins as he gathered the half ton of athlete beneath him and demanded one final lung-testing slog up the hill. This was no place for sentimental anthropomorphism. Culloty's long Killarney accountant's nose was the avenging beak of an eagle. The whip was up and Jim smacked Best Mate hard across the rump and swung his arm and his body forward to insist that destiny should have its day.

Not one yard was now simple. In desperation Best Mate and Culloty answered the crowd's roars to put Harbour Pilot behind them, but right at the death Sir Rembrandt closed to get within half a length, not three feet, at the line. It had been desperately close and the great breakers of cheers that rolled from the stands had as much relief as they did acclamation. But winning is everything. An ecstatic Culloty held three fingers to the sky. The champion's glove was raised again. Who cares if Arkle did it easier, or if next year might even prove one fight too far?

Two final images seared into the memory. First the very public one of the rippling waves of applauding hands as the amphitheatre, paddock-side crowd clapped and clapped and clapped the horse who had given them this moment to carry to their graves. Second, a much more private one a few minutes later up behind the dope test boxes.

Best Mate was being led round by Dave Reddy, as Jackie Jenner was collecting her trophy. The rain was sluicing, hair-plastering down. But it mattered not a jot. Eventually Dave stopped for a moment and we went up and patted Best Mate gratefully on the neck. For three weeks racing and my former jockey profession have been heaped with ridicule and shame as accusations of corruption swirled around the scene. For three days the Cheltenham Festival had thrilled us, and now Best Mate had given his answer. He had washed the old game clean.

The world knows how the story ends. Best Mate's tilt for a fourth Gold Cup was thwarted by a broken blood vessel on the gallops shortly before Cheltenham. His whole life was ended the following season on that dark day at Exeter when he collapsed and died in his comeback race. We explored the ghastly dilemma that all horse lovers have with steeplechasing. There is little to add about Best Mate's demise except to say that Henrietta was never kinder or stronger than in her moment of grief.

She spoke with the deepest of affection uncloyed by excessive sentiment. 'We who work with horses,' she concluded after the most moving of tributes, 'have to face the fact that if we have livestock, we will have dead stock.'

It was the most vivid and direct of phrases, and Henrietta's whole style of communication throughout her handling of Best Mate did horse racing the great service of showing that it was a game which had high things to relish – and people who could describe them.

Most vivid of all describers comes from across the Irish Sea. To listen to Ted Walsh is to think that he must have been born next to the Blarney Stone, not just kissed it. But the wonder for racing is that he is much more than a silver tongue on the airways. Ted has ridden the big winners, trained them and of course sired them too. No other participant in any other sporting discipline even runs close what he and the family did to saddle Papillon to win the Grand National in 2000 with Ruby riding and the other children leading up.

There was no better place to visit at the start of 2001.

PAPILLON

HAPPINESS is home made. Ted Walsh stands on the land his late father bought in front of the two Grand National winners he himself has trained to be ridden by the son whom he has reared to become Ireland's champion jockey. If it wasn't for me sitting on Papillon it would be a perfect family picture.

Mind you, of all the privileges in all of sport it's hard to think of a greater one than to be legged up on the 17 hands of gleaming bay muscle which is Papillon. This is the horse whom 21-year-old Ruby Walsh drove home after four and a half unforgettable miles at Aintree last April. He is big, tall and handsome, and doesn't he know it. On Friday morning he squealed with wellbeing as we filed out into the mists of County Kildare. He had won his comeback race last week over just two miles. He is chuffed to bits with himself.

So too should be Ted and Helen and the rest of family Walsh. But hustle and humour, not swagger, is more their style. To follow Papillon's English Grand National by taking the Irish equivalent with Commanche Court a fortnight later, to double Papillon's comeback victory on 27 December with Rince Ri's triumph in Leopardstown's £60,000 Ericsson Chase on Sunday would be achievement enough for a hundred-strong stable. For a twenty-horse operation run almost as a sideline by one of the most distinctive voices in Irish broadcasting, it is nothing short of unique.

'But I love it, just love it,' says Ted, who at fifty has become the ultimate Irish racing pundit, with as much energy crackling out of him on TV as when he took eleven Irish titles and a world record 600 winners as an amateur. 'My father originally had horses behind his public house in Fermoy. When he moved here [opposite the Goffs Sales arena in Kill, twenty miles down the N7 from Dublin] we had about a dozen boxes and would be doing a fair bit of dealing as well as training a few. He died, God bless him, ten years ago on New Year's Day, and while because of the dealing and the TV work I am now financially secure, we have kept it a family affair.'

Ted and Ruby after Papillon's National.

Most famously with Papillon at Aintree. As Ted and Helen embraced American owner Betty Moran in the stands, the three other children were legging it to greet Ruby in a professional as well as sibling capacity. Sixteen-year-old Katie had the leading rein, 23-year-old Jennifer had the rugs, and twenty-year-old rugby-playing Ted the muscle to get them through to hug their brother as the tears ran down. 'It was great that they were all there together,' remembers Ted, going misty eyed himself. 'That it wasn't ten years earlier when they were only nippers. They all flew home that night and the pub here was open till 3 o'clock in the morning. People came from all over. They will remember this time of their life for the rest of their life.'

But sentiment and good talking are not enough. Ted Walsh is blarney with a base. We go out into the functional concrete block yard to see the great rotating branches of the automatic horse walker. 'Three reasons why this is the best worker in the yard,' quips Ted. 'To start with, it always turns up on Monday morning. It never answers back. And it doesn't put its hand out on Friday.' Then he goes serious.

'I think walking is the most important exercise of all,' he says. 'I set it for six miles an hour and these horses do an hour and a half a day. Every one of mine do ten miles of a morning. Even in the summer Papillon, Rince Ri and Commanche Court will go out in the paddock in the afternoon, but they will walk ten miles first. I don't want them getting soft.' At the huge risk of giving hostages to fortune, it's worth noting that in an era of breakdowns these top three horses have collectively now done twelve seasons uninterrupted by major leg trouble.

But they are not without other problems, and a year ago Papillon had Ted close to despair. 'His last two runs had been bad. He seemed to be losing interest,' says the trainer before climbing on to his tractor. 'So I changed everything. Changed his feed, the time of day he went out, and where he went too. We even ran him over hurdles to sharpen him up. Vincent O'Brien once said to me that the most important thing with old chasers is to keep up their confidence. Look at him,' he added, nodding proudly at the swanky brute beneath me, 'he's a very confident yoke now.'

Which was just as well, as the fog was so thick that you could barely see the horse in front of you. Fields were passed, a river was waded, large logs and banks over which Ted regularly jumps Papillon and the rest were mercifully by-passed. There seemed to be only half a dozen of us. Ruby Walsh tried to be reassuring as he rode the smaller, lighter chestnut frame of Commanche Court alongside. 'You'll be all right,' said Ruby without much conviction. 'We're going on the sand. He'll know the way.'

The Walsh's sand gallop is apparently six furlongs round. As we lapped it blind on Friday it was better to measure by the minutes taken and arm sockets stretched. Papillon doesn't pull in the runaway sense, but he is a big, powerful, beautifully balanced horse right on top of his game. After five minutes and two lengthened arms the possibility of ringing up Mrs Moran back in Pennsylvania and telling her we had got tanked off in the fog had been a bit too close for comfort.

'He looks a lovely ride,' says Ted afterwards, 'but in a race he can just hang the latch. He is a leery old bugger at times and if he starts lugging right and putting his head up, you need to be in the whole of your health. He's given all his jockeys problems but Ruby is his master now and he could just be one of those horses that loves Liverpool.'

Rince Ri, a chestnut in a rather more powerful mode than Commanche Court, is aimed at the Gold Cup – 'He may not be good enough but he is still improving' – while Commanche Court himself will be bidding for a repeat of the Irish National and the continuation of the extraordinary big-race run he began for his trainer by winning the Triumph Hurdle in the colours of tycoon Dermot Desmond in 1997. 'That was when it all started,' said Ted, 'and to think that Ruby was just leading him up that day, and now he is a major player.'

The compliment is a careful one from a father who admits to sometimes being 'worried out' when his already grey-streaked son is riding. 'But I would not have encouraged him to turn professional if he hadn't been such a good amateur that he was champion at eighteen and at nineteen.He's a lot better than I ever was. I was only a mollicker. He is getting to be the finished article. He has four or five years of improvement in him. He could be exceptional. But as with the horses, at my stage in life, I don't take anything for granted.'

Which winds the camera back fifteen months to Velka Pardubice day in the Czech Republic, with Ruby Walsh on the floor, his leg snapped by a splintering rail. 'I ran as quick as I could,' said Ted, 'and although he is twenty years of age he could have been seven with his head in my lap and me saying, "Jaysus, Ruby, it couldn't be broken." Then he is coming back in December and we have a school over hurdles and doesn't he turn over at the last and re-open the fracture. A year ago Rince Ri won the Ericsson and Ruby was beside him on crutches. Last week he was riding again, and all the family were there.'

He thinks back. 'I remember when our oldest Jennifer began to climb out of the cot. The "tump!" as she landed on the floor and Helen and I would then hear the feet pattering, and, oh the joy of the two of us when she came around the corner and not a bother on her. All those little things you get with kids growing up. It is that great sense of pride with your own doing it. I just couldn't describe how I felt at Aintree.'

Ah Ted, you just have.

In my time one of the greatest pleasures has been to see how Irish racing, like the Irish nation as a whole, has modernised to take its rightful place among the elite. On the Flat no race has better symbolized this than the Irish Champion Stakes at Leopardstown, which has produced a whole series of encounters which you know, even as you see them, will be seared in the memory.

Nothing has bettered the renewal of 2001. This was the year of Galileo, albeit a full four centuries after history's greatest astronomer first got his telescope out in Pisa. The horse Galileo came to Leopardstown still unbeaten, having taken the English and Irish Derbies and come out best of a finishing duel with Godolphin's five-year-old Fantastic Light in the King George at Ascot. The sight of Galileo in full flight in the straight at Epsom is an image of the Thoroughbred I will happily take with me to the grave.

But Fantastic Light, not to mention his rider Frankie Dettori, was a winner too. This mile and a quarter was his preferred distance. For all these races you can only travel in hope. This time we got what we wanted – and more.

FANTASTIC LIGHT and GALILEO

DON'T DWELL on disappointment. Galileo was second. He's not quite a super-champion. But in finally conceding his six-race unbeaten sequence to Fantastic Light and an inspired Dettori, he gave us fans what we crave for. A race, a finishing duel, that we will never forget.

Of course there is a downside. The style of Galileo's Derbies had us romantics sending him to the stars. But more realistic evidence of merit was available last time at Ascot. Fantastic Light made him run near the limit. Yesterday the older horse was back to his favourite mile and a quarter and had a 5lb turnaround in the weights. Fantastic Light is one heck of a horse to start giving favours to.

The world already knows just how tough is this beautifully balanced five-year-old. In the second half of last year he ran in three time zones – not always luckily in America, finished third in the Japan Cup before closing out the Emirates World Series by winning the Hong Kong International in December. He is the most experienced top-class horse in training. Yesterday confirmed he is the best.

The anticipation beforehand was as simply, purely exciting as anything I can remember and, God help me, I go back to Aureole running against Pinza in the King George of 1953. There may have been seven runners but five of them were either pacemakers or fishing for place money. This was the Galileo-Fantastic Light rematch. This was one to watch close.

It was 3.15 when Galileo and his entourage crossed over to the crowded paddock from the anonymity of the security yard. His two stablemates Bach and Ice Dance were in front. He had two attendants at his head. Three large minders followed close behind, with the Ballydoyle farrier and his basket sweeping up the rear. You noticed that Galileo's hindquarters sank down almost pantheresque at the walk.

At Epsom and very noticeably at Ascot the adrenalin pumped white ripples of lather out through the skin. But in all the next forty minutes of preliminaries he stayed calm. A poised, elegant, lengthy model of Thoroughbred perfection. 'Aidan says he is happier with him than at Ascot,' whispered a Tipperary insider. Surely this would be the day to rank way up with Nijinsky and the top constellation?

Fantastic Light (right) gets the upper hand.

But then Fantastic Light walked past us. He is shade smaller than his younger rival but held his tautly muscled neck up proud and steady, and you realised the enormity of the challenge. Twenty-three races the older horse has run to his junior's six, £3.1 million to the other's £1.6 million. Sheikh Mohammed came up, all lean intensity. He looked across at Galileo. 'He's very good,' he said, 'but is he a great horse?'

The crowd, at 17,000 a Leopardstown record, had done a funny thing. They had fallen silent, almost hushed in the buzzing wonder of the battle ahead. Only when Galileo swept down past the stands at the close of the field, his head just yawing gently as he stretched Kinane's arms with his eagerness, did they burst out into applause of delight. They would probably never see him on a track again. The cheers were both in thanks and for more.

Even down at the start Galileo was calmness personified. In a small part of the brain a nagging voice wondered whether that King George effort might have sapped him a little. But doubts cannot linger when race gates whack open and when two pacemakers thunder off, setting a double dilemma.

Because this now became tactical. Up front Ice Dancer legged clear as if the devil was pillion. Give The Slip, Fantastic Light's leader, settled six lengths behind with Dettori, his own plans overruled by owner Sheikh Maktoum, placing himself three lengths away third ahead of Galileo. Right until the turn when the big shots began to rumble, the pattern was set.

Afterwards Aidan O'Brien felt he should have planned to have Galileo closer to his own pacemaker. But the top pair were not dawdling and a personal impression was that Michael Kinane's body never gave the super-confident signals we saw at Epsom and Ascot.

And off the turn, the cards did not quite fall his way. In a perfectly executed manoeuvre Give The Slip rolled right, allowing Fantastic Light up the inner, forcing Galileo a horse wide. Now there was just Ice Dancer ahead of him. As the top pair swept past either side of him Dettori went for everything on Fantastic Light. The older horse took three quarters of a length out of his rival.

It was the winning move. Run the replay as many times as you like. Look forward with greedy relish to the real chance of a Breeders' Cup decider at the end of October. But what happened now was what goes in the history book.

Two terrific horses, one ahead, the other trying valiantly to collar him. A hundred yards out Galileo almost got level. For a moment Dettori had to grab the reins and rebalance the runner beneath. But then he asked again and asked so much that he got an 'excessive whip' caution. Galileo stretched that long neck to its limit. But Galileo was just beat.

No, that's too good to be a disappointment.

Godolphin bested Ballydoyle that day, but in recent seasons there has been an unmistakeable shift of power towards the more integrated Coolmore set-up as opposed to the wider flung, more globally stretched ambitions of Godolphin. Much ink can be spilt on the issues involved, but this volume wants to look at the horses who, when they click, hold the whole thing together.

For Ballydoyle, one of those occasions, one of those horses, was High Chaparral taking the Derby in 2002. It followed Galileo's triumph the previous year and more than ever invoked comparisons to O'Brien's legendary namesake who had saddled Golden Fleece to be the last of his six Derby winners back in 1982. But the race and the day were a bit more than that. It brought things which, for very different reasons, you would never forget.

HIGH CHAPARRAL, HAWK WING and COSHOCTON

TWO EYES and two images for this Derby finish. In the right eye High Chapparal holds off his stamina-sapped stable mate Hawk Wing for a place in history and a million dollar future at stud. In the left

Coshocton does an exhausted chestnut cartwheel, his leg broken, only five minutes of life left to live.

In 223 Derbies you would have thought we would have had every possible drama by now. But here, with the Queen among 50,000 aghast spectators, was new one, a stricken horse in the very shadow of the post.

We had just seen one of the greatest training performances in the whole Derby story, young Aidan O'Brien following up Galileo's triumph last year with both first and second this time. We had witnessed one of the clearest cases of stamina deficit since top milers ever attempted Epsom's brutal mile and a half, Hawk Wing cruising effortlessly up to the leader before oxygen ran short and his legs became lead. But none of that mattered.

What mattered was what had happened right out there in front of us on this rain-softened grass. Coshocton had seemed to run his heart out. He had jumped first out of the stalls, jockey Philip Robinson had then hauled him back behind the leader Moon Ballad as they and Frankie's Dream set a strength-testing gallop. He had followed Moon Ballad into the straight and had continued clearly fourth best when the awesome Ballydoyle pair stormed past in their own private duel.

Watching a race down by the rails hits you in the eye. Moon Ballad's early pace had been fast almost to the point of reckless. The first uphill seven furlongs were covered in 1 minute 35.89, a clocking associated with quick rather than testing ground. The next quarter mile slowed dramatically to reach the three-furlong pole in 2 minutes 0.72, before coming home in 11.39, 12.25 and a leg-laggardly 14.32, the slowest final furlong since Shergar's victory canter in 1981. Yes, those last fractions took their toll.

It had seemed such a simple story. Johnny Murtagh on High Chapparal and Michael Kinane on Hawk Wing had positioned themselves some way off Moon Ballad's rapid early attack. But as the twelve-strong field made the Tattenham turn into the most famous downhill sweep in the galloping world, the two Irish colts powered through as if they were creatures from another planet. Visitors to Aidan O'Brien's immaculately organized operation in Tipperary would say that 'another planet' is exactly right.

High Chaparral had already won his last four races, but at least twice had seemed to kink his head a bit unwillingly to one side. Hawk Wing was hailed as the fastest horse in Europe, but his stamina in these conditions was a big doubt. The first question was answered with the most determined straight neck set for the line. And for a while Hawk Wing hovered so easily that it seemed only a matter of when Michael Kinane moved past to put a third Derby on his riding shield.

Then that 11.39 furlong bit. Kinane's lofty poise came down to a compelling crouch. Hawk Wing stretched to battle but his legs suddenly could not answer the call. A quarter of a mile out you worried, and by the furlong

High Chaparral pulls clear of Hawk Wing.

pole you could see the petrol tank had gone from green to red. Kinane was kind on him as the huge colt got home two lengths behind High Chaparral. The great mile races of the world now beckon.

But such easy reflections were shattered by a green and white blur to the left. At the furlong pole Coshocton had suddenly lurched out to his right as tired horses do. The mind registered how harsh a penalty his efforts were enforcing. Then he appeared to be coming on again to collect a highly honourable fourth when something gave and he pitched over on to his side right in front of me, hurling Phillip Robinson to the turf.

The jockey got to his knees gasping for air before stretching out flat when the pain hit in and the paramedics took over. Philip was badly shaken but should ride next week. Coshocton lay apparently equally winded. I got to him, undid the buckles on the surcingle and the girth, and pulled the saddle off his heaving, sweat-soaked flanks. You prayed that 'winded' was all that it would be.

Within seconds green screens, vets, officials and the horse's own connections were in an instant casualty ward. So often these heart-stopping moments have a marvellous revelatory end when the breathless horse recovers, believes in himself, gets up, has a shake and walks off to the spectators' cheers. This was not to be one of those.

As the vets probed they found the fracture on the near fore. Some hairsbreadth weakness in the bone had shattered under the strain. Horses don't have the understanding or the metabolism to go through human-style hospitalisation. The lethal injection had a job to do. It was the first Derby death on the course in forty years.

Just forty minutes earlier I had walked up from the stables alongside Coshocton and his groom Colin Dalton. Ahead of us were the gleaming Irish pair, but Colin was as hopeful as his trainer Michael Jarvis – who had himself led up Charlottown to Derby victory back in 1966. Colin patted this chestnut symbol of vitality with wondrous pride. 'He's in great form,' he said.

Now Colin had to take home an empty bridle and Michael and his wife comforted their weeping daughter as she tried to comprehend how the horse she knew as a galloping dream had become a mere lump of meat in the ambulance van.

If you love racing you will always remember this Derby as the finest example yet of Ballydoyle's current dominance. But if you love horses you will never forget a young girl's tears.

Time was when the likes of High Chaparral would have been off to stud so quickly that they would have been lucky to have made Ascot. But those who hark back to supposedly better days need to acknowledge that the continuing careers of so many of the major players has hugely enhanced Flat racing's offering to its committed public. Whether in these football-obsessed and multi-sport days horse racing can continue to pull its weight as a sport rather than as a mere betting game is one of the most crucial questions for its future.

For in Britain, and often worse in other countries, the coverage of racing in newspapers is little more than grids of racecards and tips to go with it. This is accepting the thesis that what is being presented as a gambling game, something stated every morning when The Today Programme ends its sports bulletin with two racing selections. Of course horse racing and betting are umbilically joined, but the current policy of trying to get newspapers to carry as many racecards as possible, however bad, is the strategy of the madhouse. For if racing is only about cards and tips, it is a mere betting diversion and belongs, at best, in the business pages.

What is needed is for stars to join battle so that the half-interested observer sits up and takes notice. On the Flat this is particularly difficult as the leading players are often one-season wonders: even football would struggle if that was all the exposure you got. But 2003 was different. High Chaparral battled on, outsmarted Falbrav in the Irish Champion, and then inched past that horse again in the greatest ever finish of the Breeders' Cup Turf.

At the end of the 2003 season the Racing Post *published a collection of essays on the leading horses. It was a pleasure to get involved, and the first one I chose was not High Chaparral but the horse he beat twice but who had every right to claim to be his equal, because after this piece was written Falbrav journeyed back across the world and signed off triumphantly in Hong Kong. He was, in the best sense of the term, worth writing about.*

FALBRAV

NOT JUST a champion but a battler too – every month in 2003, from April to October, Falbrav went to war. Nine times in all, every start at Group One level and that ninth effort in the Breeders' Cup as good a performance as any. No other top European horse in recent times has ever had a campaign to match it. And his year continued. Back in Newmarket from Santa Anita, he was immediately being readied for a final target a month away in Hong Kong.

Falbrav didn't always win; indeed, High Chaparral bested him both times they met. But even that Titan could not stand comparison for versatility and endurance. Third in the Ganay over ten furlongs, victory in the Ispahan over nine, muddled defeat over ten in the Prince of Wales, redemption over the same distance in the Eclipse, wide-running fifth in the King George over a mile and a half (or in view of the course steered, make that a mile and five).

Back to ten furlongs and total dominance at York, then total frustration over that trip at Leopardstown, down to a mile for a power display at Ascot, before going so near and yet so far over a mile and a half behind the dead-heaters Johar and High Chaparral under the hot Californian sun.

It took us time to get used to Falbrav after his move to Newmarket in January. In all of 2003 he only once started favourite, and that wasn't until the Queen Elizabeth II Stakes at Ascot, his eighth race of the year. He may have been Italian-owned and Cumani-trained, but their strategy was almost Australian in its approach. Find a big race, aim for it, run in it, then look for the next one; rest, aim and run again; and again and again and again. In our culture such no-frills campaigning is almost downgraded as desperation. It was not until Falbrav pulverised the Juddmonte International field at York that we really began to realise what a monster had developed in our midst.

For the beauty of Falbrav is that what you see is what you get – 16.3 hands at the shoulder, 540 kilos on the weighbridge, a magnificent aggressive bull Thoroughbred whose confident maturity as a five-year-old reminds us what we can miss when the Classic generation is hustled off to stud. This is an athlete without fear or frailty who doesn't suffer fools gladly. He shooed me out of his box when I visited him in early November. Yet looking at him glowering down, his bright bay coat still gleaming despite the strains of his Breeders' Cup exertions showing clearly across the ribs and loins, was to rejoice in the old maxim: that a racehorse should be there to race.

By then his career record read eleven wins and some £3 million in prize money from 21 starts in four seasons and over three continents and six countries. Uniquely he has won Group One races at eight, nine, ten, eleven and twelve furlongs, seven Group One successes in all. The trail that began with a first-time-out victory in a one mile two-year-old maiden at San Siro on 3 September 2000 is as long, honourable and eventful as that of any champion racehorse in recent memory.

That opening success was his only score in three runs as a two-year-old; at three he won three from six starts but is best remembered for his second to Morshdi in the Italian Derby. It was at four that he began to register on the international front, Luciano D'Auria saddling him to beat Godolphin contenders in back-to-back Group Ones, the ten-furlong Premio Presidente della Republica and the twelve-furlong Gran Premio di Milano, and he closed his season with that dramatic Dettori-ridden blitz finish in the Japan Cup at its temporary home in Nakayama. It had seemed a crowning triumph. Who would guess that the best was yet to come?

Even at the time, the decision during the winter by owner Luciano Salice to switch Falbrav to Luca Cumani's stable in Newmarket was clearly one of the great challenges of the trainer's career. Luca had made his name handling top horses like Arlington Million winner Tolomeo and Breeders' Cup hero Barathea, but he needed another champion to complete the climb back from the doldrums to which his split with the Aga Khan had confined him in 1998. Falbrav was a triple Group One winner, but his form would still need to improve to beat Europe's very best. Here was a training team on its mettle.

'I know the Italian system,' says Cumani himself the son of a successful Milanese trainer: 'It tends to be a bit less severe than the one I use at Newmarket so I was anxious not to overdo Falbrav early on. He is never impressive in his canters and although he worked well enough before his first run in the Ganay I felt he was a bit short of fitness, which Kieren [Fallon] confirmed. We were delighted with that run and even more when he returned to win the Ispahan impressively three weeks later.'

By now Cumani and his team were getting excited. 'I think the horse was suited by going up these hills,' said his groom Keith Ledington as we cantered up the Warren Hill Polytrack in November: 'He had a bit of a belly on him when he came, but he really began to muscle up across his loins and quarters.' Nottinghamshire-born Ledington, who did the same duties with Barathea and earlier had spells down the mines and with Securicor when his first racing dreams had come to nothing, is just the sort of quiet expert on whom men like Cumani depend. No surprise then that he won't get drawn into any recriminations about his horse's apparently lacklustre performance when only fifth behind Nayef, beaten seven and a half lengths, in the Prince of Wales Stakes at Royal Ascot.

'It was just a bit of a non-event,' says Keith: 'The jock [Marco Demuro, who had ridden Falbrav as a two-year-old] didn't know Ascot, got a bit stuck on the outside and never really got going. But he accepted things and that was good for the horse.' Without getting into silly chauvinism, a study of the video does suggest that the short-legged Demuro was unable to galvanize his massive partner in the way which Darryll Holland made a trademark in the three victories that followed, albeit punctuated by controversial and unlucky defeats.

The first victory was the Eclipse, and Ledington and Cumani's Ascot analysis was confirmed when Falbrav quickened clear two furlongs out, decisively turning the tables on Nayef. Admittedly Falbrav had a brilliant run round the inside rail all the way and Nayef was not done any favours by the Godolphin pacemaker early in the straight, but this was still a top-class performance by any standards.

It was an also an ideal start to the Holland-Falbrav partnership, which was then somewhat tarnished by a fairly nonsensical 'round the outside' strategy in Alamshar's King George VI and Queen Elizabeth Diamond Stakes at Ascot. It's one thing to take the Willie-Carson-under-the-trees route on the outside for the Old Mile course, quite another to pursue it for a full mile and a half and to stay out wide round Swinley Bottom. The ground, if softer than the official 'good', still produced a 2 minute 33 second finishing time, and Falbrav's fading to finish a nine-length fifth could be ascribed as much to his eccentric navigation as to lack of stamina or unsuitable going.

York was the ultimate in redemptions. Rarely do you get a horse race with the winner looking so dominant throughout. With no worries about the going, Holland tracked Nayef through and then put him ruthlessly to the sword when the two came to duel more than two furlongs from home. Magistretti ran on well to be second, but this was the hailing of a champion. He and his jockey had made it look easy. Three weeks later at Leopardstown for the Irish Champion, they would be made to remember how difficult it could be.

The real truth about jockeys' tactics is not what they say publicly but what they think in private when they watch the video. Darryll Holland had his best ever season in 2003, and his three victories on Falbrav in England will stay with him till he croaks. In particular the revelation of Falbrav's pure speed when returned to a mile for Ascot's Queen Elizabeth II, stalking the leader and then having far too many guns for the Classic-winning Russian Rhythm and for Tillerman. But it is the photofinish defeats at Leopardstown and Santa Anita that Darryll will continue to play in his head. Why did he get trapped in the Irish Champion's mile and a quarter? Did he go too soon in the Breeders' Cup mile and a half? It will be the first question not the second that upsets his sleep.

The final stages at Leopardstown are much more complicated than they look on TV. In the space of three and a half furlongs the runners make a 180-degree turn at the same time as the course dips and then rises again to the finish. Falbrav's one snag as a race-ride was that he could waste energy pulling too hard in the early stages. At Leopardstown Darryll Holland still had his arms out on sockets as Moon Ballad and Alamshar took over from the pacemaking France going to the final turn. Just ahead of him Mick Kinane was taking High Chaparral to the outer while Kieren Fallon was beginning to work Islington up from the back. In far less time than it takes to read this sentence, Darryll had to decide whether to go inside after Alamshar and hope for a split, or go outside and be forced to swing four wide into the straight. He went for the inner. He didn't get the split. It will haunt him.

Everything went wrong from that moment. With three Group One winners up ahead of him and another, Islington, closing the door on the outside, he was the ultimate example of being 'all dressed up and nowhere to go.' Even in the last 100 yards he was unlucky when High Chaparral rolled him towards the rail, but the stewards were surely right to rule that it was not that which cost him the race.

If Holland should criticise himself for the Leopardstown ride, he should snooze soundly over his Santa Anita efforts. Sure he committed a doubtful stayer for the line only to be run down by the stamina-stronger High Chaparral. But the season showed that Falbrav's biggest weapon was the big match-winning kick two furlongs out. That was the key at Sandown, York and Ascot.

Circumstances meant it never got played at Leopardstown. Now running to that extra-tight Santa Anita turn Holland correctly asked Falbrav to attack. Straightening up with only a furlong and a half to run, he took a couple of lengths out of his field. In the final hundred yards his fading stamina just failed to repel the dead-heaters' assault. No more need be said.

Falbrav's year gives huge credit to his connections and to himself. He was handsome, talented, tough, sound and almost uniquely versatile. He was as good at a mile as a mile and a quarter, and not much worse over a mile and a half. He preferred fast ground but won the Ispahan on soft. 'He was the best horse I have ever trained or ever will,' says Luca Cumani. For the rest of us, he will be remembered as one of the best we ever saw.

Just in case the argument had not been made well enough when the above was written, Falbrav took himself to the witness stand again when tackling the

£1.6 million Hong Kong Cup over his favoured mile and a quarter at Sha Tin on 14 December 2003. Up against him was the brilliant if headstrong Rakti, whose homework had been such that he started favourite. Hong Kong punters did not know the horse they forsook. This time Cumani put Frankie Dettori in the irons, and his former apprentice repaid him with a masterly powerhouse of a ride, beating Rakti to the punch 400 metres out and never looking back. There may have been bigger and better horses than Falbrav, but they number precious few.

Dalakhani, the little grey winner of the 2003 Prix de L'Arc de Triomphe, was certainly a lot smaller than Falbrav, but he also added hugely to the narrative in the completeness of his career's contrast to the other. But I enjoyed telling his story so much that I hope you will enjoy it too.

DALAKHANI

LEAVING Longchamp there was a sense of wonderment with a little twist of regret. It had been one of those cold, clear autumn days too beautiful to last. In Dalakhani's Arc de Triomphe we had seen a brilliant young colt fulfil what seven generations of breeding had planned for him. But now the day and his track career were ending. There would be no more clues as to whether Dalakhani was great or just good.

The Aga Khan's policy of retiring his Classic winners is so long established that it would be churlish to moan too much, especially in a year when his studs have given us two such excellent colts as Alamshar and Dalakhani. Yet Dalakhani's dazzling talents beg a wider comparison than the Prix du Jockey-Club and the six other successes amongst his own age group. The Arc was the first and only time he took on the other generations. The need now is to get the feel of him as well as the form book.

We knew his potential. His successes in all three races as a two-year-old, climaxing in the Group One Criterium International at Saint Cloud in heavy going, had left the normally imperturbable Alain de Royer-Dupré positively drooling with expectation. Dalakhani's early season was slated to take in the Prix Greffhule and the Prix Lupin en route to the Prix du Jockey-Club. It was the standard strategy, but the public as well private visitors would soon to realise that this was anything but a standard horse.

Dalakhani is not exactly short – he stands 1.64 metres (16 hands) at the shoulder – but he is light and lithe. Throughout the year he regularly checked out at 445 kilos on the weighbridge – fascinatingly almost 100 kilos (fifteen stone) lighter than Falbrav – and the impression you get both in repose and in action is of elegance and ease. He is a runner who moves with grace, an impression heightened by a peculiar white puff at the end of his otherwise grey tail which flicks in the wind as he gallops past.

His two preliminary races passed smoothly enough; a half length defeat of the unpronounceable Jipapibaquigrafo in the Greffhule and then a length victory over the Wildenstein runner Super Celebre, most notable for jockey Christophe Soumillon's boasts as to how much more his horse had in the tank. Purists get irritated at such flim-flam, but showmanship is no bad thing for a sport which still has something of a stuffed shirt image. Come the finish of the Prix du Jockey-Club, Soumillon was into a slightly juvenile taunting of Super Celebre, left arm outstretched in a sign to overtake, but much more interesting was what had gone before.

Because for many of us this was a first real look at this new star – and what a look it was. For Dalakhani in mid-event is one of the sweetest sights you will ever see on a racetrack. Soumillon rides him quite beautifully, his long body folded perfectly above his galloping partner, a full length of rein looped free to allow Dalakhani to reach out forward with his neck and forelegs as the stride skims him across the turf beneath.

Watching this, you could see what Royer-Dupré had meant when he said: 'I have never had anything like him. His movement is so elastic, there is such a flow about him. He is a very special horse.' That mid-race moment is exciting because it give you the promise of the finish ahead. All season few delivered more impressively than Dalakhani when Soumillon let him stride up to the leader that day in Chantilly.

The horse runs with his ears half back, but in the Jockey-Club there was no doubting his greyhound-type hunger for action as he coursed down the leaders then easily held Super Celebre at bay.

The old chateau skirted track was a place of sun-filled celebration, and four weeks later race fans had an unexpected bonus. The Aga Khan decided to let his French champion travel to The Curragh for the Irish Derby. It would pit him against Alamshar, his fellow graduate from the Gilltown Stud nursery only a couple of miles away, and there would be no fewer than six runners from Ballydoyle. Racegoers expected a Dalakhani treat, French turfistes a coronation. It was not to be.

Soumillon erred. The 22-year-old Belgian is a rider of tremendous gifts and, normally, of great self-confidence. But in the opening few seconds of the Irish Derby he seemed to let nervousness get to him. Drawn over against the rail, he jumped quickly out of the stalls and took up a position behind the two hell-for-leather pacemakers. It was as if he was anxious to get clear of any dastardly Ballydoyle plot to enclose him But he had the classiest horse, he could afford to play last. In those first few seconds he had thrown his best weapon away.

For straight away you could see how the race would unfold. High Country and Handel were never going to keep the gallop up beyond the final turn.

With the others happy to queue up behind Dalakhani, this meant that Soumillon was bound to be stranded in front with a good two furlongs to go. He would be a sitting duck if something was good enough and tough enough to pick him off. Alamshar was.

In a perfect world such strategic misfortunes should still not have sunk Dalakhani's chance. It was even possible to wonder just how enthusiastic he was about the closing struggle, and cynics went so far as to say this was the result that would suit his owner best. But in view of Alamshar's blossoming prowess which was to peak in the King George at Ascot three weeks later, and in view of the Dalakhani's apparently unflinching resolve at the Arc in October, the best analysis of the Curragh debacle surely comes from the trainer. 'He was ridden as a leader,' said Alain de Royer-Dupré in his shrugging, no-nonsense way, 'and he is not a leader.'

While Alamshar carried the green Aga Khan silks to King George triumph, Dalakhani took a Deauville holiday. Alamshar's subsequent lacklustre efforts in the Irish and English Champion Stakes remind you of the strain of keeping a three-year-old on the go through the season. Deauville was a delight for Dalakhani, not just a holiday but a cooler sea-breeze escape from the oven that was Chantilly during one of France's hottest ever heat waves. He was never a giant, but when he returned to action he was certainly refreshed.

First up was the Prix Niel, and once again mid race images of Dalakhani and Soumillon were a real delight. He always moved easily in the seven-runner field but then stretched with purpose to sprint home ahead of Doyen. Thanks to Longchamp's sectional timing system – how pathetic it is that in Britain only Newmarket has bothered with this essential aid to race understanding – we can put a clock on Dalakhani's athleticism. The fractions show that after an opening seven furlongs in 1 minute 30 seconds the race ran 22.5 for the next quarter and then came home in three final furlongs of 12.0, 11.3 and 11.8. Royer-Dupré said the colt could be a lot sharper. Arc rivals took note.

Then the weather threatened to turn the Arc into a mud bath. The Prix Niel penetrometer reading of 3.3 had moved down the scale by Arc day to 4.5 officially heavy. Despite his Group One win in such going as a two-year-old, Dalakhani's connections were fearful that the testing conditions would compromise the flow of their colt's wondrous stride. Punters took the hint. High Chaparral, a close and honourable if slightly ring-rusty third last year, was made favourite on the strength of his tremendous Irish Champion Stakes battle with Falbrav and Islington. Punters got it wrong.

If Soumillon seemed to lack confidence at The Curragh, at Longchamp on Arc day he positively purred with it – and his little partner purred back. Drawn on the wide outside, he broke smartly to feel the rhythm of the race, then eased Dalakhani back so that for a long way he only had one or two of the thirteen runners behind him.

Yet horse and rider looked content, looked ready to gather in this field when they wanted. With Diyapour as pacemaker for Dalakhani and with High Chaparral's stable companion Black Sam Bellamy also on the attack, the opening seven furlongs was taken in 1 minute 29.10, nine-tenths of a second quicker than the Prix Niel run on much faster going. Up front they would pay for it. Along the false straight Soumillon and Dalakhani closed, ready to pounce.

This is the stage in the Arc when the eye looks for dangers. High Chaparral may have been backed down to favourite, but Mick Kinane was already hard at work along the rail, his colt lacking a bit of the zip of Leopardstown. Behind him Kris Kin was in worse trouble, ahead Black Sam Bellamy was coming to the end of his tether, and it was the surprise packet Mubtaker who went best of all. Soumillon went after him. But he had to work.

With ears set back in effort Dalakhani coursed the leader down, got ahead a furlong out and then held on convincingly rather than spectacularly to have just three quarters of a length to spare at the line, the final furlongs being ground out in 12.6, 12.2 and 13.2. To beat a six-year-old trier like Mubtaker by so comparative small a margin hardly seems championship class. But High Chaparral and Doyen were five lengths and six and a half lengths adrift in third and fourth. All a horse can do is to beat those in front of him. A final time of 2 minutes 32 seconds showed the demands of the ground compared with Peintre Celebre's record 2 minutes 24.6 in 1997 or even Dancing Brave's rocket-finishing 2 minutes 27.70 in 1986, clocking an incredible 11.2 seconds over both the last two furlongs.

After just nine races it was to be Dalakhani's last hurrah on the racetrack, and no horse ever left a better final impression. In all the interminable preliminaries and then the protracted and ecstatic celebrations, he was the epitome of elegant composure. Much sentimental anthropomorphic bosh is written about racehorses, but here was an animal whose mind seemed to be ready for the job in hand. The demand of the racecourse tests temperament as well as physique. On Arc day Dalakhani won honours in both departments.

He was certainly a very good horse. His strict achievements do not quite rank him amongst the Mill Reefs and Nijinskys as he did not pitch at a Classic over a mile. But he probably could have won the French Two Thousand

Guineas had he been aimed at it, and he showed more natural speed than any Arc winner since Dancing Brave himself 27 years ago. For two brief seasons there was certainly a touch of 'greatness' about him. Dalakhani was what breeding racehorses was intended for. He had class in every line.

From the outside the big Flat racing battalions – Godolphin, Ballydoyle, and in this case those of the Aga Khan – look about the most exclusive and uninviting places on this earth. They are surrounded by protective fences, have the most luxurious imaginable living quarters, every conceivable pampering aid, and when they travel it is little short of a state visit – and that is just the horses.

But just because it is horses, there is a simplicity at the heart of it all. It is a racehorse, often a very young one, being readied for a physical and mental challenge that will define its future. Being part of that process makes people proud and generous. They are close to a wonder, and they want to share the experience – although the Flat racing context has the serious proviso of the preciousness of the commodity, both in the physical and in the commercial sense. The first makes connections ultra-sensitive to visitors; the second makes them extremely economical with any truth which might in the tiniest way affect the horse's value.

There is little of that nonsense in jump racing and absolutely none at all in Paul Nicholls. What incredible luck for race fans, therefore, that he should be the trainer of both Kauto Star and Denman. His direct openness was enough of a boon when he saddled Kauto Star to win the 2007 Gold Cup. It became a gift from the gods when next season he took 'Kauto' through to face the upstart Denman in a showdown at Cheltenham not bettered since Arkle squared up to Mill House way back in 1964 – and those two horses were not, like Denman and Kauto, next-box neighbours back at the yard.

The matchmaking seemed perfect. Kauto Star, the finer, swifter, more precocious athlete who as a four-year-old was rated the best young star in France. At that stage Denman was still a great chestnut lump only just beginning nursery lessons in Ireland.

Kauto Star was the reigning champion, whose faulty fencing seemed cured and who was fresh from a sizzlingly impressive success at Ascot. Denman was the massive powerhouse, the style of whose Hennessy Gold Cup victory made you recall the great ones in history and whose two subsequent wins made you believe that even Kauto might have trouble in catching him.

It was set up well enough, but on the day it was almost a mismatch. Watching Denman was still for me a moment of redemption. For it's easy to argue that sixty years of conscious following something as apparently limited as a bunch of horses thundering round a field is hardly helpful for the soul. But then you get something like Denman's Gold Cup and ask yourself if at least some of it might have been worth while.

This was.

DENMAN

THERE was beauty in the brutal simplicity of it all. Denman's whole life had led to this. He would set off to attack round Cheltenham's great anvil of dreams and gallop and jump until the best horse in the world was battered into submission behind him. It was what he had been bred and trained and raced for. It would be two circuits, 22 fences and 6 minutes 47 seconds of fulfilment on the hoof.

To be exact, the big attack did not come until they started the second circuit. Until then Denman had been tracking the grey Neptune Collonges while Kauto Star kept track along the inside about four lengths away. Until then you could not spot a chink in the defending champion. Some of us thought he looked a touch tight, his skin dull in the paddock, but maybe that was more our nerves than his. Then, just as Sam Thomas decided to play Denman from the front, Ruby Walsh had a problem. At the eleventh fence, the second last on the final circuit, Kauto galloped in and clouted it.

This happens. But you don't want it to happen too often. They came thundering towards us at the twelfth, the final fence in this Gold Cup next time round. When he had come here first time in 2007, Kauto Star had put in such a huge spring-heeled leap that he landed almost too steeply.

This time he didn't. Kauto galloped in again and clouted. It wasn't dangerous like it used to be a year ago. But he had missed it. Ruby Walsh has a poker player's stillness about him, but he now knew his hand wasn't perfect.

Not that he betrayed anything down the backstretch. Denman was piling it on up ahead of Neptune Collonges, and the lesser horses were already being driven. But Kauto was neat enough. It didn't matter that he was still five lengths adrift at the seventeenth, the last open ditch. But it did at the eighteenth, at the top of the hill. For he galloped in and clouted hard again. Denman was launching off down the hill and Ruby had the stick up. Kauto was in trouble.

There was no mistaking it. The champion had taken the equivalent of a knock-down. He was on his feet, but the contender was pummelling him. Kauto got good jumps at the nineteenth and twentieth, but he couldn't even take Neptune Collonges. There was a roar from the crowd as Denman's name was called, but also a strange muted feel. For Kauto this was not going to be just defeat, but humiliation.

Yet he had not become a fifteen-victory, six-season champion without being a battler. The game looked up as Sam Thomas crammed round the last turn for those final two fences with an ever widening gap behind him. But Ruby dug deep as he drove Kauto up the inside to that penultimate fence, and the horse's long white blaze came up with a mighty leap, finally to take second.

As Denman came towards us, the roll of his forelegs showed the strain was biting. If he was to blunder and Kauto could get another big jump there was just a chance of the equivalent of a last round knock-out.

But Denman kept his rhythm. He landed weary but running. Kauto drove in but clouted, and as he came away from the fence, he staggered slightly sideways. You should always look at the forelegs. Denman's were no longer moving easily, but at least they were rolling. Kauto's had lost their bite. It was over.

Afterwards the mind was in a muddle. Denman was the new champion. Sam Thomas well deserved his arm-punching elation. The ownership 'Odd Couple' of Paul Barber and Harry Findlay had their belief fully vindicated and Paul Nicholls's achievement of training the first three home recalled the 1983 'Famous Five' of Michael Dickinson, who was in the unsaddling enclosure to greet him. Yet this had not been Arkle-Mill House after all. That cold clear day in 1964, both sets of supporters could still believe as they swung for home and then Arkle changed it all, changed it utterly. Here the champion had been in trouble too early. We can't be really sure until the rematch.

With this bizarre, stable-companions, all-good-friends, no-edge rivalry, there was no chance of one of those, wound-licking, 'I will follow him to the end of the earth and then I will beat him' declarations which Jimmy Connors would say after another defeat by Bjorn Borg. But it seemed important to walk back to the wash-down box with the loser. Sonja Warburton has been Kauto Star's closest companion. 'The most important thing is that they are all home safely,' she said patting her horse's sweat-soaked neck. 'But I think the ground was a bit sticky for him. For me he is still a champion.'

The small knot of fans broke into spontaneous, sympathetic applause as she led Kauto out into the ring after his wash-over. They did the same in more cheery mode when lofty, grey-suited young Harry Fry came up with Denman. Away in the paddock you could hear the loudspeaker calling Jess Allen to the podium as groom to the winner. The two horses circled together with the familiarity of the stablemates they are. Kauto Star still tall and grand, Denman even bigger, but that low chestnut neck making him look slightly less than the seventeen hands that he is.

Eventually Jess Allen came up to join us. She will become a mother in the summer. 'I could feel the baby kicking on the run-in,' she said. But even that wide-eyed wonder could not stem thoughts of her four-legged hero. 'Yesterday morning,' she said, 'I put my hand on the bottom of his neck and for the first time ever it was just one slab of muscle. Paul asked me how he was. I said he had never been fitter.'

The two horses were led off to share a box home to Somerset. They don't look as if they argue, but we have to hope the debate is not over. Seven lengths was the verdict. It was decisive but not necessarily final. Next March let's hope it's not only the daffodils that are blooming.

The frailty of these hopes was brought home in September 2008 when Denman had to be treated, successfully it seemed, for a fibrillating heart. But it is just because the horses have always taken the most strain and most risk for least complaint that I have wanted to acknowledge them as markers on the sixty-year journey back to Black 47 that wet April day in 1948.

Denman's ailment has an irony about it. Because, for me, the horses have to be the heartbeat that carries us on.

L OOKING back over the lives and careers of these horses and people brings an unfortunate sense of both one's own inadequacy and impending fate. In the right mood this can spur you on to try and achieve something half decent before the grim reaper lops the poppy down. But on bad days there can be a weary echo of the line from Robert Graves: 'The dead are the lucky ones, for they are complete.'

Of course, the urge to seek wider truths as we think we hear the tolling of the bell stretches way back beyond Thomas Gray's famous Elegy in a Country Churchyard, *and it would be pretty presumptuous for this volume to try and add much now. But as racing – indeed, all sport and all life – takes more and more of its information from the television and computer screen, there is everything to be said for searching for the tangible.*

Racing is good at that. You don't just have to stay in the stand or watch TV in the bar. You can go to the paddock and move across to watch the horses canter down. You can go to the start, to the last fence, or way out into the country. You can get close. I hope that when my time comes there will always be a part of me out there in the wind where the hooves thunder and the divots fly.

INDEX